C000245672

'A veritable Rosetta Stone which reveals and deciphers a myr
mindfulness instruction in mainstream settings that are key t
mindfulness-based interventions of any kind.'

Jon Kab

'For the field of mindfulness to realise its potential, we need to take great care in training the next
generation of mindfulness teachers. They need to develop clarity of intention, theoretical understanding,
knowledge of the key research and proficiency as teachers. They need to consistently examine their
embodiment and integrity and be open to a lifelong process of learning.

This is not just a book. It is an extraordinary collection of resources developed over decades of training
many hundreds of mindfulness teachers. It is timely and will be widely welcomed.

At one level it is a practical, well-structured, skillfully curated set of training resources. At another level
it provides inspiration, a compass, as well as a road map for trainees at every stage of their learning. The
authors are generously committing to writing what they know through their extensive training experience
helps trainee mindfulness teachers. The list of authors represents some of the leading trainers in the world.

This edited collection is timely in resourcing both trainees and trainers in mindfulness-based interventions.
I can easily see this being a contribution that will evolve through many editions in decades to come.'

Willem Kuyken, *Ritblat Professor of Mindfulness and*
Psychological Science, University of Oxford, UK

'This is an outstanding book. As mindfulness-based programs enter the sphere of evidence-based
medicine, it is imperative that teacher training programs are consistent with the randomized controlled
trials that built the evidence. This book is a rich guide that invites us to travel the high road in teacher
training so that we skillfully serve learners, while fitting within healthcare delivery systems.'

Eric Loucks, *Associate Professor and Director,*
Mindfulness Center at Brown University, USA

'Mindfulness-based programs ask much of teachers who, in turn, are poised to deliver much to program
participants. This book will ably guide, support and nourish teachers in linking the implicit knowledge
embedded in their curricula with skillful, explicit means for conveying it. It should be required reading
for anyone in our field.'

Zindel Segal, *Distinguished Professor of Psychology in Mood Disorders,*
University of Toronto Scarborough, Canada

'This is a jewel of a book, reflecting the multi-faceted nature of teaching mindfulness in our present
society, the explicit and implicit aspects of curriculum, and how to nourish ourselves as its teachers. It is
the fruit of the experience of a worldwide network of experienced and committed trainers, to whom I am
very grateful for this priceless resource. I can warmly recommend it to beginning and advanced teachers,
and to teacher trainers. May it lead to even wider and tighter connections of mindfulness teachers and
their students around the world!'

Anne Speckens, *Professor of Psychiatry and Director of the*
Radboudumc Centre for Mindfulness, Radboud University,
Nijmegen, The Netherlands

'The authors of this book bring many years of collective wisdom to the process of teaching mindfulness-
based programs. As such, this book will be a valuable resource for all aspiring mindfulness-based
teachers.'

Susan Woods, *Senior Faculty at the Centre for Mindfulness Studies,*
Toronto, Canada, an international MBSR/MBCT senior level trainer/teacher and author

'What an incredible resource! Rich in depth and breadth it will surely become an essential companion for any mindfulness teacher. I am struck by the generosity and humility of the authors and the great integrity with which it is written and compiled. A tremendous contribution to the burgeoning field of mindfulness.'

Vidyamala Burch, *Co-Founder of Breathworks and author of*
Mindfulness for Health, Mindfulness for Women *and*
Living Well with Pain and Illness, *www.vidyamala-Burch.com,*
www.breathworks-mindfulness.org.uk

'This is a remarkable contribution to the field. This book delicately, deliberately and generously unfolds the architecture and essence of compassionate and competent mindfulness teaching. It is an essential companion for the experienced mindfulness teacher and a precious resource for those training to teach mindfulness-based interventions.'

Dr. Paul D'Alton, *Head of the Department of Psychology*
at St Vincent's University Hospital Dublin, Ireland, and Associate Professor
at the School of Psychology UCD where he is Co-Director of the MSc in
Mindfulness Based Interventions

'This resource is so rich. It touches upon most relevant issues the MBI teacher will come across when starting (and continuing) to use their wings after a teacher training. This book is an invitation to continuous learning. Dearly needed, for continuous learning is an important quality of embodying mindfulness.'

Rob Brandsma, *author of* The Mindfulness Teaching Guide:
Essential Skills and Competencies for Teaching Mindfulness-Based Interventions

'This book is a rare combination of rigid scholarship, practical pedagogy, and embodied mindfulness. Mindfulness-based teachers and supervisors will find the wisdom and skills in this book essential for helping not only their participants, but also their own personal and professional growth.'

Heyoung Ahn *Ed.D.,*
Executive Director of Korea Center for Mindfulness

'This book is a treasure and a generous gift to the mindfulness community and beyond. Each chapter is grounded in a deep understanding of mindfulness and it´s applications. The book reflects the profound experience of the authors in the domains of self-reflection, in practicing and teaching mindfulness and in training other to teach. A MUST for everyone involved in teaching mindfulness or training mindfulness teachers.'

Petra Meibert, *Psychologist, MBSR and MBCT teacher trainer,*
author, Head of the Mindfulness Institut Ruhr (MIR), Germany

'This book is a beautifully clear and accessible guide for potential and experienced mindfulness teachers alike. The rich history of these particular teachers, the depth and the wisdom of their contributions and their compassionate commitment to sharing what they know leaves a precious legacy to the global mindfulness community.'

Maura Kenny, *Founding Co-Director,*
Mindfulness Training Institute Australia and New Zealand,
Senior Consultant Psychiatrist, Clinical Senior Lecturer, University of Adelaide, Australia

'This is as comprehensive, detailed and inspiring as one could wish for in a handbook for mindfulness-based teaching. Infused and informed with the many years of experience of its contributors, it is a rich resource that will be invaluable for many years to come. In our institute's teacher-training programs, it will be a standard work for our faculty and trainees. At this point in the development of the field, it truly celebrates and documents the coming of age of Mindfulness-Based Programs. Well done!'

Linda Lehrhaupt, *Executive Director, The Institute for Mindfulness-Based Approaches,*
co-author of Mindfulness-Based Stress Reduction:
The MBSR Program for Enhancing Health and Vitality

Essential Resources for Mindfulness Teachers

Essential Resources for Mindfulness Teachers offers the reader a wealth of knowledge about the explicit and implicit aspects of mindfulness-based teaching.

The book focuses on how to develop the craft of teaching mindfulness-based courses and is divided into three parts. Part I addresses the explicit elements of mindfulness-based courses, such as how to offer meditation practices and inquiry. Part II investigates the subtle but powerful implicit qualities needed within the teacher to convey the essence of mindfulness. Part III is a series of chapters on the underpinnings, considerations, and theories surrounding the teaching of mindfulness-based courses, and includes a new framework for reflective practice – the Mindfulness-Based Interventions: Teaching and Learning Companion (the TLC).

The book is a core companion text for both trainees and established mindfulness-based teachers, and is a resource you will return to again and again.

Rebecca Crane, PhD, leads the Centre for Mindfulness Research and Practice at Bangor University and is an internationally renowned trainer, researcher, and writer in the mindfulness-based field.

Karunavira, MSc, teaches at the Centre for Mindfulness Research and Practice at Bangor University, and works internationally as a mindfulness trainer and retreat leader.

Gemma Griffith, PhD, is a senior lecturer and researcher at Bangor University, and is director of postgraduate programmes at the Centre for Mindfulness Research and Practice.

Essential Resources for Mindfulness Teachers

Edited by Rebecca S. Crane, Karunavira,
and Gemma M. Griffith

Routledge
Taylor & Francis Group

LONDON AND NEW YORK

First published 2021
by Routledge
2 Park Square, Milton Park, Abingdon, Oxon OX14 4RN

and by Routledge
605 Third Avenue, New York, NY 10158

Routledge is an imprint of the Taylor & Francis Group, an informa business

© 2021 selection and editorial matter, Rebecca S. Crane, Karunavira, and Gemma M. Griffith; individual chapters, the contributors

The right of Rebecca S. Crane, Karunavira, and Gemma M. Griffith to be identified as the author of the editorial material, and of the authors for their individual chapters, has been asserted in accordance with sections 77 and 78 of the Copyright, Designs and Patents Act 1988.

All rights reserved. No part of this book may be reprinted or reproduced or utilised in any form or by any electronic, mechanical, or other means, now known or hereafter invented, including photocopying and recording, or in any information storage or retrieval system, without permission in writing from the publishers.

Trademark notice: Product or corporate names may be trademarks or registered trademarks, and are used only for identification and explanation without intent to infringe.

British Library Cataloguing-in-Publication Data
A catalogue record for this book is available from the British Library

Library of Congress Cataloging-in-Publication Data
Names: Crane, Rebecca, 1964- editor. | Karunavira, editor. | Griffith, Gemma M., editor.
Title: Essential resources for mindfulness teachers / edited by Rebecca S. Crane, Karunavira and Gemma M. Griffith.
Description: Abingdon, Oxon ; New York, NY : Routledge, 2021. | Includes bibliographical references and index. |
Identifiers: LCCN 2020052864 (print) | LCCN 2020052865 (ebook) | ISBN 9780367330774 (hardback) | ISBN 9780367330798 (paperback) | ISBN 9780429317880 (ebook)
Subjects: LCSH: Reflective teaching. | Teaching—Methodology. | Teachers—Psychology. | Mindfulness (Psychology)
Classification: LCC LB1025.3 .E857 2021 (print) | LCC LB1025.3 (ebook) | DDC 370.15—dc23
LC record available at https://lccn.loc.gov/2020052864
LC ebook record available at https://lccn.loc.gov/2020052865

ISBN: 978-0-367-33077-4 (hbk)
ISBN: 978-0-367-33079-8 (pbk)
ISBN: 978-0-429-31788-0 (ebk)

Typeset in Minion Pro
by Apex CoVantage, LLC

Access the Support Material: www.routledge.com/9780367330798

Dedicated to reducing suffering and supporting the wellbeing of all who live on our earth

Contents

Figures and Tables

FIGURES

TABLES

Editors and contributors

EDITORS

Rebecca S. Crane, PhD

Rebecca directs the Centre for Mindfulness Research and Practice (CMRP) at Bangor University and has played a leading role in developing its training and research programme since it was founded in 2001. She teaches and trains internationally in both Mindfulness-Based Cognitive Therapy and Mindfulness-Based Stress Reduction (MBSR). Her research and publications focus on how the evidence on mindfulness-based interventions can be implemented with integrity into practice settings. She has written *Mindfulness-Based Cognitive Therapy Distinctive Features*, co-authored *Mindfulness-Based Cognitive Therapy with People at Risk of Suicide*, and is a Principle Fellow with the Higher Education Academy.

D. Karunavira, MSc

Karunavira left his initial career as head teacher in primary education in 1982 to pursue Buddhist studies. From 1990, he taught meditation and Buddhist studies, and between 2000 and 2010 was the spiritual director of the Brighton Buddhist Centre. He gained his MSc through Bangor University in mindfulness-based approaches in 2010. He has taught mindfulness-based courses and trained mindfulness teachers since 2005, specialising in working with carers, young people, NHS staff, and traditional Arab communities. He is also trained as a psychotherapeutic counsellor working with parents of children with complex needs as a mindfulness therapist.

Gemma M. Griffith, PhD

Gemma Griffith is a Senior Lecturer and researcher at the Centre for Mindfulness Research and Practice at Bangor University. She is director of the Master's in Mindfulness-Based Approaches and Master's in Teaching Mindfulness-Based Courses. Research interests and publications include group process and pedagogy in mindfulness-based programmes, qualitative research, the role mindfulness plays in parenting, and the adaptation of mindfulness-based programmes for people with learning disabilities.

CONTRIBUTORS

Susannah Crump, MA

Susannah was a counsellor and counselling supervisor within the NHS for over 20 years. She taught MBCT and MBSR to NHS patients, therapists, and healthcare professionals since 2005, was a member of CMRP's core training team, and was a supervisor within the Mindfulness Network. Susannah died in 2019 while we were in progress with bringing together this book. We are grateful to her husband Tim for gathering the notes she had made on relational skills in mindfulness teaching, which formed the basis for this section.

Pamela Duckerin, DipCOT

Pamela Duckerin has been a member of CMRP's training team and a supervisor with the Mindfulness Network since 2014. She qualified as an occupational therapist in 1984, working for 35 years in the field of mental health in a variety of settings and specialties in the UK and Canada. She later trained in dialectical behaviour therapy and cognitive behaviour therapy. She currently works in the NHS in a primary care mental health service as a senior therapist and clinical lead working with complex trauma, and teaching MBCT to client and staff groups.

Alison Evans, DClinRes

Alison Evans is the Executive Director and Supervision Lead of the Mindfulness Network (MN) charity. She is a mindfulness-based teacher, trainer and supervisor. She worked for some years at the University of Exeter, including being a therapist in several MBCT research trials. Her doctorate research was about Mindfulness-Based Supervision, which is a particular interest. She has been a CMRP trainer since 2017, and prior to that worked closely with Cindy Cooper (CMRP trainer who passed away in 2017), and Jody Mardula to jointly facilitate and develop Mindfulness-Based Supervision trainings and provision.

Eluned Gold, MSc

Eluned is a CMRP trainer and previously worked for CMRP at Bangor University as Director of CPD developing training pathways and curricula. She currently teaches and trains internationally in MBSR and MBCP (Mindfulness-Based Childbirth and Parenting) and is Director of Training for the Mindful Birthing Foundation. Eluned is a qualified psychotherapist and has worked supporting families for many years within the NHS and care organisations, integrating mindfulness into family care, particularly to parents who have multiple stressors. Eluned contributed to *The Mindfulness Breakthrough: The Revolutionary Approach to Dealing with Stress, Anxiety and Depression*.

Heledd Griffiths, MA

Heledd has a master's degree in Social Research and Social Policy and a particular interest in health inequalities and access to health services. She has over 10 years' experience working in research at Bangor University and has worked on multiple projects that focused on implementation. During 2014–2017, she worked as a research assistant on the ASPIRE Project: Accessibility and implementation in UK services of an effective depression relapse prevention programme: Mindfulness-Based Cognitive Therapy. Heledd was involved in conducting ten case studies across the UK to explore why accessibility to MBCT for depression was limited and helped to develop a guidance for future implementers.

Lynn Koerbel, MPH

Lynn is a trainer and teacher at the Mindfulness Center at Brown University, and served in multiple training capacities at the Center for Mindfulness in Medicine, Health Care, and Society at the University of Massachusetts Medical School. Before teaching mindfulness, she was an integrative bodyworker for over 20 years, primarily working with survivors of trauma. This work deeply informs her alignment with the ethos of wholeness and innate human capacity embodied in MBSR. She is a co-author of *Mindfulness-Based Stress Reduction Workbook for Anxiety*.

Bridgette O'Neill, D. Clin. Psych.

Bridgette is a trainer with the Centre for Mindfulness Research and Practice and the Retreat Lead for the Mindfulness Network. She is a clinical psychologist by training, worked in the National Health Service in the UK for 18 years and continues to teach and train in the NHS with the Sussex Mindfulness Centre. She lives in Brighton with her husband and two daughters.

Bethan Roberts, MSc, MA

Bethan teaches Mindfulness-Based Stress Reduction and Mindfulness-Based Cognitive Therapy mainly within workplace contexts and is a member of CMRP's training team. She is also a Mental Health First Aid Instructor and a registered i-act Instructor. Her involvement in the field of equality, diversity, and inclusion spans three decades, having worked for three UK statutory equality commissions (the Equal Opportunities Commission, the Commission for Racial Equality, and the Disability Rights Commission) delivering training, managing casework, and having commissioned research. She has been an Associate of the Older People's Commissioner for Wales and an Associate of Diverse Cymru.

Saki F. Santorelli, EdD

Saki pioneered the integration of mindfulness into medicine, health care, and broader society. He was a professor of medicine, director of the internationally acclaimed Stress Reduction Clinic, and executive director of the Center for Mindfulness in Medicine, Health Care, and Society at the University of Massachusetts Medical School. A Senior Fellow of the Mind and Life Institute, Fellow of the Fetzer Institute, and founding member of the Consortium of Academic Health Science Centers for Integrative Medicine, he teaches internationally and is the author of *Heal Thy Self: Lessons on Mindfulness in Medicine*, which has been translated into 11 languages.

Foreword

Twenty-five or thirty years ago it was not clear whether mindfulness would have much of a role to play as an approach to help people who are suffering from physical or mental pain. Jon Kabat-Zinn had set up the Centre for Mindfulness at the University of Massachusetts Medical School (UMass) and taught a stress reduction approach that would become known as Mindfulness-Based Stress Reduction. That was in 1979. His studies showing significant pain reduction using mindfulness meditation (published in 1982 and 1985) were to be later seen as a breakthrough, but as with many such breakthroughs, at the time it was not clear that they were to have any lasting significance for the wider field outside the treatment and management of pain.

In an article reviewing theory and practice of Buddhist psychology written in 1990, the clinical psychologist Padmal de Silva from the Institute of Psychiatry in London (one of the most influential scientific centres of clinical psychology research in the world), mentions mindfulness meditation (and refers to Jon's work on pain) only towards the end of the review. Most of the article talks of the many different aspects of Buddhist psychology, seeking to show how similar they were to *existing* theories and practices of behaviour modification. This included theoretical positions on motivation and 'primary drives'; the gateways of perception and development of cognition; links between concentration meditation (samatha) and progressive relaxation techniques; and links between insight (vipassana) meditation and several cognitive strategies, e.g. habituation training which we would now call 'distancing' or 'decentering' (inviting a client to bring a thought to mind repeatedly or for a long period so that the thought loses its intensity).

What emerges from this and other early reviews was a desire to map early Buddhist texts onto modern behavioural and cognitive methods, and an emerging body of specific research showing that samatha meditation was highly effective in bringing about change in the body's stress system. De Silva mentions reduction in oxygen consumption, lowered heart and breathing rate and decreased blood pressure, reduction in serum lactic acid levels, increased skin resistance, and changes in blood flow (all indicating decreased arousal in the sympathetic nervous system). He points out how these physiological changes associated with meditation were now being called 'the relaxation response'. De Silva concludes that 'it is possible to envisage that a limited integration between certain aspects of Buddhist psychology and certain parallel areas of modern psychology may fruitfully be affected' (De Silva, 1990, p. 254).

Indeed, when in the early 1990s John Teasdale, Zindel Segal, and I approached Jon Kabat-Zinn to ask what he thought of the idea of using a mindfulness-based approach for the prevention of depression, we did so because we thought that mindfulness would be a useful adjunct to existing cognitive therapy; that one might help people prevent future episodes by teaching them 'attentional control' and 'decentering' so that they might learn to relate differently to their own thoughts. This was consistent with a theory developed by John Teasdale and Phil Barnard, and observations about what caused relapse made in Zindel Segal's research and theoretical articles.

John, Zindel, and I attended one of Jon's last ever teaching sessions at UMass. It was 1993, and he was teaching a new class of participants, but was travelling too much to teach after that. We visited several times over the years, sitting in on MBSR classes at different stages of the eight-week course and with different teachers. We started to use his methods for our own personal meditation: struggling and renewing and struggling again, and gradually found a way in which personal transformation and professional practice could somehow be aligned. The results of our first randomised trial were encouraging, but how on earth could we train teachers to deliver this method to others? The answer is, we didn't know how.

In those early days, the common way of learning to teach a mindfulness-based program to your own patients and clients was to do an internship at UMass, so a trainee could sit on all classes at one go. These provided an incredible opportunity to sit alongside experienced teachers, to participate in their classes, and to sit with them after each class to reflect on what had been seen, heard, and felt in the class. We discerned that the only way forward for us in North Wales was to ensure that we had, within the area, people who had a background in both meditation and mental health, and could thus be sent to the USA to benefit from the full UMass internship. Rebecca Crane was one of the very first from North Wales (indeed from the UK) to do this programme. On the basis of her own experience of the internship, comparing her experience with my own, and that of Sarah Silverton (another UMass missionary from Bangor who had sat in with me even earlier as an assistant on the original trial and then done the internship), we were able to discern what might be necessary to begin to embed mindfulness-based training within the health and social care systems in the United Kingdom.

The landscape around Bangor makes it a good place to become a centre for training in mindfulness. It is dominated by the mountain range of Snowdonia, a place where one only has to walk for five minutes away from a road for you to become lost in its landscape and its grandeur. The lure of its compelling beauty is also deceptive. If you wish to walk much further, you need a guide who knows the landscape. This is true for mindfulness training. Meditation is simple except when it isn't. In 1999, a senior teacher at the UMass, Ferris Buck Urbanowski, was invited to offer a seven-day training retreat on the island of Bardsey off the coast of the Llyn peninsular in North Wales. Inaccessible except by a half-hour trip in a small boat, Bardsey Island became the birthplace of a new cohort of now senior teachers.

It was also the birthplace of a new form of training. For a seven-day training was relatively new even for UMass colleagues. It would become the model for training people in the United Kingdom and beyond. However, had that been the *only* method of training, there would have to be so much left out. It became clear that a pathway of learning was needed that allowed time for trainees to absorb what needed to be learned.

With a small amount of funding (£30,000 over three years) from the Worshipful Company of Drapers, a charitable institution founded in London in 1361, that had special links with Bangor University, we were able to set up a Centre for Mindfulness Research and Practice (CMRP), and Rebecca became its first Director. This would be the very first training centre in mindfulness-based approaches outside the United States. But how to proceed with training? Fortunately, Bangor University has a long tradition of training in knowledge and skills in many fields – each field needing to enable new generations to practice: in school teaching, nursing, midwifery, sports science, engineering, and clinical psychology to name a few. Each of these fields has a body of theory but is practice-based: each needs to find reliable ways to train its students, and then assess good practice. There were no university courses anywhere in the world that were providing post-graduate training in mindfulness, but there were models from these other fields, especially in the training of school teachers, and there were also staff in the Education Department who had the kindness, wisdom and interest in this new field to help.

What a training process in teaching MBPs eventually looked like is clear from this book: we see what the sequence of learning turned out to be, what balance between academic knowledge and practical skills was most useful, and, of course, how they solved the thorny issue of how anyone could assess the quality of somebody's teaching in mindfulness. The answer to these questions could not be 'drawn down from on high', and there was very little literature relevant at the time. There was only the wisdom of Rebecca and the team she assembled around her, and their willingness to reach out to colleagues including senior teachers at UMass, to enable them too to be part of building the foundation on which the CMRP's teaching and training would proceed.

Over the years, the CMRP team have been true pioneers, developing a wealth of materials that represents hours and hours of deep reflection on how best to train people to teach Mindfulness-Based Programmes. This book represents the gathering together of all this wisdom. It is extensive, it is very practical, and it touches the heart of what it means to practice mindfulness and to teach it.

None of us could have imagined in the early 1990s that it would go in this direction. Yet the evidence has continued to accumulate: mindfulness-based approaches for physical and mental suffering have taken their place alongside other evidence-based approaches in many areas of health and social care. The field continues to need teachers to teach it well and we need trainers to train it well. This book will be a vital companion and a reliable guide to all those seeking to train to teach mindfulness. I warmly commend it to you.

Mark Williams
Emeritus Professor of Clinical Psychology, University of Oxford

Acknowledgements

The voices, wisdom and spirit of all past and present CMRP training team are embedded in these pages: Trish Bartley, Michael Chaskalson, Cindy Cooper, Rebecca Crane, Susannah Crump, Pamela Duckerin, David Elias, Alison Evans, Estrella Fernandez, Annee Griffiths, Gemma Griffith, Eluned Gold, Vanessa Hope, Mariel Jones, Karunavira, Jody Mardula, Bridgette O'Neil, Ciaran Saunders, Judith Soulsby, Barbara Reid, Bethan Roberts, Sophie Sansom, Ciaran Saunders, Christina Shennan, David Shannon, Sarah Silverton, Taravajra, Sud Ubayasiri, and Elaine Young.

Some of the handouts from which this book have grown included contributions from colleagues outside CMRP including Mark Williams, Melissa Blacker, Bob Stahl, Florence Meleo-Meyer, and Alistair Smith.

Our work rests on the foundation of the developers of MBSR and MBCT. Deep honouring and gratitude to Jon Kabat-Zinn for your vision and capacity to make this real in the world; and to Mark Williams, John Teasdale, and Zindel Segal, the developers of MBCT, whose contribution to the world has been immense. Special gratitude to Mark Williams for your long-standing solidarity with and support for CMRP, and for the generous foreword to this book.

We have the profound privilege of working shoulder to shoulder with MBP colleagues in other centres and parts of the world. There are too many to name them all but particular gratitude for connection and collaborations with Nancy Bardacke, Judson Brewer, Christina Feldman, Margaret Fletcher, Fabio Giommi, Rick Hecht, Genevieve Hamelet, Gwénola Herbette, Steven Hickman, Lynn Koerbel, Willem Kuyken, Linda Lehrhaupt, Eric Loucks, Trish Luck, Petra Meibert, Helen Ma, Florence Meleo-Meyer, Saki Santorelli, Anne Speckens, Alison Yiangou, and Susan Woods.

In the UK we are grateful for the collaborative spirit that has grown between training centres – and would like to particularly to acknowledge Willem Kuyken and colleagues at the Oxford Mindfulness Centre, Vidyamala Burch and the Breathworks team, Heather Regan-Addis and the Mindfulness Association team, Robert Marx, Clara Strauss, and the Sussex Mindfulness Centre team, Kay Octigan and the Exeter University mindfulness team, and Tim Sweeney and the Nottingham mindfulness team.

Our early development was catalysed and supported by close engagement and support from senior teachers from the Center for Mindfulness at the University of Massachusetts

Medical School. We particularly appreciate Melissa Blacker, Pamela Erdmann, Florence Meleo-Meyer, Elana Rosenbaum, and Ferris Buck Urbanowski.

We would like to thank Ruth Baer, Jaqui Barnett, Gwénola Herbette, Sophie Sansom, Jem Shackleford, and Alison Yiangou for their helpful editing and suggestions to the MBI:TLC. Particular thanks to Jem Shackleford, who first suggested the TLC acronym.

Gratitude to Trish Bartley, Paula Haddock, Lynn Koerbel, Bridgette O'Neil, David Shannon, and Sud Ubayasiri, who offered detailed and insightful feedback on key sections, and to Shelby De Meulenaere for support with copyediting.

We are grateful to colleagues in Routledge – particularly Joanne Forshaw for support and advice along the way.

There is a group not mentioned yet who have probably contributed more than any other. These are our trainees, who have taught us far more than we ever taught them! Thank you to you all.

Abbreviations

CMRP – Centre for Mindfulness Research and Practice
CBT – Cognitive Behavioural Therapy
MBCT – Mindfulness-Based Cognitive Therapy
MBP – Mindfulness-Based Programme
MBSR – Mindfulness-Based Stress Reduction
NHS – National Health Service
TLC – Mindfulness-Based Interventions: Teaching and Learning Companion
UMass – University of Massachusetts Medical School

Introduction

In this book, we offer the materials and resources that we have developed over the last two decades of training teachers within the Centre for Mindfulness Research and Practice (CMRP) at Bangor University. Our hope is that this book will be a companion, a trusted resource, a 'turn to' place for both newer and more experienced mindfulness-based teachers. It may be used as a quick reference when preparing to teach a particular practice or exercise, or read more broadly to gain perspectives about how the various curriculum elements fit and work together. No book replaces the lived actuality of human engagement in the teaching and training space, but it is important to have anchor points to support us in orienting towards the skills, knowledge and qualities we are cultivating as mindfulness-based teachers.

The process of gathering these resources together has been a rewarding and connecting experience for us as a team of teachers within the CMRP. It has given us the impetus to pause and reflect on our development and process, and to appreciate the passion, care and energy that the collective gathering of CMRP teachers has poured into this work over the years.

CMRP was formally founded in 2001 following a creative development process during the 1990s, which was stimulated by Professor Mark Williams's leadership of the development of Mindfulness-Based Cognitive Therapy (MBCT) at Bangor University. Mark sought local connection with colleagues who were already engaged in the practice of mindfulness and interested in the ways in which this could be manifested in the world. Therefore, a group of us started to meet and explore together – this group became the founding CMRP teaching team. Mark was also closely linked with colleagues at the UMass where the Center for Mindfulness founded by Jon Kabat-Zinn was based. He initiated contact with senior teachers there, and invited them, over a number of years, to come to Wales to lead training, and he also supported myself (RC) and Sarah Silverton to go to UMass to train in MBSR.

Within CMRP therefore, we were immersed in two key lineages and influences within the mindfulness-based field – MBSR and MBCT. MBSR is the pioneer – the founding 'parent' of the field of Mindfulness-Based Programmes (MBPs); MBCT evolved out of MBSR and has catalysed a completely new field of practice and research that integrates cognitive science with contemplative practice. Therefore, our training processes and the resources in this book are embedded in these two models – but much of the material is highly relevant to any MBP because so much of the pedagogy and practice is generic.

In 2000, the first randomised controlled trial of MBCT was published and it stimulated a level of interest that went way beyond its particular contribution to depression prevention. There was a surge of interest in training to become a mindfulness-based teacher. At that point, in Europe no training processes were available. We began, in a modest way, and with support from UMass colleagues to offer trainings at Bangor University.

We were the first university training programme in this field outside the United States, and, in 2002, the first university in the world to set up a Master's programme focused on the study of mindfulness. We started from the ground up to discover models of practice and pedagogy that enabled our vision. We felt a deep responsibility to transmit the practice and the teachings of mindfulness into the world in ways that honoured its depth and its transformative potential. It was and continues to be important to us that trainees who engage in our training process immerse themselves in a personal practice of mindfulness. We held ourselves to high standards and asked the same of our trainees. Simultaneous to this in-depth experiential engagement with the practice and pedagogy of mindfulness, we were also keen to ensure that our approach was academically rigorous. There was at that time considerable doubt in academic circles that mindfulness was a valid arena to include in academia. Because of this scepticism, the first peer review of our master's programme validation was very challenging! However, in many ways we appreciated this push back. It ensured that we questioned ourselves, took nothing for granted, and found solid foundations on which to build the academic aspects of our training processes.

At this time in the early 2000s, we had no idea that there would be the massive upsurge of interest in mindfulness in the mainstream that we are now seeing. We were doing work that we cared about deeply and which aligned with values we wanted to manifest in the world. We responded to interest as it emerged. And of course, there was a significant lack of interest from various directions – we had many conversations with sceptical colleagues! Within this context, as we found our place within the university, and worked our way through the internal relational processes that are a necessary part of building a new organisation, we built our training processes so that they become a coherent pathway organised into two streams – a postgraduate master's route, and a continuing development portfolio building route (our Teacher Training Pathway – TTP).

What you are holding in your hands is one of the outputs of this process – the fruit of 20 years of collaborative, wholehearted work. This book contains the resources we developed to share with our MBP trainees along the way. They have been iteratively refined over the years and reworked again for this book. Of course, they are never finished – the evolution and creative process is ongoing. Currently we (along with colleagues internationally) are reflecting deeply on how world themes that are particularly strong in this moment in history can be represented and integrated into our teaching and resources – including social justice, climate breakdown, the pandemic, and historical trauma.

Things are always evolving – enabling this work to find its place in the mainstream is an ongoing exploration. The conversations we have now are different to those we were having 20 years ago. There is a hunger for mindfulness. This wider public and media interest brings a different set of challenges, though we continue to prioritise doing the slow and steady work of building something that matters in ways that can be sustainable. As part of a wider university reorganisation, CMRP has also recently restructured. Our Master's programme and research work continue to be embedded in Bangor University, while our TTP is now delivered through a collaboration with the Mindfulness Network charity. This book is a manifestation of this collaboration – the income generated from book sales will go to CMRP's training bursary fund within the Mindfulness Network charity to support people to engage in MBP training who could not otherwise afford to do so.

The book is structured in three parts. Parts I and II are rewritten by us (RC, KV, and GG), drawing from the body of materials that CMRP colleagues have written over the years. We are particularly grateful for three exceptions to this: a piece by Saki Santorelli on the essential spirit of mindfulness-based teaching; input from Susannah Crump on the relational skills section; and input from Bethan Roberts on the online teaching section.

Part I addresses the *explicit* curriculum of MBSR and MBCT – the tangible content of *what* is delivered: the formal meditation practices, the session-by-session group exercises, the inquiry process, and the organisation of all of this.

Part II addresses the *implicit* curriculum. In the context of MBP teaching *how* you teach is as important (if not more so) than what you teach. Here we explore embodiment and personal practice, the teacher's relational stance, the power of the group – and how all this meets the explicit aspects of the curriculum. Chapter 15, titled 'Integrating the explicit and implicit curriculum', illustrates how these various elements and dimensions dynamically combine to create a learning experience greater than the sum of its parts. We also address the orientation and assessment process for MBP courses, and how to teach MBPs online.

Part III examines the range of ways we can resource ourselves as MBP teachers through reflective practice, personal practice, and supervision, and through building skills and understandings needed within and beyond the teaching space. It includes a new framework for reflective practice – the Mindfulness-Based Interventions: Teaching and Learning Companion (MBI:TLC) or the TLC for short. This tool guides the process of reflective learning and development for trainee and established MBP teachers. It is an adaptation of the assessment tool – the Mindfulness-Based Interventions: Teaching Assessment Criteria (MBI:TAC; mbitac.bangor.ac.uk) that we originally developed in collaboration with colleagues in Exeter and Oxford University mindfulness centres. The MBI:TAC has become the main tool used internationally to enable assessment of MBP teaching skills in research and training contexts. However, its use is far wider than assessment. It offers a map of the territory of the skills of an MBP teacher, and so offers a framework for reflecting on skill development. The TLC is embedded within Part III of this book and a shorter version is also available online: www.routledge.com/9780367330798. Throughout the book we signpost to sections within the TLC to help you transition from reading about the skills and attitudinal qualities of an MBP teacher, into proactively reflecting on your learning process in relation to these. We are delighted to have worked with Lynn Koerbel, Assistant Director of MBSR Teacher Training and Curricula Development at the Mindfulness Center at Brown University to create the TLC. Part III also includes a range of chapters authored by CMRP colleagues exploring topics such as personal mindfulness practice, supervision, professional practice, trauma, and safety issues, the interface of MBP teaching with current societal themes, how to stay aligned with the science and theory, and how to implement MBPs in your context.

HOW TO USE THE BOOK

The book is designed as a resource that you can return to over the years. As the title suggests, the material in this book is (in our view!) all 'essential' if you are doing the work of teaching MBPs. It does not attempt to replicate great resources that are already available, so we point you to other sources throughout. As you engage with your training, we hope that your learning will be nourished and sustained by the reading and reflecting you may do on the material in this book. The book is also intended to be an ongoing companion beyond training. As you prepare for teaching certain sessions, we anticipate that it will be useful to read sections of Part I that describe the particular elements that you are about to teach; that Part II will offer some nourishment to return to when you seek to reacquaint yourself with the deeper essence that supports you to offer MBPs congruently; and that the various chapters in Part III will support a culture of ongoing reflective practice, and will expand, open, and deepen your understanding on key themes.

Our deepest wish is that the material in this book enables you to flourish as an MBP teacher, and to offer this work out into the world with skill and integrity. May many benefit from your practice and your teaching.

Part I
The explicit curriculum

INTRODUCTION

What is the explicit curriculum and how does it fit with the implicit curriculum?

In Part I we outline the underpinning intentions and teaching methodologies of the explicit curriculum (i.e. the actual *content* of what is taught session by session, such as the formal meditation practices, inquiry etc.). Afterwards, in Part II we unpack the importance of the implicit curriculum (i.e. the qualities and values that are communicated through *process* rather than content, such as the embodiment of the teacher). This section offers an overview of curriculum issues, clarifies the role of each part of the curriculum, and offers a perspective on how they work together.

There is a lot more going on in the teaching space than the actual content of the curriculum – what is immediately seen and heard. The phrase 'mindfulness is caught rather than taught' captures the sense that it is both through *what* we are taught, and through *how* we are taught that learning happens. In educational circles the implicit aspects of the teaching process are often called the 'implicit or hidden curriculum': the parts of the learning process that are often unacknowledged by students or educators yet are vital to learning. This implicit part of the curriculum tends to be conveyed through non-verbal messages: tone, prosody, affect, body language, and eye contact. It is the aspect of the pedagogy that communicates ethics, values, authenticity, congruence, and trustworthiness (or lack of these). It is through the implicit curriculum that we communicate an attuned capacity to embrace diversity and teach inclusively (Chapter 24). To enable a connected meaningful learning experience the hidden and the visible curriculum need to be congruent with each other.

In our teacher training programmes at CMRP, we intentionally give a strong emphasis on both the explicit and implicit curriculum. We recognise the truth of Maya Angelou's words: "I've learned that people will forget what you said, people will forget what you did, but people will never forget how you made them feel". We recognise that people who have completed an Mindfulness-Based Programme (MBP) course leave with a toolbox of practices (the explicit elements), *and* they will take away memories of mindful connection, of living in alignment with values, and of caring about themselves, others, and the wider world (the implicit elements). Clearly, these rest and rely on each other. If one is weaker, the whole learning process is weaker. Mindfulness, both as a *quality of being* and as a *practice*, is essentially an open and responsive stance towards internal and external experience. It follows therefore that an MBP *curriculum* is designed to enable this essential stance to be communicated. This is mirrored in the frameworks offered by the Mindfulness-Based Interventions: Teaching Assessment Criteria (MBI:TAC: Crane et al., 2018) and the Mindfulness-Based Interventions: Teaching and Learning Companion (the TLC: Chapter 19) which enable trainees to reflect upon and develop both explicit and implicit teaching skills.

In the first section of Part I, Saki Santorelli offers a piece that was originally written as the opening *canto* of the 2017 Mindfulness-Based Stress Reduction (MBSR) curriculum guide. Note that because Saki is reflecting specifically on the role of the MBSR curriculum guide, there are some references to MBSR, but the spirit of the text applies to any MBP. He reminds us both of the importance of understanding the explicit elements of MBP curriculums, and the pitfalls of overemphasising them. The following chapters in Part I are all written by the editors.

1

The essential spirit of mindfulness-based teaching

Saki F. Santorelli

Eight centuries ago, during the last twelve years of his life, the great Sufi teacher and poet, Jelaluddin Rumi, recited and wrote the *Masnavi* – six oceanic volumes about the human condition and the unfolding of the soul (consciousness) comprising 62,000 lines of poetry. Among the topics Rumi speaks about in this great work is what he calls the 'variety of intelligences' and, as well, about 'Universal Intelligence', what he refers to as 'The Mind of the Whole'. Among this 'variety of intelligences' he comments on 'personal intelligence':

> Personal intelligence is not capable of doing
> work. It can learn, but it cannot create.
> That must come from non-time, non-space.
> Real work begins there.
> (Rumi, 1994)

He speaks, too, about what he calls 'two kinds of intelligence':

> One that is acquired ... one already completed
> and preserved inside you.
> (Rumi, 1988)

In the context of reflecting on the spirit that informs the pedagogy of MBPs these 'two kinds of intelligence' are essential to explore and understand.

ACQUIRED INTELLIGENCE: THE INSTRUMENTAL DIMENSION OF MBP TEACHING

Often enough people learning to teach MBSR ask me the question, "Has the MBSR curriculum changed much in 38 years?" I am keenly attentive to the silence that usually ensues between us when this question arises. What is the answer? Yes? No? Yes and No? Neither yes nor no seems to me to be about as close to reality as I can land because any of these possible answers depends upon the perspectives of the person asking and the person responding to the question. At heart, the MBSR curriculum has remained absolutely true to the *form* that it entered the world with in 1979. For now, the basic structure of the program, the sequencing of meditation practices and underlying session themes permeating the program remain robust and intact. In aggregate, these curricular components constitute the 'instrumental' domain of the MBSR curriculum. This instrumental domain is what Rumi is referring to as 'acquired' intelligence. Acquired intelligence comes through practicing, through repetition, attainment of goals and the development of skills and competencies learned, understood, and experientially refined over time. Surely, the instrumental is of great value, comprising one domain of learning. Seen through the perspective of the instrumental, this curriculum guide is akin to an operating manual – a session-by-session handbook. Understandably, when someone is first learning to become an MBP teacher, the curriculum is often approached in this way. When viewed through the lens of the instrumental – the world of doing and becoming – then the answer to the question of whether the curriculum has changed leans towards "no"; the curriculum has not changed much at all since 1979.

Of course, herein lies one of the inherent dangers of publishing an authorized curriculum guide. Soon enough, it will be mistaken for a 'manualized protocol'. Soon enough, people will become fastened to the form, bound tightly to the instrumental, because it provides a structure, a trajectory, and a map that is easily mistaken for the territory. While valuable and oftentimes comforting, this is also problematic because it is limiting. Much of the time, we want the map to be the territory because we desperately want *constancy*. Observation would suggest that often enough it is easier for us to hold firmly to and be comforted by the instrumental, by the form. Having established some sense of the instrumental dimension of intelligence as it expresses itself in the MBSR curriculum, let's now turn our attention to another intelligence.

'ALREADY COMPLETED' INTELLIGENCE: THE NON-INSTRUMENTAL DIMENSION OF MBP TEACHING

At heart, the MBSR curriculum has remained true to the *formlessness* it entered the world with in 1979. At the most basic level, you need a room to teach MBPs, a gathering place for people. Of course, you already inhabit a room that is always with you. This is the room of your heart. Rumi calls this placeless place:

A freshness in the center of your chest.

Two centuries later Hafiz described it as:

The city inside your chest.

This 'freshness' or 'city' is outside of space and time, outside of personal intelligence, outside of needing to get anything, outside of transforming yourself or anyone or anything – no attaining, no non-attaining, no completeness or incompleteness – simply *being*. This is the non-instrumental actuality of meditation and MBPs, the intelligence that is already complete within you, and within those with whom you work. This intelligence does not need to be acquired but rather, *remembered*. This is the real curriculum, the real guide; the deep spring from which MBP teaching flows out of you and makes its way into the world. You might consider returning to this water whenever you need a reminder of who and what you are behind all the words and forms described in any MBP curriculum guide. This 'freshness' that is available to you whenever you become lost or tired, overextended or discouraged or simply in need of rest and ease; the refreshment of not needing to pursue any aim at all. I suspect that if you allow yourself the space, you'll discover for yourself that holding too firmly to the instrumental inevitably blinds you to the non-instrumental

Like Russian Matryoshka dolls, the instrumental is *nested* within the non-instrumental. If this were not the case, how could you learn anything? How could you love anyone, if love were not an innate attribute of your being? How could you ache and feel tenderness in the orbit of another's pain, if empathy wasn't inherent? Surely, we can learn to become increasingly familiar with these attributes through deliberateness and practice. However, if they were not already part and parcel of who and what you are, occluded as they may be in most of us, you would have no reference point for loving, compassionating, (as Walt Whitman says) or assuming your measure of universal responsibility for the wellbeing of the world.

Look at MBP teaching as a 'thing' and you'll miss it. See it as a pattern of relationships – a pulsating, ever-changing expression of life unfolding and you'll discover it. If MBPs are worth anything, their worth lies in their aliveness. Their aliveness rests in the basic *ungraspability* of the curriculum. Seen from this vantage point, the vantage point of the non-instrumental, then the answer to the question, "has the curriculum changed?" is "yes". The curriculum has changed because, like everything else in the world, it is constantly changing. Likewise, who and whatever you think of as 'you' is also continually changing. This dynamic flux is none other than the creative nature of Rumi's 'universal intelligence' reflected *through* you and embodied *as* you. And, of course, as you grow and deepen and surrender more fully into what you are behind the occlusions, the curriculum changes quite naturally, deepening and expanding into new expressions, endlessly ....

Ultimately, and in a very palpable way, the 'curriculum' of MBPs are none other than *your* life intersecting and comingling with the lives of the people you will have the privilege of sharing in and engaging with week by week in the teaching space. The suffering, the inconstancy, the lack of a solid, concrete 'self' – the wish for relief of suffering and the longing for wellbeing that you carry within you, and all the people you will ever work with carry within them – *is* the curriculum, the vital life of MBP teaching.

Now, as you enter into the stream of learning and teaching MBPs, my invitation to you is to realize that the real guide for teaching any MBP curriculum is always available inside of you, always awaiting your attention, always resting in your completeness outside of any notions of here and now, past and future, time and space.

2

Curriculum considerations

Before exploring the explicit curriculum elements, we offer some perspectives on the evolving context of MBP curriculums and the question of which MBP curriculum you choose to anchor your learning into. This is an important prelude before moving on to 'how' to teach the explicit curriculum, as it balances Saki's section by underlining the importance of curriculum adherence, and clarity about what you are teaching. The issue of curriculum adaptation for particular contexts or populations is briefly introduced below with pointers to helpful resources

As Saki so eloquently communicated, any MBP curriculum is a 'principle-led' curriculum – as opposed to a fixed treatise or a list of edicts, whether these are based in historical sources of authority, contemporary science and thinking, or our collective wisdom and experience as MBP teachers and trainers. A 'principle-led' curriculum relies on the teacher cultivating a clear and deep understanding of the principles themselves. Embodying the underlying principles of an MBP curriculum draws from our lived experience of mindfulness practice, from our teaching experience, and from our study and understanding of theory and research. This means we make any changes to the curriculums we have inherited with great care and humility!

When we first started training teachers at Bangor University in the early 2000s, curriculum choices were simple. MBSR was the original MBP, and MBCT was a tailored adaptation for a specific population and clinical context. MBCT was situated clearly in the clinical context. MBSR made sense for all those who were not clinically trained, or who wanted to teach a curriculum for people with chronic pain, or with a broader focus on human challenges. Since then, the range of clinical applications for MBCT has grown, it has moved out of the clinic into a diversity of settings, and a version of MBCT for general populations has been developed (e.g., MBCT for Life). The MBCT development process pioneered the integration of mindfulness training with cognitive science and this has paved the way for the development of many other MBPs and a whole body of science and literature. The pedagogy and science of MBSR has also evolved – it continues to be an approach that is exquisitely suited to general populations with a diversity of life challenges, and alongside this, there are many well thought through and empirically tested adaptations of MBSR for specific populations and contexts. There are a vast range of other MBPs developed for different contexts and populations from the 'DNA' of both MBSR and MBCT. There is also enormous pressure in some fields for teachers to offer shorter programmes.

The dynamic evolution of this young field is something to celebrate. The energy and enthusiasm to adapt the MBP teaching process and content to different contexts and populations is enabling this work to become available to a wider range of people. Alongside this there is also some caution needed. In their analysis of the science of the MBP field, Dimidjian and Segal (2015) pointed out that there is a plethora of 'one-off' feasibility studies of multiple MBPs offered in a diversity of contexts and populations, but that this work then tends not to be built on.

In this fluid context, within CMRP, we take a clear stance within our training process of encouraging our trainees to embed their learning in curriculum forms that do have substantive underpinning evidence. We also recognise that MBCT and MBSR are not ideally suited to every population and context and that skilful adaptation is, at times, needed. However, we believe that this adaptation process is best conducted from an in-depth familiarity with established MBP forms. In the context of this evolving process, the Center for Mindfulness (CFM) that Jon Kabat-Zinn founded at the University of Massachusetts Medical School (UMass), published the first MBSR curriculum guide to enable the field to re-anchor to MBSR as it is intended (2017). This has offered the field greater clarity about the true form of a program that is labelled 'MBSR' – though as Saki Santorelli eloquently writes in the prologue to the curriculum guide (Center for Mindfulness, 2017; see Chapter 1), there are 'edges' to pinning down the subtleties of MBP curriculums in writing. The MBSR curriculum guide has subsequently been updated (Kabat-Zinn et al., 2021).

Both MBCT and MBSR were the anchor points to our development in Bangor as a training centre. MBCT was being developed and researched at Bangor University by Mark Williams. Our primary teachers, guides and colleagues in the early years of our development were senior MBSR teachers from the CFM at UMass. This did result in the early dissemination and training in the UK context becoming a merging of the curriculum forms of MBCT and MBSR. More recently, in response to the plethora of programme forms that are out there, and the resulting potential for confusion and loss of integrity that this causes, we are more clearly delineating MBCT and MBSR in our training processes. We continue to train in MBCT and MBSR alongside each other while being clear about the distinctive features of each program. Our aim is thus to enable our trainees to know each curriculum in its original form, and to anchor their early teaching experience into one or other of these. If trainees then choose to adapt the program at a later point, we can be confident that they are adapting from a place of lived experience of the curriculum as it was originally intended to be.

There are many advantages to training in MBSR and MBCT alongside each other: it emphasises the coherence of the MBP field as a whole, and with this, a clarity about the generic knowledge, skills and attitudes needed for MBP teaching practice. The generic defining features of MBPs are laid out in the warp and weft paper (Crane et al., 2017). This paper describes the distinctive features of any program that is *mindfulness-based*. However, in the midst of clarifying the shared ingredients of MBPs (i.e. the 'warp') it is also important that we are clear what distinguishes different MBPs from each other (i.e. the 'weft'), so that we become clearer of the ground we stand on as teachers, and of the particular contribution that each programme has to make to the whole. Next, we describe the key distinguishing features of MBSR and MBCT.

MINDFULNESS-BASED STRESS REDUCTION (MBSR)

The MBSR programme was developed as a form of participatory or integrative medicine. The programme intends to enable participants to access their own inner resources for growing and healing, and so to empower them to become active participants in their own journey of engagement with medical services and with their lives (Kabat-Zinn, 2013). MBSR has a culture of education rather than therapy, and is an integration of various theoretical and pedagogical underpinnings (see Figure 2.1).

MBSR is underpinned by an understanding of the general vulnerabilities shared by all humans that relate to our patterns of reactivity to difficult experience. These understandings draw on Buddhist psychological frameworks that map the causes of human suffering, the ways to ease this, and also draw on contemporary theories on stress physiology, psychology and resilience (Williams & Kabat-Zinn, 2011; Kabat-Zinn, 2013; Chapter 25).

MINDFULNESS-BASED COGNITIVE THERAPY (MBCT)

The MBCT programme is an integration of MBSR with the theories and principles of cognitive behavioural therapy (CBT) (see Figure 2.2). It was developed as a depression prevention programme for people who are vulnerable to repeat episode depression. It developed in a culture of research, theory development and with a pragmatic awareness of the realities of implementing in clinical settings. It pioneered a theoretically driven methodology for carefully tailoring MBP teaching to particular populations and contexts that catalysed many other MBP developments.

Figure 2.1 The pedagogical influences that make up MBSR

Figure 2.2 MBCT is an integration of MBSR with CBT

The CBT contribution to the integration takes two broad forms:

1 An underpinning psychological framework/model which describes how general vulnerabilities (inherent challenges shared by all humans), and specific vulnerabilities (particular challenges shared by the population that the programme may be targeted to), are triggered and maintained.
2 Curriculum elements that are drawn from CBT practice. The main MBCT curriculum guide is Segal et al. (2013). There is a useful summary in Crane (2017).

THE DISTINCTIVE FEATURES OF MBSR AND MBCT

There is enormous overlap between MBSR and MBCT. The structure of the course, the approach to pedagogy, and much of the content is the same. There are also differences. As you build your understanding of the curriculums, allow some room for ambiguity and confusion even whilst you have an intention to build clarity about distinctiveness!

One key difference between the two programs is culture. MBSR arose out of a culture of experiential education and thus has a strong emphasis on the importance of non-instrumentality, emergent learning, allowing room for the unexpected and for connecting to the mystery of experience. There are aspects of the program that are core and are always delivered, but within this, the teacher uses the course structure and curriculum flexibly, and prioritises immediacy and the capacity to be responsive. MBCT arose out of a culture of clinical delivery, and developed within the context of a structured research trial. The curriculum therefore has always been available in manual form. MBSR historically prioritised the implicit. MBCT historically prioritised the explicit. Both are clear that both are important!

Another difference is that the MBCT program and teaching process is framed by an underpinning psychological model, which implicitly guides the learning. The MBCT teacher has studied and integrated frameworks of theoretical understanding, and weaves these into the teaching process as appropriate and relevant. This may be quite subtle (for example, leaning the guidance of the body scan towards the development of 'decentering skills' by emphasising the capacity to both experience and clearly see experience), or more explicit (for example, offering a short didactic piece on cognitive understandings of avoidant mechanisms which are implicated in depression maintenance).

WHAT INFORMS MY DECISION TO TEACH MBCT OR MBSR?

At a certain point in our training program process – usually following the early stage engagement with building generic MBP teaching skills – we encourage our trainees to choose either MBCT or MBSR as a primary anchor point within which to develop their early teaching experience. The themes that influence this choice are as follows.

Context

The setting in which you are working may influence the choice of curriculum. For example, in the UK health service MBCT is better known and therefore may have greater acceptability.

The population who are coming to the course

For example, the title MBSR may have more meaning and be more appropriate for a general public population than MBCT. MBSR was designed for general populations so is naturally suited to this context – though the MBCT for Life programme is also now taught for general populations.

Teacher experience and knowledge

MBCT teachers have training in relevant psychological processes, have a working understanding of the psychological theories which describe general vulnerability, and an understanding of the psychological model which describes the particular vulnerability of the population attending the course (if it is a course for a specific population e.g., people with chronic fatigue). Note that when teaching any MBP in a clinical context, a relevant professional clinical training is required, or the MBP teacher should work in collaboration with a clinical colleague.

Teacher preference

The more open fluid culture and style of MBSR teaching may suit certain people; or the anchoring into cognitive science and theories that is part of MBCT may be more suited to others.

Research

If there is an evidence base for a certain MBP with the population or context you are working with, then this is a strong guide on curriculum choice.

Making a choice to anchor into one curriculum from the beginning enables trainees to have the space to study the curriculum guide carefully, and through this to build understanding of the layers of intentionality underpinning each curriculum element, each session, how everything builds on what has been before, and lays the ground for what is coming next. Supervision is a particularly important resource to help develop curriculum understanding throughout your development as a teacher (Chapter 21). Many trainees later expand their development and practice by building their understanding of and practice skills with both MBSR, MBCT, and other MBPs. As trainees take their first steps into teaching, we encourage them to stay close to the form of the program they are teaching as it is laid out in the curriculum guide. There is an integrity to the form – and no space to add things in without compromising what is already there.

CONSIDERATIONS FOR ADAPTING MINDFULNESS-BASED PROGRAMMES

MBCT and MBSR are designed to be responsive to the particular group, and a particular moment. Therefore, adaptation already happens as a moment-by-moment process in every course. However, further tailoring the programme to certain populations and contexts through adaptation can be important. It is important to seek input from others before adapting, for example from professionals who have expertise with the population you are adapting the course for, and in mindfulness supervision. The delicate process of adapting can involve the curriculum content, course structure, course length or teaching style. The 'warp and the weft' model (Crane et al., 2017), offers a perspective on adapting the curriculum, the 'warp' being the unchanging structure that holds the various individual textures and colours of the 'weft'. For a curriculum to remain defined as a 'mindfulness-based program' clearly knowing the difference between the warp and the weft is essential, the weft being adapted skilfully to meet the needs of particular populations or contexts. Thus, in clinical contexts if you have training and experience with a particular population for whom there is currently no evidence base on MBPs, the careful development work needed prior to embarking on adapting the 'weft' includes:

- Considering, from your knowledge of your clients and your experience of mindfulness, the different ways that mindfulness training is likely to affect people with their specific clinical diagnosis;
- Formulating how mindfulness training could best be used with this client group, including length and kind of meditation practices; how meditation practice is likely to interact with their specific needs or challenges; didactic material that would enhance and support their use of mindfulness;
- Embarking on cautious pilot trials, evaluating carefully, and using this evaluation to improve or cease the adapted course (Sanghvi, 2019).

In non-clinical contexts adapting the 'weft' may be linked to responding to the requirements of, for example, organisational, cultural, socio-political, or religious considerations. The standard curriculums (i.e. MBSR and MBCT) have a solid evidence base and every attempt should be made to find ways to deliver them intact. At the same time, responding to the particularities of context or population may involve adjustment, if so, consider the following:

- Carefully explore the issues and perspectives that seem to require adapting the program with your supervisor. There may be a need to seek out information from other teachers and researchers to inform this discussion.
- Perhaps employ a 'cost-benefit' analysis to each element of the program that seems to need adapting (i.e. what might be lost through adaptation and what is gained).
- Consider how an element changed in one session may have implications for later sessions; the whole is greater than the sum of its parts.
- Refer to key resources that support this process including McCown et al. (2016), and Sanghvi (2019).

SUMMARY

The curriculum, the explicit dimension of teaching MBPs, needs to be responsive to change whilst remaining protective of hard won, evidence-based integrity. The experienced leaders of this emerging field and the ever-evolving evidence-based science *together* offer a steady compass direction in the seas of uncertainty and ever-increasing rates of change. We, as developing teachers and trainers embrace, with humility, the task of steering the craft using this compass, negotiating change with skilfulness, courage and energy. The chapter on adapting to online teaching in response to the Covid-19 pandemic is illustrative of this careful balance, using the clarity offered by MBI-TAC to help check that 'adherence' is sufficiently maintained (Chapter 17).

3

Guiding the formal practices
Overview

The upcoming chapters (Chapters 4–7) focus on the four formal practices of MBPs – the body scan, mindful movement, sitting meditation, and the short practices, such as the MBCT Three-Step Breathing Space. Guiding these practices is the most explicit skill or craft of being an MBP teacher. Confucius once said 'The first act of government is the rectification of terms' and this is important to remember when teaching the formal practices. Terms can often be confused, for example 'attention' with 'awareness' or 'mind' with 'thoughts'. As we pay *attention* intentionally to the breath in the present moment, non-judgmentally, we develop *awareness* of the object of our attention – i.e. *attention* is not of the same order as *awareness* although this term is sometimes used in this sense. Likewise, 'mind' is of a different order to 'thought'; so, saying, "noticing the wandering mind" is less specific than, "noticing wandering thoughts" (i.e. thoughts are one category of 'objects' *in* the mind along with perceptions, impulses etc.) This section first outlines core principles that are applied across all four formal practices, and then takes each of the formal practices in turn, exploring first *why* they are taught (the learning intentions), and then *how* they are taught (practical teaching considerations).

A core support to learning how to teach MBPs is engaging in reflective practice. We invite you to use the Mindfulness-Based Intervention: Teaching and Learning Companion (called the TLC for shorthand) from Chapter 19 as you read these sections, to assist you in journaling any new learning or points you wish to reflect on in your teaching practice. There is a lot of information contained in this section, which may feel overwhelming, especially if you are new to teaching MBPs. Allow all that emerges in your learning process (including doubt and uncertainty) to be included in your reflective practice, and trust that new learning takes time – give yourself space to read, digest, practice, and reflect.

THE CORE PRINCIPLES: INTENTION, ATTENTION, AND ATTITUDE

The common principles underpinning guidance of mindfulness practices are wide ranging and complex but they can be helpfully organised using Shapiro et al.'s (2006) model of the three axioms of intention, attention and attitude. (Note that much of the below goes beyond what is described by the IAA model, as we are using the model as a useful organising framework):

13

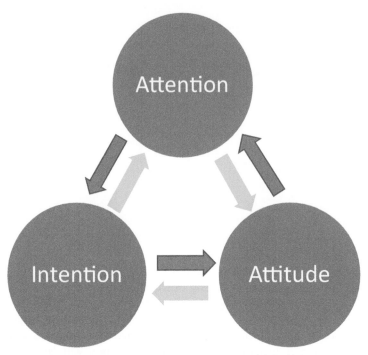

Figure 3.1 The Intention, Attention, and Attitude model (adapted from Shapiro et al., 2006)

- *Intention*: Intention can be at different levels, and can be thought of as having two aspects: our broad and deep values and aspirations for our lives, connected with the question of why we are practicing mindfulness (for example for emotional regulation, personal wellbeing, to cultivate a caring, altruistic orientation); and more specific intentions for a particular task or time. Often this is linked to the question of what and how we practice when we settle for a period of formal practice (for example patience or present moment focus). Intentions are a support to us rather than goals to achieve against which we judge ourselves; connecting with our intentions is like setting our compass or the rudder of our boat to point in the direction we are choosing to steer.
- *Attention*: Attention to moment-by-moment experience as it is, both internally and externally. Our experience is shaped by what we attend to and how we attend. Without training, attention tends to be caught without our choosing, and hijacked by reactive preoccupations and cognitive biases (Britton, 2016). One research study suggests that our attention is wandering away from what we are doing 47% of the time (Killingworth & Gilbert, 2010). As our practice develops and we become more able to stabilise and direct attention, we can start to pay attention in a less reactive way to experience as it arises both externally in the environment and internally from within the body – heart – mind. As we practice, stability of attention grows, as does the ability to stay with and attend to instability. In this way, mindfulness practice differs somewhat to a 'concentration' practice, which has an aim of stilling the attention (see learning considerations below).
- *Attitude*: Attitude is the *way* in which we approach practice. Attitude is the 'how' rather than the 'what' of attention. Mindfulness involves a friendly, curious attitude rather than a judging, critical way of paying attention. We can have a strong sense of this if we consider how we might pay attention to a person and see that it is possible to pay

Table 3.1 The seven attitudinal foundations. Summarised from Kabat-Zinn (2013)

Attitude	Description
Patience	A recognition that things can only emerge in their own time
Beginner's mind	A mind that is willing to see everything as if for the first time with fresh curiosity and vitality
Trust	A faith in the validity of our experience; and allowing the process of bringing awareness to experience to unfold in its own way
Non-striving	An attitude of willingness to allow the present to be the way it is without trying to fix things; responding rather than reacting
Non-judging	Assuming the stance of impartial witness to your experience
Acceptance	A willingness to see things as they are; bringing openness to, kindness towards, and welcoming of experience just as it is in the moment
Allowing/ Letting be	Seeing the possibility of moving out of the perpetual human tendency to want to hold on the pleasant and get rid of the unpleasant

attention with a range of orientations – friendliness, criticism, or impatience. With these different attitudes, our experience of the person's same actions or speech is likely to be quite different. Noticing how we are paying attention to inner and outer experience, and deliberately developing particular attitudes is central to mindfulness practice. Kabat-Zinn (2013) outlines attitudes that he considers foundational to mindfulness (see Table 3.1).

Together, these three axioms of mindfulness, when practiced, can lead to a shift in perspective known as *reperceiving*. By facilitating participants exploration of attention, intention, and attitude during the course – this often (or perhaps inevitably?) leads to the ability to develop a decentred awareness that allows us to step back from being caught up with personal narratives. Other terms for this include de-fusion, witnessing, decentring, or holding our experience (Segal et al., 2013; Hayes et al., 2012).

Note that attention, intention, and attitude are interlinked, operating together and influencing one another. Although they are presented as separate axioms for clarity; there is no clear line between them, nor should there be. It is impossible to pay attention without some kind of attitude being present in the act of attention – even to have a neutral attitude is to have an attitude. To pay attention in a kindly way is to infuse attention with the attitudinal qualities of mindfulness. Therefore, the IAA model provides us with a handy way to think about how the formal practices are guided. For example, if you notice you are offering a lot of guidance around attention, you can recall from the model that attitude is equally important and lean towards some guidance around attitude.

CORE PRINCIPLES FOR ALL FORMAL PRACTICES

In this section we detail the core principles of attention and attitude, discussing them in terms of the following: 1) learning intentions, and 2) teaching considerations. Note that it is important to refer back to these principles when reading later sections specific to each practice. These are the core principles that underpin how to guide the core formal practices, which are:

- body scan
- mindful movement
- sitting practice
- short practices (which include STOP, the pause, the Three-Step Breathing Space).

Paying attention: key intentions

Paying attention, when approached with clear intention and a supportive attitude, is the means by which awareness is cultivated in mindfulness practices. Awareness is the *main* thing! Steven Covey's adage is helpful here: "The main thing ... is keeping the main thing ... the main thing!" (1989, p. 145). This is different to the role of attention in many 'concentration practices' which, for example, regard mind wandering as something to be managed or avoided in order to arrive at a stable focused state of mind and body. Mindfulness regards mind wandering, meandering, racing, dreaming etc. as a significant part of the process to bring attention to, and that our overarching intention is not to keep attention one-pointedly on the breath – or other anchors of attention such as touch or 'sound' – but to use such objects of attention to develop and maintain awareness. This includes awareness of the activities of our mind as we patiently and repeatedly invite attention to come back to one particular object. The metaphor of the object of attention being an anchor conveys this very well; an anchor safely holds a boat in place whilst allowing some flexibility of movement so as not to be damaged by storms. With this in mind, the various practices during an MBP aim to make attending to present moment sensations an enduring and accessible anchor from which awareness and all its benefits arise. Thus, the core learning intentions for the formal practices are as follows.

Connecting to direct experience of sensing

This is a key intention. Our body travels with us at all times and so is a reliable, accessible and immediate source of sensations to anchor into; an access doorway to our unfolding moments. Participants learn to pay attention and experience sensations directly. This allows them to learn to become more anchored in the here-and-now sensations within the body. Sensing *is* present moment awareness. Attending to various sensations (body, breath, sounds, sight, smell) allows participants to stay close to the actuality of experience, rather than being caught in thought-based interpretations and assumptions. We then begin to *see* and bring awareness to the extra layers we habitually add to experience.

Essentially, formal practices teach a way to shift attention from a mode of 'thinking-doing' to a mode of 'sensing-being', in which we can relate directly to whatever our experience is and so *respond* from this basis. This also allows participants to pay attention to the 'flux and flow' of moment-by-moment experience. Feeling stuck is a common source of distress, so sensing the flow and change of ordinary experience – breath sensations, sounds, thoughts, and feelings – can be a very helpful, implicit message conveyed in formal practices.

Choosing to shift attention

Participants learn to deliberately engage, disengage, and shift attention to different parts of experience, which 'trains the muscle' of moving attention purposefully. This helps participants to develop flexibility and fluidity of attention, and sustain moment-by-moment awareness. A core skill that is being cultivated is the capacity to deliberately widen and narrow attention. For example, during the sitting practice, participants may be invited to attend to narrow aspects of awareness (e.g. sensations of the breath or the touch of the feet on the floor), and then to expand attention to sensations in the entire body and breath, which leads to a widening of attention and a related expansion of awareness. Thus, noticing particular aspects of bodily experience (narrow angle attention), and then noticing the experience of the entirety of the body (wide angle attention) cultivates the skill of deliberately shifting attention. This skill enables participants to direct attention to their experience more evenly, rather than overemphasising some and under-emphasising other aspects of experience. This skill is particularly important for when difficulty is experienced in a practice, and is the basis for choosing to shift attention either towards the difficult to explore it, or away from the difficult if it is overwhelming and there is a need to self-regulate (Treleaven, 2018). When strong difficult thoughts and emotions are present, shifting attention to the body can offer a safe way to work, acknowledging and allowing them to be experienced, understood, and possibly let go of. This allows natural changes in intensity to occur and be felt, increasing a sense of safety within an experience that may previously have been overwhelming. This is one way to 'ride the waves' of powerful internal experiences, whilst neither being overwhelmed by nor suppressing them.

Developing awareness of pleasant, unpleasant, and neutral sensations

By paying close attention to experience, it becomes possible for participants to read the early signals that the body communicates in relation to perceiving aversion, attraction, and neutrality. Through this awareness of the immediate *feeling-tone* (the Pali word for this is *vedana*) of pleasant, unpleasant, and neutral in reaction to a stimulus, we can begin to learn to be mindful of these reactions. The knowing of feeling-tone happens before conscious control or thinking about it. For example, stubbing a toe is experienced viscerally as an unpleasant sensation even *before* the mind has identified it as 'toe-stubbed'. An important aspect of mindfulness practice is to gain an experiential knowing of the implications of feeling-tone on reactivity. Because it is natural to feel aversion to the unpleasant, unwanted aspects of our experience, the teacher can helpfully direct participants to sense aversion or unpleasant sensation as contraction, bracing or holding in the body. We can then offer guidance inviting curiosity, kindly acknowledgment and perhaps an allowing of these sensations – letting be – rather than maintaining distress through denial or fighting. We thus start to build foundations for relating to difficult thoughts and emotions in the mind. This skill is a foundation for *decentring* – gaining objectivity – so as to choose more wisely and foster well-being. All the formal practices support this skill by including guidance towards noting and working with pleasant or unpleasant experience – and to acknowledge neutral experience.

Knowing how to use attention to work skilfully with the natural tendencies of mind

Mindfulness practice invites and develops *stability* of attention rather than concentration as a primary intention. Because of this, the various instructions to 'come back to the breath' or 'to the body' when the mind has wandered are given in a way that allows participants to first become interested and aware of what 'the mind' is doing – wandering, dreaming, planning etc. The ultimate task is to develop a steady awareness of all our experience including the 'play of the mind' (the varying thoughts, images, sensations that come into awareness). Then, by noticing recurring patterns or reactions, we learn to observe how things shift, change, and recur within our body and mind. Regular experience of practice offers the possibility of developing a wider perspective on the underlying patterns and processes, which drive the content. Thus, loosening the tendency of overreliance on a content focus. In this way, we can work with letting go of maladaptive tendencies to ruminate or suppress thoughts.

Learning how to build stability and calm

We can use sensations of breath and body to build stability and, at times, calm. One effect of mindfulness is likely to be increased concentration, although this is a useful effect and helpful, it is not a goal-oriented aim. Although we are not teaching a 'concentration' practice, this ability to find mental and bodily stability is crucial to create the conditions within which we can 'see' our more subtle experience, and learn from this seeing. Stability of attention builds the basis for sustained awareness and insights arising from this. It is also a source of simple pleasure, and over time, can contribute to resilience.

Attitude: key intentions

Learning how to approach experience – the attitudinal foundations

The attitudinal foundations we bring when paying attention to our experience are a crucial act of befriending our experience. A core aim of formal practice is for participants to develop helpful attitudes towards their experience. Thus, it is not just about the act of 'coming back' to the practice per se, but about *how* we come back. So without unhelpful *judgement*, without *striving*, and with *patience*, *trust* in the process, *allowing* and *letting* experience be what it is, *accepting* and starting again with a *beginners mind*!

Allowing experience to be just as we find it is fundamental to mindfulness. This skill of noticing direct experience with no other agenda teaches participants how pervasive the goal of 'getting it right' can be. Acceptance of the present moment is key here: the implicit learning is that participants can simply allow whatever arises to be here, now, in this moment; this helps them learn acceptance of all experiences, whether pleasant or unpleasant.

Developing a spacious quality of mind

The attitude of remaining *open* to all experiences as they arise and pass away develops the skill of remaining spacious with the whole range of human experience. This spaciousness allows participants to observe thoughts and emotions with interest and kindness, and gives opportunities to notice recurring thinking patterns, how these develop and play out within the mind. It is not about making the thought or emotion go away, but by acknowledging its presence and effects as if it were a 'weather pattern' we can step back from and observe. This attitude is the basis for *reperceiving*, thus preventing the 'stepping back' from becoming unhelpful avoidance or denial.

Working with reactivity

Formal practices often illustrate to participants how *automatic* judgements are (e.g. thoughts of "I'm not good at this, I can't focus" etc.) which can lead to unhelpful inner dialogue and rumination. Instead, we learn to acknowledge where our attention has wandered to, and bring it back gently and clearly. *How* this is done is important, bringing the attitude of patience and compassion when working with a busy mind or judgements helps participants work with the natural unruliness of the mind.

Reperceiving/decentring: key intentions

Paying *attention*, when approached with clear *intention* and a supportive *attitudinal context*, is the means by which 'reperceiving' arises, which is a 'fundamental shift in perspective' (Shapiro et al., 2006, p. 377). Decentring allows for the experiential realisation that 'thoughts are not facts' and that emotions come and go as aspects of our experience rather than defining truth. So, key intentions include the following.

Cultivating being fully with experience from a decentred perspective

It is very important to offer guidance that encourages a decentred, objective, stance while not encouraging dissociation or alienation from the unwanted or wanted object in attention. Learning to 'step back' and see thoughts and feelings from the perspective of the 'interested kindly observer' must be clearly differentiated from avoidance. Beginning to notice thoughts and feelings as passing mind-states rather than 'holding onto' them as facts can lead to freedom from negative, self-critical judgements. This spacious quality of mind allows perspective and reduces the power of unhelpful automatic thoughts. This fundamental skill is based on developing a curious and kindly attitude towards our moment-by-moment experience.

Seeing more deeply into the nature of human experience

Clear seeing into the 'way things are', whilst often challenging, is ultimately a doorway to greater sense of integration, freedom and well-being. Seeing even glimpses of the ground of awareness within which all experience arises offers the potential for radically altering one's perspective. Practice enables us to perceive both the space within which experience arises, and the experience itself.

KEY TEACHING CONSIDERATIONS FOR THE FORMAL PRACTICES

Here, the 'core' practical teaching considerations common to all formal practices are outlined. These are tips for how to bring in the learning intentions when guiding practice. It is useful to use the TLC (Chapter 19) to help you reflect on your learning strengths and learning needs when guiding formal practices.

Attention: key teaching considerations

Establish an anchor point

An anchor point is a place in the body where the attention is easily shifted to and grounded; one that feels clear and safe for the participant. Individuals may change their 'anchor point' according to what is most helpful at that moment, it is an alive, conscious choice arising as an aspect of 'intention'. Therefore, while it is important to settle on a particular anchor for any given period of practice, it may change over time. The role of the teacher is to invite clear attention to this choice and underscore its immense value. In many practices, a helpful suggestion for the anchor point is the breath as it provides a continuously renewed source of moving sensations that both assists attention and reminds us of loss of attention. Whilst this is helpful for many people, there are some for whom the breath does not feel like a safe place or a helpful anchor point (e.g. participants with asthma, trauma, or particular medical histories). It is therefore important, when guiding participants to choose an anchor point, to include various options (e.g. "Going back to the anchor point whenever you have lost touch, this could be the sensation of your hands, or feet, or the breath"). It may be helpful to explicitly check during the inquiry in early sessions, that all participants have found an anchor point they feel comfortable using.

Use clear and accessible language

When guiding a practice, clear and accessible guidance of both where and how to place attention needs to be offered. Metaphors such as the "torch beam of awareness" or "sunlight playing over" can convey where the attention is directed. Remember the language of discovery helps frame attitudes and involves the participant in the process, generating interest and engagement.

Offer clear guidance on mind wandering

The task is not to stop the mind wandering but to invite attention to what is actually happening in a way that does not strengthen the default habits of judging and striving. Thus it is helpful to:

- Acknowledge attention has wandered and perhaps note where it has gone before returning
- Gently bring the focus back to the chosen anchor of attention
- Repeat this process as needed, with acceptance and notice any judgement or striving
- Offer silent spaces in the guidance to allow participants to practice this process independently
- Increase or decrease the unguided, silent, spaces depending on the attentional experience in the group and/or their level of vulnerability
- Remember that the mind gets 'lost' more easily when the 'object' is more subtle, such as open-awareness practice, so adjust the guidance as needed.

Attitude: key teaching considerations

Modelling from the teacher

The implicit, attitudinal dimension of formal practice begins with the teacher's attitude. The attitudes modelled through tone, clear invitational language, attention to comfort and so forth, speak volumes about *how* we wish participants to practice mindfulness. In this way, we can introduce non-conceptually a flavour of care, compassion, and warmth. The choice of words and metaphors, silences between phrases, tonality, speed of delivery, and volume are all utilized to convey the attitudes imbued within the practice. This cannot be scripted or faked but relies on the teacher being directly in touch with these attitudes within their own being as they guide. In this way each teacher will develop their own congruent voice.

When guiding practices

It is important to infuse guidance with multiple and clear invitations to be aware of attitude. Balance guidance which gives a *receptive* flavour of allowing and accepting, alongside that of an *active* flavour of exploration, curiosity, aliveness, adventure. More specifically:

- Prioritise the use of present participles – i.e. attend*ing*, bring*ing* attention – giving a sense of invitation rather than command can reduce resistance, and encourages participants to be more involved. Avoid language that might feed into a sense of striving: words such as "trying", "working", "see if you can"
- Offer *choice* and *safety*: the guidance really is guidance, not instruction – e.g. reminding participants to "remember you have choices to let go of the guidance or adapt it, keeping your well-being always to the fore"
- Offer guidance on the spirit to bring to the practice: a gentle, light, curious attention, inviting interest in our experience, and in a similar tone encourage clarity of intention
- Consider framing the attitudinal aspect of the practice in relation to the particular population you are introducing the practice to – e.g. fast-moving businesspeople may need more guidance on *non-striving* and *trust*; parent groups more guidance around *patience* and *allowing* or *letting be*
- Remind participants there is no goal, no right or wrong way to practice
- Normalise all experiences: offer guidance to recognise and normalise our wandering minds, boredom, restlessness etc., and repeat this regularly. Allow and normalise the absence of feeling (e.g. "noticing perhaps the absence of sensation in the foot, allowing this to be as it is")
- Periodically through the practice offer attitudinal guidance on responding to distraction – i.e. "if your awareness is caught up in thoughts, clearly recognise this and let them be, coming back *gently* and *clearly* ... if this is possible ... to a direct awareness of sensations"
- Offer guidance which invites participants to move into a direct and, if possible, a kindly 'being with' what is arising in the body or mind, rather than looking at it coolly from a distance
- Invite a gentle approach to the practice, invite patience and non-striving to perceived obstacles – such as boredom, judging thoughts, noise, dreaminess, striving, planning-mind, restlessness, doubts etc. Offer guidance to bring kindly interest to ourselves, attending with care and compassion, and a sense that 'perhaps it is okay not to feel okay'
- Introduce all formal practices explicitly – as well as implicitly, through tone and spaciousness – in terms of letting go of wanting the practice to achieve anything in particular; a popular misunderstanding of mindfulness practice is that it is about concentration and attainment! Remind participants there is no goal – no right or wrong way to practice – it is simply about developing awareness. *Any* object arising in the mind can be a means to grow awareness. This is the task!

Noticing aversion and how to safely approach unwanted experience

This is a key attitudinal skill which helps develop participants' ability to decentre. Once they become aware of unwanted experience – ranging from boredom to pain, to contracted thoughts and emotions, we can offer guidance to approach it safely as felt-body sensations so as to limit unhelpful proliferation of thoughts *about* the unwanted experience. The breath can be directed – metaphorically – towards these sensations to 'flow alongside' or 'around and through' so as to 'hold it in kindly awareness' – i.e. acknowledging and allowing. This noticing is already a shift in perspective that offers greater choice about what happens next, and allows participants to let go of tendencies to go numb, fight or fret about what has arisen; perhaps saying "it's okay to have this feeling" – whatever it is. It is about learning acceptance.

4
The body scan practice

The body is happy (like any other living being) when we pay kindly attention to it.
(Ajahn Sumedho)

The body scan is the first formal mindfulness practice of the eight-week course, and extends the theme of paying attention to sensations (which is first introduced in the raisin meditation in session 1). Mindfulness of body sensation is a foundational skill, taught in all MBPs as a basis for building mental and emotional stability, and to facilitate a safe way to work with the vulnerabilities that are rooted in over-thinking. It is taught as the formal practice in the early weeks of MBSR and MBCT, and then at the end of the course in session 8 – and in MBSR is usually a 45-minute practice.

This first formal practice invites us to experience what the definition of mindfulness offered in session 1 means: 'The awareness that arises when we pay attention in a particular way: on purpose, in the present moment and non-judgmentally' (Kabat-Zinn, 2013). It is through practicing the body scan that important but subtle distinctions between mindfulness and either concentration-focused meditation or relaxation practices are experienced and made clear to participants.

Many participants comment on how challenging the body scan practice is compared to mindful movement and sitting practices. So, why is it the first practice in most MBPs? The rationale is essentially two-fold:

- It trains the skill of paying and moving *attention* in a grounded way
- It facilitates a clear, grounded means by which crucial *attitudes* can be developed through the way we pay attention.

The body scan practice overtly seems like a body awareness practice but it is much, much, more than this: it is a training in how to relate with more skill and kindness to ourselves, and by extension, to our world and those in it. Keep the core principles of the formal practices outlined above in mind and refer back to them when reading the section below, where we draw out the specific intentions and teaching considerations.

LEARNING INTENTIONS – THE BODY SCAN

A key intention of the body scan practice is to bring awareness and gentle inquiry to the sensations directly felt as the participant focuses attention on one part of the body after another. This explicitly trains attention and, just as significantly, cultivates the attitudes essential to mindfulness. In the body scan, the attitudes of non-judging, non-striving, allowing, and letting be are explicitly and implicitly foregrounded. The body scan teaches a way to shift from modes of 'thinking-doing' to a mode of 'sensing-being' and illustrates how we often judge ourselves harshly for loosing attention, which can lead to unhelpful inner dialogue and rumination. Instead, we learn to acknowledge where our attention has wandered to, and then bring it back gently and clearly to relate mindfully to whatever our experience is. Over time, the body scan helps to develop awareness of how the experience of the body changes moment-by-moment. It allows participants to sense 'where' and 'how' rather than becoming stuck in the default of 'why'. We are training to notice '*where* do I feel frustration in my body and *how* is it felt'. This way, participants can allow related thoughts and emotions to pass without additional rumination. It shows us that *how* we handle difficulties that arise during practice (sleepiness, discomfort etc.) is what makes the difference. Thus, the body scan begins the important work of being able to deconstruct complex experiences (i.e. sensations, thoughts, and feelings), and to learn to relate to them more objectively and safely.

The body scan practice illustrates how over-identification with our body image can lead to self-criticism; being connected to the direct experience of sensation can help us 'feel more at home in our body'. It can help integration, and give rise to an experience of wholeness and well-being. Participants may experience integration in many ways – from sensations of lightness, or even 'transparency', to sensations of pleasant heaviness. In addition, participants may experience how observing and letting go of thoughts/emotions associated with a particular body part can encourage the muscles to begin to release chronic tension.

A unique aspect of the body scan is that participants are invited to imagine they can breathe into parts of the body. This aspect has a number of learning intentions. The breath can act as a vehicle for directing and maintaining attention in the body. Developing the skill to imagine directing the breath into regions of the body prepares participants for using this when working with difficult thoughts and emotions later in the course. Breathing *into* a place of difficulty can help participants who suffer from pain to learn to 'move through' the area of maximum intensity without 'drowning or blocking' (Burch, 2010). More generally, many participants enjoy this aspect of the body scan, as it can be felt as a 'nurturing' in-breath and a 'letting go' out-breath. Then, in the final phase of the body scan, participants are invited to breathe into the 'whole body', which may become a metaphor for, or lead to a felt sense of, wholeness and integration itself.

TEACHING THE BODY SCAN: GENERAL CONSIDERATIONS

Setting up the body scan

As this is the first long formal practice, how the teacher sets-up the body scan conveys a strong message about the nature of the course and mindfulness itself. Participants will notice the presence – or absence – of important themes woven into the introduction such as 'invitation' and 'choice'. Hence, offering choices to lie down or sit up, and getting blankets or cushions for comfort become much more than postural guidance. Implicit self-care and self-compassion can be communicated in a grounded way by the teacher's actions and words.

The physical space – an opportunity for subtly conveying the theme of care

- Check the size of the room with people lying down in mind – participants need some personal space around them
- Providing, and/or asking participants to bring blankets or covers helps participants feel less exposed, as well as keeping warm. Provide mats, or ask participants to bring them, especially if the floor is hard or uncarpeted. Be prepared to clean the floor if necessary!
- If the room is too warm, people are more likely to fall asleep – opening windows can help, though may increase noise levels
- If teaching online, these considerations need to be built into the guidance for participants on how they prepare their space.

Posture – an opportunity to convey grounded self-compassion

- The body scan posture resembles the start or end of a yoga or relaxation class and so it is important to clearly name the intention of the lying down posture. The intention underpinning this posture is to physically support moving into 'being mode'. Also, as opposed to a yoga class, where specific instructions to place the "hands palm upwards at the sides of the body" are given in order to open the shoulder, in the body scan, encourage participants to place the hands and arms in whatever way allows most comfort; another opportunity for discovery and choice!
- Before starting to teach the body scan offer various choices of posture with brief rationales for each: lying down may help with 'letting go' and 'letting be'; astronaut position (lying with the back on the floor with the lower legs up and resting on a chair which has been drawn in close to the buttocks), or lying with the feet flat on the floor with knees pointing up towards the ceiling may help with specific pain issues; whereas sitting up may be better in office workplace contexts, for those with a history of trauma, or for people with mobility issues.
- Despite encouragement to 'fall awake' in the body scan, some people are likely to fall asleep; you could suggest that those likely to sleep have their feet flat on the floor and the knees raised, or a forearm raised vertically. Encourage a non-judgemental attitude towards sleepiness – if it arises, it is simply what is arising.

Safety – operationalising ground rules outlined in the orientation session

- If you are teaching alone, we recommend that you sit up while guiding to ensure you are able to see what is going on in the room. However, this is not a rule – discern what feels most appropriate and supportive. If you normally close your eyes when guiding, remember to glance around at participants every few minutes, listen out for signs of restlessness and visually check participants who may be fidgeting. Such observations can helpfully inform the guidance, demonstrating aliveness and responsiveness as well as simple empathy. If you wish to guide from a lying down posture yourself – i.e. from a physically embodied posture – you may need an assistant who is able to see and interact with anyone getting into difficulty. If you have an assistant, train them to know potential signs of distress to look for and what to do about this (Chapter 23).

Simultaneously, it is also important not to be overly vigilant or cautious, which can cause participants to worry, so keep a light touch to your awareness of the group during the practice and balance vigilance with skilful awareness. How you orient at this early point in the course will depend a lot on your knowledge of the participants particular vulnerabilities that you will have attuned to during the assessment process.

- Some participants may have distress associated with areas of their bodies, from disability, chronic pain, or experience of abuse or other trauma, so bringing attention to the body may be triggering (refer to Chapter 23 on trauma and safety for more information about this). Also, reassure participants it is fine to sit rather than lie down, to move during the practice, to leave eyes open rather than closed, and overall to prioritise making choices to take care of themselves (which may include not following the guidance).
- Offer reminders about what participants can do if they wish to move during a practice. Establish an anchor point at the start of the practice and remind participants they can come back to this if they need too, or if they get 'lost' in the practice. They can then re-join and follow the body scan when they are ready.

Guiding the body scan practice

Here are some guidelines around how to guide the body scan practice, remember that these build on the core principles on attitude, attention, and decentring outlined earlier. A detailed account of delivery considerations can be found in Chapter 15 where session 1 of a typical eight-week course is outlined.

 Summary of guiding considerations – body scan

1. Skilful use of language
2. Clear structure for the practice
3. Moving attention: wide and narrow focus
4. Normalising what may well be occurring in the practice
5. Using the breath as an anchor and a *vehicle* for moving and sustaining attention
6. Conveying attitudinal foundations
7. Giving guidance on working with difficulty

---

1. Skilful use of language

- Invite particular attention to the detail of body sensations, using words describing sensations such as warm, cold, tingling, numbness, texture of clothing etc. Detail creates interest – and interest is the basis of sustained attention, encouraging attentional resources to be taken up with the fullness of the experience, which may naturally reduce wandering thoughts.
- It can be helpful to use words belonging to different senses, as participants have different ways of experiencing sensations – such as 'feeling the toe', 'the shape of the toe', 'listening to the whispering of the toes'. Some words are general across all of the senses and can be used often, such as noticing, experiencing, sensing.

2. Clear structure for the practice

- Start and end the practice by bringing attention to the whole body. At the start this establishes a secure sense of the body held by ground beneath. At the end we can offer a helpful emphasis on feeling whole, and simply "allowing ourselves to be just as we are"
- Offer a systematic, clear progression through the body parts -from the left big toe all the way up to the top of the head. The rationale for starting at the toes is that it is the place furthest from the head and 'thinking', but it also offers a narrow angle focus (i.e. the toe) modelling *how* to pay attention to detail which can then be applied to the rest of the practice
- Be clear in inviting participants to *let go* of the last body region before moving awareness to the next. The capacity to let go and reengage attention is an important foundational skill. This can be synchronized with the breath, for example "as you next breathe out, letting go of the left knee ....and moving your attention upwards to the thigh".

3. Wide and narrow focus of attention and moving attention

- In the first part of the body scan practice, pay particular and detailed attention to body sensations – e.g. "the big toe of the left foot ... its nail ... the coolness, perhaps between it and the next toe". This communicates what is being asked for, and enables participants to know what to do, which allows you to guide more spaciously, with periods of short silences, later in the practice.
- At times guide attention in a focused, small area of the body such as the toes, and at other times open up to a wide awareness of a region – e.g. "the whole length and weight of the legs". This ability to narrow our focus and see detail, and widen to a broader perspective is another foundational skill.

4. Normalising what may be occurring in the practice

- Early on in the practice (within first five – ten minutes), offer guidance to recognise and normalise participant's wandering thoughts, boredom, restlessness etc., and repeat this regularly.

5. Using the breath as an anchor and as a vehicle for moving and sustaining attention

- Early in the body scan give participants the option to come back to the breath or other chosen anchor, at any time to stabilise attention – remind them of this regularly during the practice.
- Offer suggestions of breathing into regions of the body as an invitation, for example, "playing with a possibility" rather than an instruction. Remember that some participants may find metaphorical guidance unhelpful, so offer suitable additions such as: "bringing awareness to the length and weight of the legs as we breathe in ... as we breathe out".

6. Conveying attitudinal foundations

- Balance the guidance by inviting a flavour of open receptivity (e.g. letting be, allowing, and accepting), alongside guidance that invites active participation (e.g. exploring, curiosity, aliveness, and adventure).

- Offer guidance which invites participants to move into a direct and if possible, a kindly 'being with' body sensations rather than looking at them coolly from a distance.
- Ensure the guidance includes clear reminders to stop the practice if this feels the right thing to do, or to not follow the guidance, feeling free to self-guide in a way that feels safe and appropriate.

7. Giving guidance on working with difficulty

- Offer choices about working with or being with pain or discomfort in the body. Remember that at the early stage of the course, participants do not have the foundational mindfulness skills to safely move proactively towards difficulty – so the emphasis is on acknowledging experience and on self-care. For example, "if pain or discomfort is arising remember to take good care of yourself ... gently acknowledging the experience, and then with kindness bringing the attention back; and feeling free at any time to shift posture, to move the body with awareness, sensing the impact of the movement as it is happening".
- Using the opportunity that discomfort can offer to demonstrate how we can bring self-care and compassion into our body, and by extension to our lives.
- Consider making particular reference to discomfort in the areas of the body that often 'store' tension and so pain – i.e. lower back, neck etc.

SUMMARY

The body scan is a highly significant and rich practice. It helps build the foundations for all the subsequent practices and exercises. Attentional skills and essential attitudes are developed in a moment-by-moment grounded way. The awareness that arises when we do this has the potential to transform habitual ways of relating to ourselves that limit our potential or cause us harm.

5
Mindful movement

Movement practices formally make their entrance in week three of the eight-week programme. Though it is recommended that the teacher guide short movement practices from the beginning and throughout the course, particularly in transitional moments to shift energy in the group within the session, or as a prelude to sitting practices. In MBSR session three, participants are guided through a lying down yoga-informed practice (40–45mins) and in session four, a standing yoga-informed movement practice (30 mins). In session three of MBCT, participants are invited to use a lying down yoga-informed practice as part of the home practice for the following week and in class are guided in a "stretch and breathe" practice that uses some standing yoga postures followed by a sitting meditation. Yoga-informed movement practice is assigned for home practice, alternating with the body scan. In addition, in both curriculums, walking meditation practices also often form part of sessions three and four.

Before moving on, it is important to be clear what mindful movement practice is not. It is not yoga, at least not as this physical discipline is traditionally delivered. Rather, it uses some of the simpler forms of yoga-based movements as a means to develop mindful awareness of moment-to-moment experience. "As we carefully move up to our limits in a stretch … we practice breathing at that limit, dwelling in the creative space between not challenging the body at all and pushing it too far" (Kabat-Zinn, 2013, p. 101).

The introduction of mindful movement coming after the body scan is an evolution. The evolution consists of foregrounding body sensations arising from movement rather than stillness. As such mindful movement can be viewed as a 'body scan in motion' where "The focus is on maintaining moment-to-moment awareness of the sensations accompanying our movements" (Segal et al., 2013, p. 240).

It is particularly important with mindful movement to have experience in the practice you are basing your teaching on, thus it is important that mindful movement is part of your regular personal practice. Firstly, this is because participants could sustain physical damage from being taught postures or movements incorrectly and, secondly it is important to teach with confidence and authenticity. It may be helpful to take additional training that supports you to build confidence in guiding mindful movement. Bear in mind that you may be introducing the participants to a physical discipline that they may well continue with through their entire life. This perspective may change the way we teach in session 3!

Much of this section relates to all forms of mindful movement (i.e. Yoga-based or Chi Kung-based and walking practice). However, there is a predominance of emphasis in MBSR and MBCT on movements drawn from hatha yoga, as this embodies a gentle, accepting but determined persistence in working with physical intensity and boundaries. If another movement approach is used it is important to ascertain if it meets all the required 'learning intentions' just as well as a yoga-based approach. The core principles of the formal practices (attention, attitude, reperceiving) outlined at the start of this section are fundamental to mindful movement. As you read the specific learning intentions and teaching considerations related to mindful movement, keep in mind these general principles.

WHY IS MINDFUL MOVEMENT INTRODUCED IN SESSION THREE?

It is common for many participants to find paying attention to the body in movement much easier than during the stillness of the body scan. This is frequently a very fruitful mindful movement inquiry theme; participants may ask – why don't we start with the mindful movement practice from session one? Although it is important to resist a 'fix-it' answer, there are several reasons for this to bear in mind because they point to the underlying intentions of this practice:

- First, if mindful movement practices were introduced before firmly establishing the basic foundation of paying attention to simply 'what is'- i.e. with no additional goal attached – it would be understandable for participants to assume its aims are more akin to those of yoga (such as flexibility and strength), and miss the fundamental intention of developing awareness. Without the attitudinal foundations offered by the body scan ('letting things be' and acceptance – 'opening to our experience, just as it is') – the subtleties of the intention of mindful movement can easily be lost. The attitude and skill of receptivity (non-striving/being) is an essential foundation.
- Second, because movement can create stronger, more apparent sensations, having a frequent body scan practice for a couple of weeks helps cultivate the necessary receptivity and sensitivity to the more subtle end of the spectrum of sensations, including the absence of sensations.
- Third, mindful movement invites participants to practice in visual relationship to each other, which can feel physically exposing. Previous practices (i.e. the raisin exercise, body scan, and shorter breath meditations) are practiced lying down or seated, often with eyes lowered or closed. Up to this point the main formal practice has not required any obvious visual comparison. This new group experience creates new learning opportunities and challenges for participants, as some may compare themselves negatively to others in the group, or feel compelled to quietly demonstrate to the group how flexible they are. By session three there is hopefully sufficient safety in the group to allow these comparisons to be held in awareness. This can elicit learning about the attitudinal foundations of non-striving and non-judgement. One of the main learning outcomes of mindful movement practice is to notice striving and the layers of judgment that can orbit this striving.
- Fourth, for vulnerable participants it is absolutely crucial before being led in mindful movement to have begun to embody the 'invitational' stance introduced by the teacher, and to feel comfortable exploring *not* taking part in some aspects of mindful movement. This began with the raisin exercise – i.e. the invitation to not participate or not eat – and becomes fully developed in the body scan and indeed in every aspect of inquiry over the first two – three weeks.

Mindful movement: learning intentions

Mindful movement can help participants learn to experience sensations directly from the 'inside'. This enables them to become more anchored, in here-and-now sensations within the body, allowing a greater sense of 'who we really are' in the present moment. Note: remember to refer back to the start of the chapter for *core intentions* around attention, attitude, and decentering which are central to mindful movement and are to be used in conjunction with the information here. The specific learning intentions for mindful movement are as follows.

Movement practices offer the invitation to work with physical boundaries in a particular way

1 *Honouring and respecting the boundary* of what is ok for our body in each moment. Discovering how the edge of our comfort zone actually feels and how boundaries move and shift over time and from day to day without the application of 'trying'.
2 *Discovering the actuality of these boundaries* using moment-by-moment awareness of direct sensations to discover these – rather than any perceptions, thoughts and feelings about them; dwelling at the edges of what feels ok in each moment.
3 *Working with acceptance* of the experience of our limits in each moment. This prepares participants to later explore working with difficult thoughts and emotions in a similar way: the 'felt' experience of working with the 'edges' of physical sensation offers an experience of what may also be possible within emotional and cognitive experience. Participants can thus begin to open to the possibility of moving in close to emotional intensity in the same accepting, present-centred way that is encouraged in relation to movement in the movement practices.

A felt experience of working with processes within the movement practices can offer parallels and insights into personal habits in daily life

1 *Balancing postures* – experiencing how balance does not happen through staying still, but through constantly wobbling and recovering oneself; we discover there is no end to the number of times we can wobble out of a posture, and simply start again
2 *Transitions* – the phases in the practice between moving from lying to sitting, standing to lying offer the possibility of developing awareness of being in the present *alongside* a future intention. Many times in daily life, we lose awareness of the present because we are focused on where we are heading rather than the process of getting there.
3 *Seeing the effects of 'trying' too hard* – experiencing how often we tense up parts of our body that are not actually engaged in what we are doing in the present moment; and how over time this can become habitual and entrenched. Conversely, we may discover habit patterns relating to non-engagement and passivity.
4 *Seeing 'doing mind' in action* – it is easy to engage with this more active form of practice with a 'doing mode of mind', wanting to achieve certain things, hold postures a certain length of time, be competitive with ourselves and others; striving is experienced at a concrete level and so more readily observed and worked *with* as a mind state.
5 *The group context* brings awareness to how we relate to our body and its movements in terms of comparisons/judgements. Thus, mindful movement practice can offer

a bridge between practice experience and daily life by creating a felt experience of judgements and comparisons in the body.

6 *The link between body and mind* – mindful movement can help participants make the link between how positioning our body in certain ways can have immediate effects on one's mental and emotional state. For example: standing upright, taking our full height in 'mountain posture', can offer a felt experience of holding one's own and of approaching life with a sense of inner dignity, respect and of feeling empowered. Whereas, 'child posture', in which participants kneel down and gently lower the upper body onto the thighs, can offer a felt experience of quietening the mind, resting and protecting oneself.

Participants working with chronic illness and physical difficulty

It is important to note that for participants working with chronic illness and physical difficulty, becoming aware of their boundaries or any limitations in this way can be a means of disentangling their physical limitations from the emotions connected with them. In this way a moment-by-moment openness and responsiveness to experience is cultivated, rather than remaining fixed in preconceptions of what may or may not be possible in any moment. Increased awareness can bring a recognition of the changing and fluctuating nature of pain and so builds capacities in allowing here-and-now experience. This can allow participants to loosen any identification with pain or illness. This is tender work. Safety remains paramount and is ensured by 'knowing your craft' which means seeking additional advice and/or training when working with participants with acute or chronic conditions. Bodywork can stir deeply hidden hurts and habits, and great care needs to be exercised throughout the guidance and the following inquiry.

Mindful movement teaching considerations

 Key teaching points

1. **Safety:** ensure that participants engage in practices in a way that is safe and respectful to their body
2. **Clarity:** ensure guidance is given in ways which is aligned to the core intention of movement practices in MBPs, and invites detailed awareness of the moment-by-moment experience
3. **Attitude:** ensure the guidance is invitational, and reflects the seven attitudinal foundations

1. Safety

- Before starting the practice: Encourage participants who know they have a particular health challenge to receive guidance from their doctor/physiotherapist before starting the course. Note that some illnesses/limitations require particular care, for example, not bending forward fast or taking the upper body past right angles to the lower body if there are problems with blood pressure or the heart etc.; not doing stretches if there is an inflammatory condition of the joints or muscles; if pregnant, generally twists and forward bends need to be adapted or deleted and in the last months, all stretching has to be done with great caution – seek expert advice if you have a participant who is pregnant during the course. Some areas such as the neck require care for everyone – tipping the head backwards can, over time, result in harm. All of the above should be ascertained in the orientation and assessment phase of the course (Chapter 16). It is important to check these issues out before the course starts so as not to have to ask such questions in the public space.

- Check the physical space for hazards, warmth, privacy and ventilation, ensure that you have enough mats for everyone.
- Clear choices: Give clear and precise guidance on ways of working with physical boundaries at the beginning of the practice, such as "If you have any injuries or if a posture isn't right for your body, making choices within the practice to take care of yourself, which may include not doing a particular movement".
- Empowerment: Encourage participants to err on the side of caution and to listen to the wisdom of their own body and allow this to override any guidance you give. Underline that it is okay not to do a posture or movement – perhaps say that they could visualise doing it.
- Respect: Take care not to touch participants unless permission is explicitly requested, and even then, it is not advisable and not necessary as we can make mirrored demonstrations of the areas and directions we wish to draw attention to.
- Group pressure: Even when reminded to take care, many people will follow whatever they are told to do by the teacher, therefore give frequent reminders about working within safe limits for "your body today".
- Normalise guidance on adaptations of postures or movements: Incorporate adaptations into the guidance (it is helpful to plan adaptations beforehand). For example, if the cat/cow posture is challenging on all fours, an alternative could be participants sitting on the knees or cross legged on a lift and moving the spine in a similar way to the cat/cow posture.
- Timing: Give reminders to hold postures/movements only for as long as feels okay. If guiding movement coordinated with breathing, take care not to imply holding a posture or the breath longer than is comfortable.
- Striving foregrounded: Frequently remind participants to notice if they are being competitive with themselves or others; that mindful movement is a practice designed to develop awareness and not intended for developing strength, agility, flexibility etc.
- Breathing: It is helpful to encourage participants to breathe fully and freely in whatever way feels most natural to them, especially when 'holding' a posture, as people can also habitually hold their breath at the same time.

2. *Clarity*

- Detail and discovery: Help participants cultivate a sense of discovery, exploration and curiosity through guidance that gives attention to specific detail that may be happening – e.g. "sensing the weight of the arms" or "small movements in the feet standing here". Be guided by what is happening in your own body whilst teaching. Also use open questions such as: "what can be sensed in the legs right now?"
- Time to notice details: Give plenty of space within the practice so, remember to hold the postures or movements long enough to allow awareness to grow, and pause in between postures to enable time for the effects of the movement to be sensed.

3. *Attitude*

- Balancing receptivity and activity: encourage participants to explore and discover the creative edge between exploring/ discovering, and accepting/ being with experience just as it is.
- Language and tone are crucial: avoid language or tone which might feed into a sense of striving: words such as "trying", "working", "see if you can ... ?"

SUMMARY

As with the body scan, mindful movement offers vast, although often quite subtle opportunities for training attention and cultivating helpful attitudes. If guiding this practice without a formal training in the approach being used, it can be especially important to attend classes for yourself in the approach, and support your development through supervision and engagement with the TLC (Chapter 19).

6
The sitting meditations

Sitting practice makes a gradual entrance into the eight-week MBP curriculum, and is first introduced, as a longer, formal practice, in session four in MBSR and session three in MBCT. The sitting practice is introduced in a way that builds upon the foundation of skills and attitudes participants have developed via the body scan and mindful movement. Over the eight-week curriculum, the sitting practice further becomes a vehicle for operationalising the key themes of each session, enabling participants to work with specific and/or general vulnerabilities (see Crane, 2017, for more details), and building helpful attitudes and resilience. Box 6.1 below illustrates how the building blocks are gradually put in place in MBSR by expanding the length of the practice and the range of objects of focus. The principles are similar for MBCT with some minor differences of emphasis (i.e. more explicit working with thoughts and with difficulty).

Box 6.1 MBSR sitting meditation: progression over the eight-week course

Session 2: Brief sitting meditation (5–10 minutes): introduce sitting meditation with awareness of breathing as primary object of attention – or alternative attentional anchor.

Session 3: Longer sitting meditation (10–20 minutes): sitting meditation with awareness of posture and breathing as primary object of attention – or an alternative attentional anchor.

Session 4: Sitting meditation (at least 20 minutes): with focus on breath, body sensations and whole body; introduction of guidance on ways of working with difficult or unwanted physical sensations which may be present in experience.

Session 5: Sitting meditation (45 minutes): attending to breath, body, sounds, then thoughts and emotions as events in the mind; then inviting an open-awareness.

Session 6: Sitting meditation as per session 5, but with fewer instructions/more silence (45 minutes): breath, body, sounds, thoughts and emotions, then inviting open-awareness/open-presence; return to breath at the end.

Session 7: Sitting meditation with more silence (45 minutes): open-awareness practice, using the breath as an anchor if lost; also possible to include aspects of Mountain or Lake meditation; more silence.

A typical sitting practice seeks to cultivate awareness using a particular *sequence* of 'objects' of attention. This sequence moves from the more concrete objects of posture and sensation-based anchors such as the breath, to more abstract objects in the mind – sounds, thoughts, and emotions. Having traversed these progressively subtler objects of attention, sitting practice finally arrives at a 'choiceless' or 'open' awareness. 'Open' is perhaps more accurate because there *is* a *choice* in choosing to develop and maintain a 'choice-less' awareness!

It is said that 'close enemies' are the most dangerous – it is important to emphasise that mindfulness-based sitting practices have differing intentions to concentration-based practices. Both use the same posture and both may use similar objects of attention such 'breath and/or body'. In a mindfulness sitting practice, focus is directed towards a suitable sense-based anchor such as the breath. This builds sufficient stability and calm to be able to *meet* or *know* our experience more generally, just as it is, so as to more deeply understand our inner patterning. Mindfulness prioritises training in relating to whatever is arising in the mind-body in particular ways. In *concentration* practices the emphasis is to develop calm, peaceful states. Put metaphorically, mindfulness is about finding peace *within* the storm, whilst concentration practices are about becoming gradually storm-free. It is very possible that in any group you teach there will be several participants with previous experience of meditation and it is important to sensitively, and without implying one approach is better than the other, clarify the particular differences of intention between these two approaches to sitting practice (meeting our experience 'just as it is' as distinct from developing calm states).

The next section gives an overview of intentions common to all MBP sitting practices and then briefly summarises how specific intentions may be linked to particular formats. The common and more specific learning intentions are intrinsically interrelated, but it is helpful to track the evolution of the learning intentions in the sitting practices and note how this maps onto the developing themes of the curriculum. For example, in MBCT session 4 guidance about noticing thoughts as passing events in the mind supports various other exercises focused on noticing, decentring, and working with unhelpful and stress inducing thoughts in sessions 5 and 6. In session 7, the emphasis in the sitting practice on self-compassion and self-care supports the subsequent exercises about lifestyle choices and the impact of actions on mood. The sitting practice is anchored firmly into the general principals of practices explored earlier in Part I; ensure you are familiar with and include these core principles in awareness as you read the next section.

LEARNING INTENTIONS: SITTING PRACTICE

- *Familiarity with 'the play of the mind'*: Knowing how to work skilfully with the natural tendencies of the mind is a key learning intention, and participants are invited to develop *stability of mind* rather than concentration for its own sake. Because of this core intention, the instructions to "come back to the breath" … or "to the anchor in the body" are given in a way that allows participants to first become aware of what 'the mind' *is* doing – wandering, sleeping, planning, re-playing and other common and natural forms of 'habit mind'. The key is to cultivate an orientation that this is part of the practice, rather than a mistake. Participants also learn the difference between unintentional drifting and intentional clear seeing of the flux of moment-to-moment experience. Feeling stuck is a common source of distress, so sensing the flow and change of ordinary experience during a sitting practice (breath sensations, sounds, thoughts and emotions) can be a very helpful, implicit message conveyed via the guidance. The ultimate intention is to develop and maintain awareness of all our experience including this 'play of the mind'. This enables participants to see more deeply into the nature and patterning of human experience and life: the intention is for this skill to be underpinning all mindfulness practice because clear seeing into the 'way things are', whilst often challenging, is ultimately a doorway to greater sense of integration, freedom and well-being.

- *Noticing aversion and how to safely approach unwanted experience*: Learning about the 'play of the mind' is a fundamental skill as it enables participants to recognise their recurring patterns, in particular, aversion to unpleasant experiences. Once aware of unwanted experience (e.g. boredom, pain, contracted thoughts and emotions), participants can explore how to approach them safely as *body-felt sensations* so as to limit unhelpful proliferation of thoughts *about* them.
- *Use of the breath*: The breath can be directed – metaphorically- towards difficult sensations to "flow alongside" or "around and through" so as to hold them in kindly awareness.

SITTING PRACTICES: A SUMMARY OF TEACHING CONSIDERATIONS

Note that the sitting practices generally go through various stages, from a grounded start (body), with some then moving to less tangible aspects of experience (sound, thoughts). Below is a general guide to each stage, which can be used to support teaching – be aware of the particular curriculum you are offering, and align the form of the practice and your guidance to this. An important consideration concerns the use of the breath as *the anchor* in sitting meditations. As is discussed in the chapter about trauma sensitivity (Chapter 23), the breath may not be suitable for all participants. Past trauma or problems with breathing may make another sense-based anchor (e.g. hands, feet, sounds, sights etc.) more suitable. The breath is an incredibly helpful anchor for many because of its natural dynamic-movement quality, but it is important not to make the assumption that it is suitable for all. So when guiding participants remember to help them choose a suitable *anchor* with examples other than the breath. Box 6.2 offers the general order of presentation, but some practices may miss out or emphasise some stages.

Box 6.2 Sitting practice

1 Mindfulness of posture

a) Set up the posture; grounding – the felt sense in the present moment through body sensations

b) Learn how posture can supportively influence attitude, mood and energy

2 Mindfulness of breath or an alternative anchor

a) Cultivating present moment awareness and stability via a simple and specific real-time focus on sensation – reducing thought proliferation

3 Guiding awareness of the 'wider body'

a) Noticing aversion and learning responsive choice and the possibility of acceptance in relation to pain, tensions etc.

> b) Building a foundation (for later) relating to difficult thoughts and emotions *within* the body. Learning more subtle connections between the body and mind activity
>
> **4 Guiding mindfulness of sounds**
>
> a) Learning to give attention to a subtle sensation that can seem less physical, more ethereal.
> b) Learning the skill of simply receiving experience rather than trying to make sense of it.
>
> **5 Guiding the 'mindfulness of thoughts and emotions' practice**
>
> a) Relating to thoughts as events passing in the mind rather than as defining facts (much as we did with sounds; decentering/reperceiving)
> b) Relating emotions and thoughts to physical sensation
>
> **6 Guiding 'Open Awareness' (choiceless awareness)**
>
> a) Developing a spacious, non-doing, quality of inhabiting the mind-body
> b) Offers a bridge between practice and daily life

1. Mindfulness of posture

Set up the posture; grounding – the present moment, felt sense of the body: Begin the practice with practical information about how to set up a supportive posture. In the earlier sessions this guidance can be rich in detail and attitudinal emphasis. For example, "inviting a comfortable, upright posture ... the height of the body rising gently upwards ... the head balancing on top ... with the chin tilted slightly towards the chest so that the back of the neck is long and open ... hands supported on the legs or lap so the shoulders can be at ease". Convey that no sitting position is better than any other: encourage participants to experiment with different sitting options and remind them that standing and lying down are also options. It is helpful to demonstrate how to use a meditation stool or cushion the first time they are offered as options, with tips around what might be a comfortable posture (such as ensuring the knees are below the hips, padding for the knees etc.). If sitting on a chair, generally encourage the spine to be self-supporting, away from the back of the chair, or, if this seems too much of a strain, support just the very lowest part of the back with a cushion. Remember that what *we do* as the teacher may be interpreted as the best posture to use. So, if anyone is likely to be uncomfortable using stools or cushions, make sure you, as teacher, use a chair for as many sessions as it takes for the group to be able to make independent choices. Offer early guidance to normalise discomfort or strangeness linked to sitting in what may be an unusually upright posture for some, whilst also offering suggestions to find ease. Also offer guidance to make informed choice about the eyes, leaving them open or closed is a real choice. If eyes are open, invite participants to rest their gaze softly on a neutral place a short distance in front of them.

Learn how posture can supportively influence attitude, mood and energy: A deliberate upright posture offers support for the broader intention to be awake and sensitive to all experience. Inviting the body to a posture which is both upright and relaxed offers a 'felt sense' of an embodiment of the attitudinal foundations (e.g. acceptance, non-striving etc.) that are being cultivated. Help participants make parallels between posture and supportive qualities – such as an upright spine and alertness. Occasionally bring participants' awareness back to their posture throughout the practice: in particular inviting participants to notice how a slump in posture can often indicate a slump in awareness!

2. Mindfulness of breath or an alternative anchor

In this stage of the practice, participants are invited to anchor their attention to a specific sense-based part of their experience, such as the breath, part of the body (e.g. the feet or hands), or if these don't work for a participant-sounds or a specific visual focus can offer an external anchor. The focus on breath is helpful to many because it *changes* moment-by-moment and – for most people – gives the mind a helpful (i.e. dynamic) sense-based anchor point. The key point when leading this practice is to offer detailed guidance on the breath, whilst also giving open options for people for whom the breath is not a helpful anchor point. Points to bear in mind:

> *Cultivating present moment awareness and stability via a real-time focus on sensation*: From the relative stillness of the posture, give participants options to find their own stable anchor point, and then invite them to discover the small movement sensations arising within the anchor. Note that observing the repetitive physical act of breathing, or sensations in the feet can lead to disengagement and vagueness, quickly filled by mind wandering, so it is helpful to guide an exploration of the chosen anchor point offering *tentative* suggestions to help recognise these sensations – e.g. "the rising and falling of the abdomen" or "the sense of weight and firm pressure in the thighs and buttocks". The use of tonal questions support discovery of, and curiosity towards different dimensions of the experience; discovery supports attention. Offer guidance to encourage steady attention to the anchor as this can lead to a sense of calm as thinking slows and quietens; allow enough spaciousness in the guidance to encourage settling and steadiness – at the same time briefly acknowledge and normalise any unsettled states that may also be present.

> *Encouraging curiosity by inviting attention to detail*: Noticing the minute *detail* and *variations*, moment-by-moment, within the anchor. If participants are with the breath they may automatically try to control the breathing – it is worth bringing attention to this possibility and offering guidance to let the breath "breathe itself". Explore different dimensions of the in and the out breath: i.e. to help participants settle: "noticing perhaps the *duration* of the breath is it ... long ... short?" or "the location where sensations are clearest".

3. Guiding awareness of the 'wider body'

In this stage of the practice, participants are invited to open out from the focus on the anchor to a wider attention to the body as a whole, with its range of sensations and 'feeling-tones'. This helps participants learn how to consciously broaden and narrow attention and bring helpful attitudinal foundations to the fore. Awareness of 'feeling-tone' and learning how not to habitually react to unpleasant and pleasant experience, is a crucial foundational skill. This stage of the sitting meditation augments the various exercises designed to develop this skill. Thus, in sessions 3 and 4, the work on pleasant and unpleasant events augments the guidance to notice areas of physical challenge and to offer them kindly awareness: "not to change or fix but, breathing alongside them to hold them gently in awareness". In session 4 of MBSR, the guidance goes on to suggest we can take a similar approach to difficult emotions and thoughts; in session 5 of MBCT this work is made more explicit by deliberately bringing a difficulty to mind during the practice. Skilful guiding includes:

Noticing aversion and learning responsive choice and the possibility of acceptance in relation to pain, tensions etc. Through tone of voice and invitational language we can invite participants to gently become aware of difficult experience – pain, tension, dullness etc. – as it arises; then, offer guidance on *how* participants might choose to approach this experience, which may include:
- If participants are working with physical pain, remind them that they can mindfully change posture, noticing the intention to move, the movement itself, and the after-effects of the movement.
- Shifting the attention towards the difficulty as it manifests in the body, inviting kindly curiosity to the direct sensations. Offer possibilities for a gentle exploration of these sensations, such as inviting participants to explore the felt-shape and texture of the difficulty, noticing if it shifts with the breath or remains static etc.
- Offer participants options to "breathe into and out from" the place of discomfort. It can be very helpful to use the breath as a metaphor for carrying gentle attention "to hold in kindly awareness". This is a shift in perspective that offers greater choice about what happens next, and allows a letting go of tendencies to go numb, fight or fret about what has arisen.
- Remind participants they can shift attention away from the area of difficulty and focus on a stable anchor point – moving back towards the difficulty later if they are ready to do so (see also Burch, 2010).
- Cultivate an orientation of kindness and allowing: "it's okay to allow myself to feel what is here".

Building a foundation for later relating to difficult thoughts and emotions within the body. The invitation is to use attention to move into and directly sense the resonance of difficult thoughts or emotions *in the body* rather than getting entangled in more thinking about it. From session 5 onwards, participants are invited to notice difficult thoughts or emotions and to ask 'where might I feel this in my body?' This body and anchor stage of the sitting practice offers a crucial early training ground to safely approach difficulties that otherwise could be overwhelming. This learning around sensations arising in the body sets the stage for later in the course when exploring thoughts and emotions.

4. Guiding mindfulness of sounds

In this stage of the sitting practice, participants are invited to shift attention from the body and breath anchor, to the sensation of hearing sounds within and around them. Points to bear in mind include:

Learning to give and maintain attention on a subtle sensation that can seem less physical, more ethereal. Receiving and attending to sound prepares the ground for recognising and staying with the even more abstract and subtle experience of thoughts and emotions. To help participants first anchor their attention to sounds, offer guidance on noticing sounds both inside and outside the room, and to explore the experience of sound itself: "noticing the pitch, tone, volume ... or rhythm of the sounds arriving to the ear and whole body", if there is little sound happening, you could invite participants to notice "the silence between sounds".

Learning the skill of simply receiving experience rather than trying to make sense of it. During this stage of the practice, invite participants to "receive sound just as it is, noticing the sound arriving at the ears" as an experience. It can also be helpful to offer guidance to notice "just how little effort is required to notice sounds arriving to our ears". Emphasise learning to *receive* experience: directly hearing, receiving, and perceiving sounds as distinct from making mental labels or stories about it. This offers insights into our automatic tendencies to get caught up in our personal take on experience. This can be an opportunity for participants to notice how often automatic reactions occur – e.g. "I like it, give me more" or, "I hate it I can't practice with this racket going on". This learning gives a grounding for understanding the similar (though more complex ways) we perceive and react to thoughts and emotions.

5. Guiding the 'mindfulness of thoughts and emotions' practice

In this stage of the sitting practice, participants are invited to let go of paying attention to sound, and to shift attention to noticing thoughts as phenomena that "come and go", just like sounds. It can be helpful to participants if you use imagery such as "imagine you are watching your thoughts like passing clouds in the sky – notice how they appear, might stay around, and then are replaced by new thoughts". Points to bear in mind include:

Relating to thoughts just as they are, as events in the mind (decentring/reperceiving). Building on the skill developed within the mindfulness of sound practice, guidance is offered to shift the attention towards awareness of the coming and going of thoughts as events in the mind. Just as sounds arise and pass away and are not seen as 'us', so thoughts can be experienced as events in the mind. This involves standing back and seeing thoughts and emotions from the perspective of the interested kindly observer. This enables us to develop a different (decentred) and more helpful relationship to our thoughts – relating *to* them rather than *from* them. This spacious quality of mind allows perspective and reduces the power of thoughts; we can now experience them as 'just thoughts' rather than as facts, seeing and making clearer decisions about how to work with them. The attitudinal qualities are very important when exploring decentering; offer guidance on observing thoughts and emotions with interest and kindness, lightly inviting participants to notice recurring patterns in thinking and feeling, and how these develop and play out within the mind. It is not about making the thought or emotion go away, but acknowledging its presence and effects as if it were a 'weather pattern'.

Relating emotions and thoughts to physical sensations. Guide participants to recognise physical sensations arising in relationship to thoughts and emotions. If strong difficult thoughts and emotions are present, bringing attention to the body can offer a new way to meet difficult thoughts – allowing the body sensations triggered by them to be experienced and acknowledged. For example, "notice if you have been drawn into thinking, and if any physical sensations in the body are related to these, for example tension in the jaw". This allows natural changes in intensity to occur and be felt, increasing a sense of safety within an experience that may previously have been overwhelming. This is one way to 'ride the waves' of powerful internal experiences, while neither being overwhelmed by nor suppressing them. It is also important to offer guidance around safety at this stage of the practice, reminding participants they can return to their anchor point at any point during the practice, or simply pausing the practice at any time.

6. Guiding 'Open Awareness' (choiceless awareness)

In this last stage of the sitting practice, participants are invited to bring an open, non-specific awareness to whatever experience arises in the foreground of attention moment-by-moment – this could be sounds, thoughts, body sensations or emotions; essentially to have an awareness of the flux of experience. The intention in this final stage is to attend spaciously to whatever experience is unfolding moment-by-moment. It is in this rich territory of simply observing our naturally unfolding experience, that we can begin the work of truly meeting and understanding ourselves, our world, and others. In this meeting and understanding there is potential for wholeness, health, and creativity. Points to bear in mind include:

Developing a spacious, non-doing, quality of mind and body. Open-awareness practice allows participants to further recognise recurring patterns of thinking, sensing, feeling, and the sense of 'meeting ourselves as we are'. By observing recurring patterns/reactions in the mind and body participants can learn to see and experience how things shift. Regular experience of practice in this way offers the possibility of developing a wider perspective on the underlying patterns and processes which *drive* the content. In this way we can let go of tendencies to ruminate or suppress, and develop a spacious quality of mind. Remaining *open* to all experiences as they arise and pass away develops a skill of remaining spacious, and perhaps fearless, with the whole range of our human experience.

Offering a bridge between practice and daily life. Open-awareness practice has close parallels with daily life experience which is often simply a flow of changing experiences. For example, at times awareness is broadly focused on the body sitting (i.e. posture, pressure, air on skin), in another moment awareness is caught by a sound, then a stream of thoughts move to the foreground, and body sensations connected to these thoughts. We are learning to naturally notice and be with this flux in the formal practice so that we can bring greater awareness to the flux of daily life. Open-awareness practice enables participants to perceive and feel both the space within which experience arises and the experience itself. Seeing even glimpses of the ground of awareness within which all experience arises offers the potential for radically altering one's perspective.

GUIDING ALTERNATIVE SITTING PRACTICES: 'THE MOUNTAIN' PRACTICE IN MBSR

In later sessions of the eight-week curriculum, it can be helpful to lead sitting practices that use the power of symbol and metaphor more comprehensively in order to convey important skills and understandings. The mountain meditation uses a body-felt sense of being like a mountain to encourage stability that allows one to 'see' contents of the mind forming and flowing past like clouds or weather: i.e. "difficult thoughts and feelings like harsh storms surround the mountainside, but the mountain remains ... still, unmoving". It is important to understand the intention behind using the mountain in this way so as to not get lost in a visualisation or concentration practice. The fundamental intention is to help the participants feel the stability of a mountain so as to decentre from thoughts and emotions or difficult bodily sensations.

7
The short practices

Short mindfulness practices (the Three-Step Breathing Space [3SBS], the STOP practice, the pause) are taught in MBPs as a means to help participants move from doing into being mode, and to bring the skills gained from longer practices into everyday life. Short practices are taught in two main ways. First, participants are guided in short practices as part of the assigned curriculum and are also given short practices as home practices. The second is by example, such as when short practices are spontaneously used by the teacher at appropriate moments during the sessions to support participants to reconnect to their direct experience (i.e. being mode). Short practices may be movement based (mindful walking, standing yoga or Chi Kung-based stretching), or, more commonly, short sitting practices using a chosen anchor as a focus of attention.

MBCT regards the short practices, specifically the 3SBS, as a core element of the curriculum. They are used to explicitly help integrate the various session themes into practice outside the sessions. There is extensive guidance on the 3SBS in the MBCT manual (Segal et al., 2013).

In MBSR, equivalent short practices are generally a loosely structured 'pause', using a chosen anchor to encourage participants to drop into being mode or, a more structured practice based on the acronym STOP (Stop, Take a few deep breaths, Observe your experience, Proceed). Some MBSR teachers may include the basic form of the 3SBS.

THE SHORT PRACTICES: TEACHING CONSIDERATIONS

General considerations: 'what' form of short practice and 'when' to do it

Which short practice to choose

In any given moment this choice of which short practice to introduce will be influenced by the people in the group, the session in hand, and what is occurring in the group. Thus, for some groups, in early parts of the course, when the teacher wants to move the group into an experiential mode a short sitting or standing body scan (more of a body sweep) may be appropriate. Or, following the session where mindful movement has been introduced and/ or when the group seems agitated or sleepy, a brief walking practice or guided standing stretch may be a wiser choice. Often though, a simple sitting with breath or other part of the body as an anchor is a helpful choice in bringing the group to an experiential mode and/or when modelling responsivity to difficulty.

The basic safety issues and guidance principles used in the longer practices outlined earlier all apply. These are even more important to bear in mind due to the brevity of the practice because they can be easily overlooked in this time-limited practice. For example, if a short breath-based sitting practice is chosen the teacher needs to remember to mention i) the same principles of choice regarding the anchor, ii) the same sequence from grounded in posture, to other foci, iii) the same normalising guidance about mind wandering and so on. Remember that the short practice is used in a given session should not be a surprise to participants in terms of skills or understanding. Thus, it is not helpful to use it to invite working with a difficulty until this theme of working with a difficulty has been introduced in sessions 4 and 5. Therefore, if a difficulty arises in an earlier session the emphasis during a short practice might simply be to acknowledge it and use the body senses to become more grounded.

When to bring in a short practice

When to introduce a short practice is dependent on context. Helpful or appropriate moments include: transitions, energy lulls, moments of crisis or intensity – including when this largely concerns the teacher, moments to absorb new learning and of course, and the start and finish of a session. An example of when *not* to use a short practice is to control or seem to 'fix' strong emotions that have arisen in the group; before introducing a short practice at such times it is vital to explicitly acknowledge and normalise the presence of the emotions so that the suggestion to 'pause' arises non-reactively with an intention to 'allow' it to be just as it is.

8
The 'all-day' of practice

In the week following Session 6, participants are invited to a full day of guided practice held mostly within a container of silence. This is often referred to as the 'all-day' and is generally offered on the weekend to make it accessible. Comprehensive information for this all-day can be found in Segal et al. (2013 p. 332) and in the MBSR curriculum guide (Kabat-Zinn et al., 2021). Here we first outline specific learning intentions, followed by practical considerations.

Learning intentions specific to the all-day:

- To consolidate skills and deepen experience in the formal practices
- To model stepping back from the volume, pace, and complexity of everyday life
- To experience sustaining awareness over a period of time and through transitions
- To model the use of mindfulness across a variety of life situations (for example the silent lunch or the 'fast-slow' walking practice); building skills in applying mindfulness beyond the end of the course.

PRACTICAL CONSIDERATIONS

1. Preparation of participants

- At the orientation inform participants of the practical details of the all-day (date, venue etc.)
- Prepare participants before the all-day: explain what it is about, encourage questions and concerns, allay anxieties appropriately.
- Ask that they bring along their own lunch, which means they can maintain mindful awareness during lunch and not have to go out to buy some.
- If not able to attend, encourage participants to attend an alternative in the future.

2. Support and safety

- It is recommended that you have an assistant, preferably known to the group, available to go out with a participant if they need support. Tell participants about this beforehand, and at the beginning of the all-day.

- Remind participants at the beginning of the all-day that it is fine to take time out, go to the toilet etc., ask them to let you or the support person know if they are going and intend not to come back. Check if anyone needs to leave early and communicate this to the group.

3. Silence

- Decide how much silence is appropriate for the group – including during lunch, and whether this includes reducing eye contact and other non-verbal communication. Introduce the rationales for silence at the start of the day, such as to regard silence as a support to the group and the practice, rather than something imposed.
- Acknowledge the unusualness of eating together in silence. Encourage curiosity towards this experience.

4. Intentions and attitudes to encourage

- It can be helpful to guide an initial reflection and suggest they find their own intention for the day.
- Attitudes to encourage: beginner's mind, staying in the present moment-by-moment, opening to whatever experience comes with friendly curiosity, looking after ourselves, non-striving, working with edges, not avoiding, not pushing through, and bringing kindness and compassion to ourselves whatever happens. As teacher you need to be particularly permissive and invitational throughout the day.

5. Schedule and practices

- Intersperse still meditations with moving ones (participants can get stiff and painful).
- Stay flexible about the schedule – e.g. if energy in the room has dropped you can introduce a short and lively movement practice.
- Useful to do a mixture of practices that participants are familiar with, and new ones (such as mountain). All-days usually omit inquiry.
- Encourage participants to stay with their experience during transitions, when our attention is often lost. Lots of permissions and reminders about 'wandering mind'.
- Appropriate poems and stories between the practices can give a lovely depth and different perspective to the day.

6. Befriending practice

- The all-day can be a good opportunity to introduce a befriending meditation, although be aware that some participants can find this challenging. Carefully read the chapter on this in Segal et al. (2013, pp. 137–144). This practice can be sensitively adapted to be more familiar and grounded (i.e. based in the breath or other 'anchor' but with a strong 'kindness' intention throughout). As with all other practices only guide a practice you are familiar with yourself.
- Ensure all guidance is permissive and invitational throughout, and keep reminders of self- care and kindness to the fore.

7. Coming out of silence

- It is helpful to do this gradually – e.g. by inviting participants to share their experiences of the day by talking softly in pairs first, then joining with another pair, then coming into the whole group.
- Encourage participants not to talk until ready, and say it is fine to fall back into silence.
- Invite participants to share all and any experience including difficulties and delights.
- Offer guidance on taking care of self in the period following the day.
- Congratulate everyone on completing the day!

9

Inquiry

Conveying course themes
through interactive dialogue

Tell me and I forget.
Teach me and I remember.
Involve me and I learn
       (Confucian School, 300 BCE)

These succinct words from around 300 BCE aptly describe the very particular role *inquiry* plays in MBPs. True learning happens when we are involved (Kolb, 1984; Piaget & Inhelder, 1969). In MBPs, inquiry is a process designed to involve participants directly in their learning. A significant part of the MBP sessions are devoted to this interactive process of inquiry – namely:

- After a formal meditation practice
- When asking about participants' experience of home practice
- When drawing out experience during and after group exercises
- When offering didactic teaching, stories and poems in an interactive and participatory manner.

Inquiry is often a process that new MBP teachers can find particularly daunting, as it can feel quite exposing. These parts of the sessions are based on participant contributions, and are responsive to what is going on in the room, so cannot be minutely pre-planned. Segal et al. (2013) wrote: "This is the single area of teaching in which both trainees and experienced instructors are most likely to express concerns about their skills. Yet it is potentially the area in which learning can be enriched enormously" (p. 250).

Inquiry is how the teacher conveys course themes through interactive dialogue (Crane et al., 2013). How to use inquiry is described by Domain 5 of the MBI:TAC and TLC (conveying course themes through interactive inquiry and didactic teaching). Implicitly, this fundamental emphasis on learning through active participation is supported by qualities described by other MBI:TAC domains. In Domain 2 for example the 'relational stance' carefully avoids an unhelpful expert-novice dynamic; in Domain 6 the group is carefully cultivated to form a collegial learning container with the teacher sitting in the circle, alongside the participants.

Course themes are sometimes explicitly drawn out by the teacher, and at other times emerge implicitly. This exploratory way of approaching experience illuminates the habitual tendencies and patterns of the human mind and offers a way of investigating and working with experience that can become a lifelong support. In particular, participants' difficulties (e.g., avoidance, distress, emotional reactivity) in sessions are crucial opportunities to convey course themes. The way the teacher works with these moments is of vital significance. This section on inquiry is about the fundamental approach to learning found in all MBPs. It first outlines, the *why* of this approach – learning intentions and theoretical underpinnings, second the *how* – the craft of inquiry, and third, the *when* of inquiry is explored in a thumbnail guide to themes that generally emerge in each session.

THE 'WHY' OF INQUIRY: LEARNING INTENTIONS AND THEORETICAL UNDERPINNINGS

 Summary of learning intentions

1. Inquiry empowers participants to know they can learn from within.
2. Inquiry models in dialogue the way we wish participants to relate to their own inner experience and to life in general – i.e. with openness, curiosity, and reflectively.
3. Inquiry demonstrates how participants can pay attention to, and perceive, their experience in detail.
4. Inquiry is a powerful, grounded way to convey important, helpful attitudes towards one's own experience such as kindness and compassion.
5. The group context normalises experience that may otherwise be distressing, confusing or misleading.

1. Inquiry empowers participants to know they can learn from within.

The intention of inquiry is, wherever possible, to create conditions for participants themselves to discover the significance of their own experience. The content of the learning is important, but of more importance is the actual experience of self-discovery and learning. All the example dialogues in this section are composite exchanges drawn from our experience of inquiry. The first example is almost the first inquiry of the eight-week course and so the intention is not to delve too deep in a way that might cause reticence in future inquiries, but to convey attitudinal qualities fundamental to mindfulness and to foreground self-discovery. (Note: Teacher 'T', Participant 'P'):

P: I hate raisins ... I hate the taste and I hate the texture ... uggh

Group: (*laughter*) ... (*silence*)

T: So you '*know*' you '*really*' don't like the taste *or* the texture of raisins but you ate it anyway ... ?

P: Yes ...

T: When you saw it was a thing you didn't like, did you notice anything happening in your body ... your posture?

P: I'm not sure ... perhaps I made a face ... maybe pulled up my shoulders like a shrug

T: Can you describe the kind of face you made ... ?

P: It was like this (*participant makes a 'face'*)

T: I am wondering what was that moment like for you ... can you recall the feelings?

P: Disappointed ... not wanting what I am being given ... but taking it anyway ... I guess I wanted to get the most out of the exercise

T: That sounds interesting ... not wanting to miss out, but not really wanting to eat it either?

P: Yes! I felt that dilemma but I think I just acted on automatic and ignored my feelings

T: So, on 'automatic' as you call it we may at times ignore our feelings? (*Looking around the whole group*) I can see 'nods' around the circle, perhaps this is quite common. Would anyone else like to say something about the raisin meditation?

2. Inquiry models in dialogue the way we wish participants to relate to their own inner experience and to life in general – i.e. with openness, curiosity, and reflectively.

The way the teacher relates to participant's experiences acts as a model for how participants might learn to relate to their own internal experience. In the example below, the teacher models interest in what seems to be a failure, asking how it felt to be falling asleep in the body scan and then about the detail of this. In essence the teacher models interest in *whatever* experience is actually happening, with a sense that it is valid and has its own significance beyond *why* it might be happening. In learning to be more open to the *process* of experiencing rather than just the *outcome* of a practice, participants can learn to be less attached to getting things right or wrong and more engaged in 'the thing itself'.

P: I couldn't do it at all ... I just fell asleep ... your voice was so soothing ...

T: I wonder what that was like for you ... to fall asleep during the practice?

P: (*chuckle*) I don't know cos I was asleep

T: I mean how did you feel when you woke up?

P: No, I woke up when you were saying 'breathe into the whole body' ... I'm not sure ...

T: Take some time ... is it ok to ask some more about this ... I can see from the nods around the group you were not alone in feeling sleepy ... (*participant nods*) ... perhaps close your eyes and remember back ... that moment ... what was it like ... that moment of waking up?

3. Inquiry demonstrates how participants can pay attention to, and perceive, their experience in detail

The inquiry into falling asleep in the body scan (session 2) demonstrates this intention of helping the participant (and by extension the others witnessing this in the group) develop curiosity and interest in the detail and begin to see the various dimensions within the moments of experience:

T: *Maybe we can all join in with this ... if it feels ok ... .rest our eyes down or close them ... and remember back to how we felt towards the end of the practice ... ?*

T: So, any sense of what that waking moment was like ... ?

P: I felt 'Oh no ... I have missed it' ... I think I felt a bit embarrassed ...

T: Ok, so you noticed a thought about missing it?.. and perhaps a small feeling of embarrassment?

P: Yes, I really was looking forward to it and then ... just sleep *(shaking head)*

T: Is it ok to ask a bit more? *(pause ... looking at the participant)* It sounds as if quite a lot was happening when you woke up ... ?

P: Yes ... I was cross and embarrassed and felt stupid, like I can't do it ...

T: It sounds as if you were telling yourself off ... can you remember the actual thoughts?

P: Not sure ... something like 'Why am I so tired? What is wrong with me? Did anyone notice? Was I snoring?'

T: That is careful noticing ... I can really sense that moment ... feels sharp? Did you notice any sensations changing in the body ... tightening ... loosening?

P: Not sure ... well yes ... my jaw was aching ... and my eyes and face were kind of screwed up ... I remember cos you said breathe into the head and face and mine was so tight

T: So, you noticed feelings of embarrassment and anger and a whole string of thoughts and your body sensations ... the details of tension ... all happening together ... brilliant noticing!

T: *(looking around the group)* Maybe for you there was something similar? Or maybe something quite different?

4. Inquiry is a powerful, grounded way to convey important, helpful attitudes towards one's own experience

We can speak about the importance of kindness and the attitudinal foundations (Kabat-Zinn, 2013), and how these link to stress reduction or prevention of depressive relapse. However, when the teacher *models* this in the group and involves the participant experientially in a more compassionate approach to themselves, a completely different order of learning takes place. This excerpt illustrates this:

T: I wonder what we are learning from all this ... about trying to pay attention ... on purpose ... in this particular mindfulness way?

P1: There were a lot of judgements *(laughter)* ...

T: Yep! Some quite strong ... some quieter but still sharp ... what else are we noticing?

P2: Maybe I don't need to be so unkind towards myself

P3: You keep saying on the audio at home ... 'there is no right or wrong way to do this' ... maybe I get this now ... maybe I can just learn from all of it ...

P1: I feel a bit sad ... I think I have been pushing myself all my life ...

P3: Getting it wrong is so interesting! *(laughter)*

T: Can we sense the feeling of all of these words ... right now ... as we think about giving ourselves a slightly less hard time of it in the body scan ... ?

5. The group context normalises experience that may otherwise be distressing, confusing or misleading

This point is also illustrated in the excerpt above. The teacher needs to keep the whole group in mind and perhaps flicker their eyes around the circle as significant feelings and thoughts are reflected back, the group can also helpfully provide an alternative view of the same experience, breaking illusions of an absolute or fixed perception.

THE 'HOW' OF INQUIRY: THE PRACTICAL CRAFT OF INQUIRY

Facilitating experience-based learning requires the teacher to develop a range of qualities, skills, and clear intentions. Inquiry is like casting a pebble into a pond – we do not know how far the ripples will reach. In this section, we will explore the difference between horizontal and vertical inquiry, and the three-layer model of inquiry (see Figure 9.1).

There are two broad ways of inquiring – vertically and horizontally. Horizontal inquiry is a group-based inquiry, where the teacher deliberately looks around the group, and asks something like "Did anyone experience mind wandering?", then acknowledging nods or murmurs coming from across the group. You could imagine this type of inquiry as a circular line sweeping around the group from person to person, hence the term horizontal inquiry. Vertical inquiry is when the experience of a single participant is inquired into in more depth – this could be as much as a sentence or may be around five minutes exploring one person's experience. You could imagine the inquiry as a line going into and down a single participants' experience – hence the term vertical inquiry.

Using both horizontal and vertical inquiry facilitates involving everyone in the room. The intention with horizontal inquiry is to gather a lot of responses from the group without going into depth about them. This can include what we call 'pop-corning' where you ask people to speak about their experience into the group if they feel like doing so, and hold that space until everyone who wants to speak has done so. This form of harvesting experience can be used with different intentions:

- To immediately involve everyone, and so can bring the whole group alive;
- To explicitly normalise issues and experiences;
- To explicitly demonstrate the diversity of experience in a group;
- To help rebalance an overly intense atmosphere that may limit involvement. The teacher may return to a particular comment to inquire of one individual more deeply, once they have indicated an end of this horizontal process, making sure to ask the participant's permission to do so.

Inquiry can thus have a wide (horizontal inquiry) or narrow (vertical inquiry) focus. The teacher can implicitly balance these two aspects by drawing out from the particularities of an individual, generalities that might relate to the rest of the group. This can often be

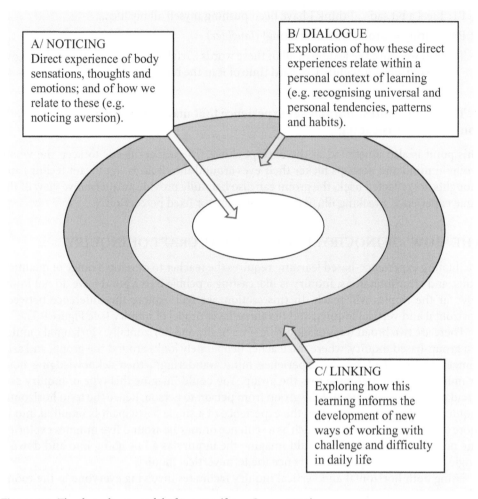

A/ NOTICING
Direct experience of body sensations, thoughts and emotions; and of how we relate to these (e.g. noticing aversion).

B/ DIALOGUE
Exploration of how these direct experiences relate within a personal context of learning (e.g. recognising universal and personal tendencies, patterns and habits).

C/ LINKING
Exploring how this learning informs the development of new ways of working with challenge and difficulty in daily life

Figure 9.1 The three-layer model of inquiry (from Crane, 2017)

done discretely by briefly looking around the whole group and saying something like: "I can see a number of nods around the group ... you are not alone in this". This cultivates a sense of engagement and safety. At times the teacher will guide the focus very clearly to one particular aspect of experience, going deeper, and at other times widen it, to encourage opening to new possibilities which may affirm or contrast the experience. For more practical tips on how to reflect upon and develop your inquiry skills, see the TLC in Chapter 19.

THE THREE-LAYER MODEL OF INQUIRY

A helpful model is the three-layer model of inquiry which offers a map of the territory of experience into which we are inquiring (see Figure 9.1). At any one time in inquiry the teacher may be guided by one of these three dynamically interrelated intentions:

1. Layer 1 – Facilitating exploration of the detail of the participants *direct experience* of a practice or exercise – i.e. direct experience of sensations, emotions and thoughts.
2. Layer 2 – Facilitating dialogue *about* this direct experience to encourage personal meaning to emerge. This includes exploration of our relationship to experience (the felt sense that is associated with experiencing pleasant and unpleasant).
3. Layer 3 – Linking themes from inquiry dialogue to general themes in the programme.

Layer 1 – Facilitating exploration of the detail of the participant's *direct experience*

This is the raw data, the ground from which learning can emerge. The skill of the teacher in this layer is to value the direct experience of the participant with genuine curiosity and interest. In layer 1, there is an emphasis on the exploration of the actuality of experience – which is so often overlooked or undervalued in a rush to understand 'why is it happening'. The clearest way to help steer the dialogue towards this is to give primacy to exploring the participant's physical sensations – including posture and any energetic sense in the body. Thoughts and emotions are also direct experiences, but the teacher guides the inquiry towards how these mental events were experienced in the body – or energetically – and so, steers interest away from their causes or consequences. The transcript below illustrates this in relation to the perception exercise in session 2 of MBSR:

T: Wow ... quite a lot happening from just looking at black and white shapes on a page! You said you couldn't make sense of all the shapes at first? What was that like?

P: A bit of giggly-panic ... I thought there was another picture in it ... I just couldn't see it

T: So, 'giggly-panic' ... what did that feel like?

P: Like I was back in school having to hide the shaking

T: Shaking?

P: Yes ... like bubbling-up in my body ... I thought it wasn't allowed ... so holding it down

T: And you said you suddenly saw the old woman and got excited?

P: Yes, I sat right upright and ... you know ... smiling with my whole face

T: It looks like you can still feel this now?

Layer 2 – Facilitating a dialogue about this direct experience to allow personal meaning to arise

This layer is a small step away from direct experience (such as 'my feet and hands were cold'), into reflection about the direct experience (such as 'It made me anxious about getting chilblains again'). This layer of questioning is targeting the feeling-tones that arise about *how* we are feeling – at its most basic it is a sense of pleasantness, unpleasantness or neutral. It can be further understood by considering the example sequence of teacher questions and prompts listed below:

- How did you feel when your mind kept wandering off?
- Did you notice any emotions – annoyance, amusement, judgement?
- What did you notice in your posture or body sensations when you tried to 'push the thoughts away to get back to the breath'?
- What happened when you brought awareness to the frustration?

Layer 3 – Linking themes from inquiry dialogue to general themes in the programme and wider life

The teacher can weave verbal and non-verbal prompts to facilitate the emergence of broader understanding from layer 2 inquiry – such as how it may link to wider experience of (for example) anxiety. This is a process of the teacher drawing out connections that emerge from the participant, and at other times offering information which supports this integration. There is an important edge here that makes inquiry a 'craft' and not a science. The potency of mindfulness-based learning rests on the direct experiential knowing that is *felt* by participants. The process of linking this learning with a context of understanding can have the effect of consolidating and validating this experience or of closing things down. Layer 3 dialogue therefore needs to be worked in with skill and sensitivity. As teachers we need to bring awareness to how much this process is generated by the participants and how much by us. It is important to allow enough time for the actuality of experience (layer 1) and the relationship with experience (layer 2) to be explored before sensing into layer 3. Exploration of Layer 3 is likely to be more prevalent in the second half of the course, once foundational mindfulness skills are in place.

The relationship between the three layers

The relationship between these three layers is dynamic and not hierarchical. The teacher has an intention for layer 3 learning about course themes to be grounded in direct experiencing, but layer 1 inquiry, in and of itself, can give rise to equally valuable, if less explicit learning. Likewise, layer 2 inquiry arises from the soil of a participants direct experience and has its own value regardless of whether it 'links' to the more generalisable learning of layer 3. The skill of proficient inquiry is based on *flexible* movement between these layers rather than knowing how to climb from 1 to 3 to make prized teaching points! The proficient teacher may invoke patience and wisdom by *not* moving to a layer 3 'teaching point' because the ground of experience in the group is not sufficiently prepared. Likewise a proficient teacher may repeatedly move from layer 2 'back' to layer 1 in order to consolidate an important theme early on in the 8 week curriculum. The important guiding principle being, is the participant – or the group as a whole – sufficiently *involved* for the learning to be internalised through direct experiencing? The example below of a session 5 MBSR inquiry illustrates this:

    T: So, thoughts! 'This is useless?' 'I can't do this?' ... well noticed ... I am wondering if you also noticed this feeling ... of being useless? Was it only thoughts or was there a sense of this feeling in your body ... or face ... or hands perhaps? *(layer 1)*

P: *(long pause)* Yes, definitely a feeling in my face ... it was sort of tight and a bit screwed up and I think my jaw was clenched

T: Is that a familiar feeling in your face?. ... you seem to recognise it quite easily? *(layers 1 and 2)*

P: Oh yeah ... common ... I grind my teeth at work over my keyboard and often end up with a headache if the day is very frustrating ... difficult people on the phone ... they just don't bother reading the information!

T: Is it ok to ask a bit more about this frustration? *(pause)*

P: Yes

T: Have you noticed any other milder sensations ... when there is frustration ... disappointment? *(Layer 1)*

P: I think I get scrunched up in my guts ... I think its most of the time

T: Was that scrunched feeling happening in the practice? *(layer 1)*

P: Yes, it was all up my back into my shoulders as well

T: *(Looking around the group)* ....I wonder if anyone else can relate to what is being said? So a reflection for us all here ... remembering back to last week, when we looked at the physiology of stress, what do you sense is happening to cause this kind of feeling in the body? *(layer 3)*

THE INTENTIONS OF INQUIRY CHANGE AND EVOLVE

At the start of the course

When participants are first learning how the mind wanders, it is helpful to emphasise layers 1 and 2 of inquiry. Inquiry aims to convey the main themes of each session which evolve as a 'spiral curriculum' (Bruner, 1966). Thus, non-judgement, patience, beginners mind and perhaps non-striving are likely to emerge in sessions 1 and 2. These four particular themes occur repeatedly in new contexts throughout the 8 weeks, but, in session 3 non-striving moves into pole position in relation to inquiry of mindful movement.

During the middle sessions

The emphasis shifts towards deeper investigation and particularly towards acceptance. Layer 3 of inquiry becomes more significant, linking learning through meditation to daily life and its challenges, remember to allow this to emerge from the participants themselves and not to 'engineer' it. In session 4, acceptance and trust may become helpfully dominant and in sessions 5 and 6, in relation to the theme of 'working with difficulty', allowing, letting be, and acceptance are helpfully encouraged to emerge.

Towards the end of the course

The themes move to taking the learning into everyday life. It remains important not to let links to layer 3 learnings suggest an end of fresh discovery; for many participants the learning will continue to develop long after the course has ended. Inquiry can be more finely tuned to individual participants as the teacher gets to know them better – i.e. being gentler or more challenging according to perceived needs.

THE 'HOW TO' PRACTICALITIES WHEN LEADING INQUIRY

There are general considerations and perspectives to be gently held in mind when leading inquiry, no matter which layer you are working with. These include:

Embodied mindfulness – learning is relational and so embodiment is crucial

Although the process of inquiry might seem complicated, at its core it is a simple way of being present with another in an open and compassionate way, while embodying mindful attitudes. It is a mutual process of investigation in which the participant is perceived as the expert in the field of their own experience and the teacher is offering service in the form of simply facilitating discovery. The process of discovery is often more helpful than what is discovered. In addition, because of the way group process works even though the dialogue is often with just with a few participants, the whole group is exposed to and involved in the learning.

Specific embodied qualities supportive of effective inquiry

- Curiosity – natural human interest based in the uniqueness of this person, and their experience
- Openness – body posture, tone, expression, and words convey there really is no agenda
- Responsive-aliveness – to opportunities arising in the person, group or environment
- Trusting – no need to 'fix,' compassion begins with empathy; solutions arise through awareness
- Spacious – opening up and maintaining space through pace and tone
- Respectful – asking permission, sensing when to inquire, and when to simply listen
- Humility – the other person really is the expert of their own experience
- Informed patience – interest in present moment content, avoid pushing or fishing for a particular outcome

Use of expression, gestures, non-verbal body language, and tonal tools in inquiry

As with ordinary life much of what is said between people is visually and tonally mediated; the words spoken and the questions asked are important but the accompanying gestures and tonality are incredibly significant. So too with inquiry. Use of body language, expression, alive silences and tone of voice may be more significant to a participant exploring their experience than the actual words spoken. Effective inquiry requires use of the complete range of communication skills available. Trying too hard to get the right questions or comments in response to a participant can stifle ones more natural ways of communicating interest and a desire to understand. A hand gesture or a tilt of the head or a small interjection can often be all that is required to encourage a person to continue their story and find meaning.

Facilitating a balance between delivering the curriculum and responding to whatever arises in the group

The teacher knows which themes are likely to emerge in each session and this knowing discretely informs the way participants are encouraged to give attention. If these are held as an agenda, the participant may be diverted from experientially based learning. Conversely, if themes are not clearly articulated, the inquiry may not encourage the emergence of important session themes. Clear intention and focus with an open and responsive teaching process is called for, responding to the unique opportunities of each moment.

SKILLS TO FACILITATE PRESENT MOMENT EXPLORATION – PROMPTS AND QUESTIONS

- Ask 'open' questions: Closed questions requiring a yes/no answer close the dialogue; open questions open up the dialogue – i.e. "What was that difficulty like?" rather than "Was it difficult?"
- *Ask permission to continue:* If unsure whether the participant is comfortable with the inquiry, it is important to check: when participants feel safe, and are in control of the process they can be more open.
- *Use of reflection and summary:* Reflecting back the main aspects of what has just been said communicates understanding and an encouragement to continue.
- *Recognise participant questions as a process linked to curiosity:* Instead of answering a question about practice, it can be fruitful to inquire into the curiosity behind the question – e.g. 'So, you are wondering how long the practice was ... was this question in your mind during the practice ... what was it like?' Prize the fact that a question has been asked; any questions represents interest and engagement.

SOME UNHELPFUL TENDENCIES IN INQUIRY

Effective inquiry can also be understood by reviewing what reduces its effectiveness, here are a few common examples:

- Becoming formulaic: allow real curiosity and respect to lead inquiry
- Talking too much – linked to a need to 'teach': this can arise from internal pressure to ensure everyone understands a teaching point, rather than trusting in a more emergent process, which might be a slower and less explicit
- Resorting to a more didactic style: when we become unsure of what we think we should be doing we can revert to 'teaching' as a more familiar and safer mode. This can keep participants in thinking-doing mode
- Becoming attached to, or excited by, participants insights: getting excited by the 'good student' can blind us to the bigger picture and sometimes indicate a 'right' way to be which creates an automatic 'wrong' way to be for many others in the group!
- Problem solving and/or rescuing: this can happen quite understandably, especially in moments of participant distress, but at such times we may communicate a need to fix problems rather than investigate them through approaching them with curiosity.

SUMMARY

Learning about inquiry can sometimes be a process of 'un-learning' ingrained personal and teaching habits. It can take considerable inner discipline at first to not introduce particular teaching points, but to be genuinely open to what emerges from participants during the sessions. Inquiry is a skill that is an ongoing learning process. Reflective practice around inquiry is supported by using the TLC (Chapter 19), and engaging in supervision (Chapter 21).

10
Conveying session themes
Group exercises and didactic inputs

Having covered the explicit curriculum elements of the formal practices and inquiry, this section is about the other explicit aspects of the course, the various group exercises and other inputs. Mindfulness-*based* programmes are so-called because mindfulness is fundamental to *all* the elements within them, including the group exercises which demonstrate the core session themes (e.g., teaching on the stress reaction cycle, perception, pleasant and unpleasant experiences). As with the formal mindfulness practices and inquiry, effective teaching of the core session themes relies on the teachers' embodiment of the attitudinal foundations. Individual teachers may choose to vary the way they are delivered in response to personal teaching style and the particular population they are teaching, but, whatever the variation, *how* they are taught is very significant. The various curriculum guides detail possible group exercises that are carefully selected to perform the task of developing the themes of each session alongside the formal practices. Box 10.1 offers a general overview of commonly used exercises to demonstrate session themes.

Box 10.1 Overview of common exercises used to demonstrate session themes

Session 1:
- Intentions exercise
- Raisin practice

Session 2:
- Mindfulness of perception (MBSR); 'Thoughts and feelings' exercise (MBCT)
- Setting up the pleasant events calendar

Session 3:
- Processing pleasant events exercise
- Setting up the unpleasant events calendar

Session 4:
- Processing the unpleasant events calendar
- The territory of depression (MBCT)
- Recognising stress (MBSR)

Session 5:
- Responding vs reacting: sea of reactions; stress mechanisms; physical barometer; 'Guest House', or Rilke's (2012) letter to the young poet, or other poem/story

Session 6:
- Exercises to demonstrate applying mindfulness to particular vulnerabilities:
  i) MBSR, interpersonal/stressful communication
  ii) MBCT, 'thoughts are not facts' and 'working with thoughts' exercises

Session 7:
- Applying mindful awareness to lifestyle choices – habits, actions and behaviours
  i) MBSR: Lifestyle choices exploration
  ii) MBCT: Nurturing and depleting, and behavioural action exercises

Session 8:
- 'Consolidating our learning' – reflection and discussion
- Preparing for the future – reflection and discussion; letter to self
- 'Closing the group' process

To demonstrate how the key principles, learning intentions and teaching considerations apply to teaching group exercises, we have selected session 2 of an MBSR course as an example. Illustrations of the exercises found in sessions 1, 5, and 8 are described in Chapter 15, where the emphasis is on demonstrating how the implicit and explicit aspects of the curriculum work together to form a whole greater than its parts. Here, we intend to illustrate the importance of bringing awareness to our choices of teaching methods, with a particular inquiry into how they may support more implicit elements of the curriculum. We highlight relevant domains of the MBI:TAC by marking them in brackets – e.g., 'D3' is shorthand for Domain 3, embodiment of mindfulness.

INTENTIONS AND PRACTICAL TEACHING CONSIDERATIONS OF GROUP EXERCISES IN SESSION 2

Perception/thoughts and feelings exercise

Intentions

Session 2 expands on the theme of session 1, which is to be more awake to our moment-by-moment experience/autopilot, and how we perceive direct experience. The rationale for the theme of 'perception' is to help participants experientially understand how perceptions and interpretations are just that – not necessarily facts! The exercises and discussions around perception aim to help participants become aware of perceptual process, and hold interpretations more lightly in a way that allows curiosity, openness, and through this, greater choice about how to respond.

Teaching considerations

To explore the theme of perception, MBSR commonly uses a perception exercise based on an exploration of optical illusions (Trompe-l'œil) and/or, the 9-dots puzzle (2020, para 4). At this early stage of the course, the learning and content of this exercise may be of less overall importance than the attitudinal qualities embodied and demonstrated by the teacher (D2, D3).

Whichever approach is chosen, there are three principles to be considered:

- The group process is still mostly in the 'forming' phase where paired or small group work is highly valuable (D6).
- The theme of the first session which supports the idea that mindfulness is natural, every day and ordinary, can be further consolidated by making this exercise light, open and fun! (D2, D5).
- Choose a methodology that best foregrounds just how 'normal' it is to have differing perceptions of experience (D5).

What follows is an example that bears these principles in mind. To prepare, print or otherwise make available around 5–8 different optical illusions (available on the internet). In the session, give one optical illusion to each person and guide a short reflection about what they are noticing whilst looking at it. Then, the group can be invited to find a partner who has a different optical illusion to discuss what they noticed. Then, open up for feedback in the whole group. This approach often induces very lively, often humorous, paired connection and the subsequent group discussion illustrates often very differing perceptions. This also serves the 'forming' stage of group development and strongly consolidates the normalising of just how differently we each may perceive our world (D1, D5, D6).

In MBCT the 'thoughts and feelings exercise' is used to explore a similar theme – how we interpret experience and how this influences thoughts, emotions and behaviours. The rationales and methodology are well outlined (Segal et al., 2013, pp. 160–164). However, there are some additional teaching considerations:

- At this stage of group development, paired discussion can be very helpful, once the main 'teaching points' have been explored collectively (D6).
- The principle is choosing a method of engagement that bears in mind the importance of the 'forming stage' of group process (Tuckman, 1965; D6), and of building a helpful relational stance with participants (D2). So, for example, if using a flip chart, positioning it 'in' the group circle rather than 'outside' can be helpful. Or, the flip chart can be used towards the centre of the circle on a low table, to enable a closer connection with participants. Also, the format used for recording the various thoughts, feelings, and body sensations need not be tabular, but can be captured within a divided circle, pre-empting any tendency for an implied hierarchy of these elements of experience.
- The exercise can leave some participants feeling that they may be negative or pessimistic by *nature* (i.e. not simply a current passing mood), and because it is so early in the course the group may not be sufficiently 'formed' to allow this to surface and be explored (D6).

Introducing the pleasant events calendar

Intentions

Towards the end of session 2, the teacher introduces the home practice for the coming week, which includes the pleasant experiences calendar. This is the first time we explore how participants bring attention to the way perceptions divide into likes and dislikes;

pleasant, unpleasant, and neutral. These are crucial building blocks for the later work on reactivity and response, and the development of skills to safely approach and work with the difficulties in our lives.

Teaching considerations

It can be very easy to underestimate the importance of introducing the pleasant experiences calendar as part of the home practice, and so squeeze it into the last few minutes of the session. It is good to put aside around 10 minutes to describe the exercise using the participant workbook and then ask if anyone has an example of a pleasant moment they could share from today. The use of the idea of a pleasant *moment* helps to describe what is meant by the term 'experience', and, what emerges is often uplifting for the group to hear and illustrates clearly what entries might be put into the calendar under its various headings. A common error, especially with more vulnerable populations, is thinking the experience needs to be special or big. Thus, if a participant offers an example that is quite special there is the opportunity for the teacher to add "Has anyone else got an even simpler example, something really very ordinary that happened today that felt just relatively pleasant?" The use of the term 'relatively' can be very helpful when met with the participant who says "I never have pleasant experiences!" (D1, D2, D5, D6)

SUMMARY

Skilful teaching of the group exercises and didactic inputs rests on having a clear intention for the exercise which then guides the teaching methodology. This is arrived at by developing a well-formed understanding of the underpinning rationale for the exercise. What is its main purpose within the overall curriculum? How does it fit both within the particular session and within the arc of the learning process across the MBP course? What needs does the group have at this stage in its development? Furthermore, each MBP group is different. Some groups are energetic, lively and forward; some are quieter and more subdued; some have individuals with particular vulnerabilities, needs and sensitivities etc. The teaching process is thus also attuned to the particular unique characteristics of *this* group. The MBP teacher will therefore over time develop a range of methodologies for approaching the same learning theme. It is an ongoing creative iterative engagement which also serves to keep the learning process alive for the teacher.

Part II
The implicit curriculum

INTRODUCTION

Our experience of training mindfulness teachers has taught us that the *explicit* learning elements are the areas in which trainees first gain competence. These logistical aspects of the teaching process necessarily take up attentional space in the early stages of learning to teach. As familiarity with these grows, it then becomes possible to give attention to the more embodied, intuitive, non-instrumental aspects of the teaching process – what we refer to here as the *implicit* curriculum. These include embodiment, relational skills, and group process work. Embracing the implicit aspects of MBP teaching includes the capacity to inhabit the deeper truths of the realities of being human. Developing our capacities in this area does not involve acquiring new knowledge per se – rather it is an engagement in processes and practices that allow us to re-connect and remember this inner intelligence. An engaged process of reflective practice particularly supports developing skills in the implicit curriculum. The TLC in Chapter 19 offers you a reflective structure for cultivating and deepening these implicit qualities – and enables you to lean into exploring one of these areas at a time.

In the next four sections (Chapters 11–14), we explore the interconnected and interwoven qualities of embodiment of mindfulness, relational skills, and holding the group learning container. Our capacities as MBP teachers in the implicit curriculum underpin the potential to be responsive to the moment-by-moment opportunities and choice points that emerge within the MBP teaching space, and through this to create learning spaces that catalyse growth, transformation and increasing depths of wisdom. In Chapter 15 we explore how the implicit and the explicit aspects of the teaching interweave and support each other. This interweaving of the implicit and explicit continues into Chapter 16 which describes how to approach the process of assessment and orientation for an MBP course. Finally, in Chapter 17, we offer a section on how to teach MBP courses online in a way that integrates the explicit and implicit aspects of teaching – skills that quickly became necessary during the pandemic lockdown of 2020 as we were writing this book.

NOTE

All chapters in Part II are written by the main editors.

11
Embodiment

The teachers' embodiment of mindfulness is a key quality which imbues the entire MBP teaching process. Although it is represented within the MBI:TAC as a domain alongside the others (Domain 3), it is perhaps better framed as an underpinning quality on which all other skills and qualities rest. Indeed, it is not really a skill or a competence that can be deliberately practiced like many other skills in our life. Our work instead is to create the conditions within ourselves that naturally enable deepening into inhabiting this way of being. We are cultivating the capacity to be inside our mindfulness practice in such a way that it becomes our natural default and thus is tangible in how we are in the world. The attitudinal foundations of mindfulness are one expression of embodiment – these qualities (i.e. non-striving, curiosity, trust etc) become expressed in the teaching space through the atmosphere the teacher creates. Another expression of embodiment is the quality of mindfully attending, and the resulting responsivity to the unique emergence of each moment – within the teacher's own being, with individual participants, the group, and the curriculum process.

It was challenging to describe embodiment when we were developing the MBI:TAC. Indeed, in our early research on the tool we discovered that this is the domain that assessors tended to have least agreement on. The work of embodying mindfulness is the inner work of mindfully relating to experience – much of which cannot be directly detected by an observer. Thus, what the MBI:TAC aims to do is to capture how the teacher makes these inner qualities tangible to their participants – through the human qualities and presence they bring forth. These tangible expressions of mindfulness practice are an important foundation to the MBP learning process. As teachers we aim to offer our participants the opportunity to directly taste an experience of mindfulness just by being in the teaching space; simultaneously, they are invited to experiment with bringing these qualities into how they relate to themselves through mindfulness practices.

There are two integrated arms to the process of embodiment. One is our capacity to align ourselves to the practice of mindfulness, and the other is to be our natural selves. Each of us will have our own unique way of being that becomes expressed in our lives and teaching process. McCown et al. (2016) speak of this as 'the person of the teacher' and 'being the person whose story you have lived' (p. 92). We can all recall the potency of being alongside people who were naturally authentic to their own personhood *and* aligned to a clear set of ethics, wisdom and values. One of the expressions of embodiment is that there is a natural continuity between the way the person shows up in the MBP teaching space and how they show up in life (of course we take on different roles and responsibilities, but we are not putting on a 'persona' in the teaching space). This points to why it is hard to describe what embodiment of mindfulness exactly looks like: thankfully there are as many expressions of it as there are people in the world – but within this there are some common threads and principles. It is not random.

In our paper on group process we called embodiment 'inside out embodiment' to capture the interface between the connectivity within our own being (inside), and how this then supports relational connectivity with individuals, the group and the teaching process (out).

> Inside out embodiment is the arising of non-judgemental present moment awareness within the teacher. The 'inside' encompasses phenomena arising within the boundary of the body of the teacher, such as thoughts, the felt sense of the body, and emotions, and 'out' refers to phenomena arising outside the body of the teacher, such as what is seen and heard in the group while teaching. In a sense, these boundaries are arbitrary and in constant flux, and the main point is that the teacher is able to be aware of and purposefully direct attention to the range of phenomena that arises while teaching.
>
> (Griffith et al., 2019a, p. 1318)

An example of 'inside' is the awareness of the felt internal landscape of the teacher. This includes recognising and being aware of the constant moment-by-moment flux of experience and being able to notice this without identifying with it too closely. For example, when I (GG) am teaching, I try to keep both feet flat on the ground. As this is not how I normally sit, I often want to cross my legs or curl up somehow, and have frequent impulses to do so when teaching. Instead of automatically responding to this impulse by moving, I maintain my deliberate posture of feet on the floor. This helps to anchor my awareness within my body, and also helps me tune into body-felt emotional resonances which I usually experience in my torso. From this steady posture, I also feel like I am more aware of any self-focused thoughts, and related reactive emotions and body sensations. For example, automatic self-judgemental thoughts such as 'Well that was a rubbish inquiry', with the attendant sinking feeling in my belly, to self-congratulatory ones 'That went great!' with attendant feelings of fizzy uplift in the chest. The point here with 'inside' awareness is to allow these natural moments of experience to flow through as we teach – and to be deliberate about what we give our attention and energy to. For example, if we give priority of attention to this commentary of thoughts about the process of teaching that may be arising within (either self-critical or self-congratulatory), we will disconnect from the immediacy of felt experience within ourselves and the teaching space. We will be caught in habit and self-identity and will have lost touch with the wider sense of things. This will happen. At this point, to re-connect with embodiment, we need to first notice we have got caught up in thoughts, and then purposefully re-orientate attention to what is going on in the session – akin to the process of working with the wandering mind during a formal meditation practice. Embodiment of mindfulness is thus a dynamic, 'in-the-moment' engagement with experience – a repeated reconnection and responsivity to how this moment is expressing itself within and without. It is mindfulness practice in action. When teaching, we intend to be present, the mind wanders (perhaps planning what to do next), we notice this movement, escort attention back to the present moment, and do this, as best we can, with compassion and care.

An example of 'out' is that at the same time as maintaining 'inside' awareness, the teacher is connecting to the moment-by-moment arising of what is seen, heard, and sensed with individuals, the group, and the surrounding space outside the body of the teacher. To continue the example above, I may notice that my mind is busy planning what to do next when a participant is talking, and so I end up giving a vague verbal response once they have finished speaking. The participants' non-verbal cues then tell me they noticed that I was not 100% listening to them: this both happens simultaneously inside (my felt sense of noticing the participant noticing my distraction), and out (I can visually see the participant in the room). The boundary between inside and outside is, in a sense, arbitrary. The key point of inside out embodiment is that the teacher has an integrated and inclusive awareness of processes emerging within and without the boundary of their body, and is attuned to the interplay between them. This process of deliberately moving attention towards and away from aspects of experience as we teach is illustrated in Box 11.1.

Box 11.1 The flow of embodied connection as we teach

Perhaps your personal patterns are to hold back in relationships – and one consequence of this is that during inquiry you tend to let the dialogue move away from the core focus of exploring immediacy and integrating this with teaching. As an experiment you might play with gently but firmly re-directing a participant mid-flow to bring them back to the core intention of the teaching process in that moment. This is likely to evoke a strong emotional response within you, which you acknowledge, but then choose to give primary attention to the connection of your body with ground, and the immediacy of what is arising within the teaching space.

Meeting our present moment experience via embodiment is not always comfortable. Part of the path of mindfulness practice is to be willing to meet the truths of experience and life. This involves allowing ourselves to be open to heartbreak, setback, and disappointment – alongside the joys, the wonder, and the beauty of life. We are engaged in a path that encourages us not to brace against our inner and outer experience. In practice as a teacher, this means being willing to be in touch with our inherent vulnerability – because this is what we are asking of our participants. When I (RC) look back at the mentors and teachers who have inspired me along the way, they are people who have been willing to show up in the fullness of their humanity – including with their imperfections. One expression of embodied mindfulness is the capacity to be open to moments of 'wobble' and uncertainty and to allow this to be a gateway to connection. We are cultivating our capacity to acknowledge the natural arising of (for example) fear, and to hold this with an awareness that is imbued with kindness, compassion, and curiosity; to allow this to be a platform for a relationship with experience that goes beyond self-identification – to recognise this as *human* rather than *my* experience. From this relationship with inner experience we are naturally more able to be attuned with what is arising for our participants through a lived connection to what it is like to be human. This asks us to access the courage to show up when we cannot predict the outcome. This theme is central to our journey as mindfulness teachers. We are not helping our participants or ourselves if we try to reach out towards some ideal of how we would like ourselves to be, instead of inhabiting who we actually are. We are thus embodying a willingness to befriend experience as it is 'beyond ideas of wrong doing and right doing' (Rumi, 1995, p. 36), rather than an attachment to a certain way of being. Embodiment involves inhabiting the paradoxes, contradictions, inherent tensions and the awkwardness of being human. MBP teaching is an exploration of the potential for freedom and ease *in the midst of* uncertainty, pain, fear, doubt, discomfort, and so on. Embodied practice is the lived expression of this. This goes to the heart of the challenge and opportunity of MBP teaching.

CULTIVATING EMBODIMENT

When first exploring embodiment, it can be common for trainee MBP teachers to focus on how they *convey* embodiment to others: with the prevalent question being 'how do I demonstrate that I am being mindful?' This triggers us into a self-conscious, vigilant 'outside in', rather than a mindful spacious 'inside out' awareness. The gateway to embodied practice is to connect to the immediacy of experience as we teach, with an emphasis on visceral sensory experience, as well as being somatically attuned to thoughts, emotions, and to what is going on in the room. Deepening our own mindfulness practice (and with this an understanding of the underpinning teachings), will naturally lead to a deepening of our capacities to mindfully inhabit our own being. This is an emergent process, and it is important to be patient with ourselves. It is an engagement in our own journey of experiential discovery, through which we come into deeper understanding of ourselves and our behavioural patterns. The TLC in Chapter 19 is a useful tool to support reflective development in cultivating your own sense of embodiment.

12
Relational skills

Others suffer just like me,
Others feel alone, just like me.
Others have to manage the business of living and dying, just like me.
Others can rest in the beauty of the world and be free, just like me.
  Mindfulness: A Kindly Approach to Being with Cancer (2017)
  by Trish Bartley

This quote from our colleague Trish's book speaks to one of the key themes that we connect to as we engage in mindfulness practice – we are deeply interconnected with each other and with all living creatures; we share patterns and processes with all other beings; and we are not alone. We have been relating all our lives, from our first gaze into our caregiver's eyes. We are relational beings. Relational skills are key capacities within MBP teaching, and are represented by Domain 2 in the MBI:TAC.

Embodiment and relational skills are deeply interwoven. Mindfulness practice is a relational practice – we are discovering a skilful way to relate to inner experience, and this becomes the ground from which we move into connection with others. The nature of the relationships cultivated in the MBP group mirrors the way of being we are cultivating within. Our relational task as teachers is to offer a climate of warmth, acceptance and kindly curiosity; an inclusive quality of listening that goes beyond the words spoken. It includes the hidden influences of the teacher's inner reactivity, the participant's way of being, and the wider energy of the participants. The quality of welcoming is important, which begins with a literal welcome of participants as they enter the teaching space, and expands to create a climate where it isn't possible for participants to have a 'wrong' experience – whatever experience is showing up is valid and genuinely welcome.

A key orientation that we embody relationally is one of 'non-fixing'. We communicate (mostly implicitly) that all participants' experiences are valid and are opportunities for learning. This transforms participants' reports of practice about, for example, the wandering mind (often assumed by participants to be 'wrong') into fruitful objects of investigation for the whole group. Our role is to create a container within which participants can inquire into experience and make their own discoveries. How can I (as teacher) build a relationship that enables them (as participant) to be open to their relationship with themselves moment-to-moment? We aim to create a relational container

71

in the MBP session that is spacious and safe enough to enable participants to explore difficulty. We hold the process in a way that puts them in the driving seat of discovering their own process. We encourage participants to discern and respect their own boundaries – deciding when to move attention in closer towards difficulty, and when to step back and steady themselves. Without the relational connection with a teacher, this tender work of proactively meeting difficulty with mindful awareness is difficult to sustain. This is the key difference of an MBP taught by a teacher compared with self-taught mindfulness (perhaps digitally or with a book). The reality is that most people are unlikely to sustain the practice when it becomes difficult without the holding relationship of the teacher.

It is essential to our survival to be in connection with others. Paradoxically it is also a place of fear – a place where we touch our vulnerability and can get hurt. As humans, we both long for and fear connection. When we gather at the start of an MBP course, as teachers we know that nearly everyone (usually including ourselves!) will be feeling some threads of fear and uncertainty. As the teacher, our role is to know this, sense it, and to also hold the process with confidence and trust in both the reliability of the learning arc of the MBP structure, and in bringing kindly attention to experience.

Our past experience and conditioning shape how we are in relationship. Our reactions to other people are frequently the product of habit, as is their response to us. Relational reactive habits that we have built up may include a movement to quick judgement and categorisation of others which then shapes how we are with them, or a fear of intimacy which leads to relational patterns of distancing. The MBP teaching process is shaped around enabling us to see these (usually off-radar) patterns – to discover the water we are swimming in. The relationships the teacher cultivates, creates the holding space within which we can support and prize participants' emerging insights into their own process. The relational work that takes place between the MBP teacher and participants is inherently edgy. As Palmer (2007) wrote – we are creating spaces that are safe enough for us to feel challenged in. We are courageously engaging together in a tender, delicate exploration of what it is to be human.

Humour and lightness is an important ingredient in MBP teaching, and helps engagement with learning. Humour helps us to align to a recognition of common humanity. We see with a smile the craziness of our own mind's activity and realise that all humans are living within this. However, humour is inherently edgy and we need to attune to when it is in the service of supporting learning and when it has tipped into something unhelpful.

Similarly, self-sharing by the teacher is helpful in enabling participants to recognise that mindfulness does not inoculate us from challenge. Mindfulness teachers can easily be idealised and placed on a pedestal by participants. It can be a great relief for participants when we share our humanity (perhaps with our own experience of working with our habits), and when we allow the shadows as well as the light into the space, stepping into the territory of being less than perfect practitioners.

Relationality is an emergent moment-by-moment process that is impossible to predict or plan. We instinctively adjust our relational styles to attune to different people and different cultures and contexts. Sometimes the moment will call on us to be more directive, and in other moments a receptive way of being is called for. We can deliberately cultivate our relational capacities, but it is important to acknowledge that relational engagement is often driven by our unconscious patterns and biases. Key to our work as MBP teachers is an engagement in training and ongoing awareness building of our conditioning, cultural context and biases so that we can deliberately practice holding learning spaces that are as inclusive and as safe as possible (see the chapter on social context in Chapter 24, and an example of a simple reflective exercise to support bringing blind spots onto our radar in Box 12.1).

Box 12.1 Reflective aid

A useful exercise to support reflection on our relational process as teacher – to be used in conjunction with the MBI:TLC in Part 3.

One practical practice (that our colleague Bethan Roberts introduced us to) is to pause after a teaching session and write down the names of all the participants in our course. Then reflect:

- Whose names came most easily to memory?
- Whose name do I tend to forget?
- Who is on/off my attentional radar?
- Who am I drawn to?
- Who do I find challenging?

This practice can give us helpful pointers in seeing and understanding our relational patterning and our unconscious biases, which can then guide how we deliberately recalibrate our relational attention.

   As teachers we will at times be clumsy and make mistakes. Our work within and around the sessions is to reflect, examine our own practice, bring live issues to supervision, learn from experience, and proactively engage in reflective practice (see Chapter 19 for guidance on reflective practice). Discomfort is a natural part of all this, as we humbly bring awareness to our blind spots, discover our relational habit patterns, and gently but persistently point ourselves in the direction of greater relational sensitivity, attunement and responsivity. It is the work of a lifetime.

BEFRIENDING

Befriending is integral to all relational levels – within our own being, within our connection with participants, and how we hold the wider space of the group. Befriending is one of three 'capacities' that make up the Inside Out Group (IOG) model (Griffith et al., 2019a).

Befriending ourselves

Teaching MBPs is challenging work. Having this fact in our awareness as we teach can be helpful in navigating challenging teaching moments, as it normalises and de-personalises our experience as teacher. At the heart of befriending ourselves is the emotional work of discovering ways of relating to difficulty. Befriending involves recognising habitual patterns of reactivity, and cultivating a gentle turning towards and opening to experience. For many teachers this may well include feelings of 'imposter syndrome' – a feeling of not being quite good enough to teach. There may also be moments of reactivity to participants in the group. These are natural aspects of being human. Befriending supports us to acknowledge these feelings and wisely attend to them, without trying to push them away or hold on to them. In these ways we are offering a model of bringing care and compassion to ourselves. Participants will learn a lot simply from seeing the teacher take care of themselves in small ways – how we set up our seat, how we take pauses, how we acknowledge our own tenderness etc.

Befriending participants

As teacher, we practice coming alongside whatever experience arises for participants, without judging or trying to change or fix what arises but rather, co-exploring with curiosity, non-judgement, and non-striving. We implicitly communicate that we do not have an agenda towards a preferred outcome. At the same time, we are directive about process – we repeatedly redirect the exploration to experiential engagement with the current teaching theme.

Befriending the group

Including the group in our attentional field when teaching helps us to responsively and skillfully navigate the dynamics that arise. Bringing a quality of befriending to this also helps us to fluidly meet the moment with fewer complications created by the judging mind. This area is the theme of the next section.

13
Holding the group learning environment

Mindfulness-based programmes were designed to be taught in a group context. Within the MBP group there are many relationships: the teacher relating to each participant; the teacher relating to the group as a whole; participants relationship to the teacher; and participants relationships with others in the group. This is a complex web to navigate and much of it – no matter how influential it is – tends to lie underneath the explicit teaching in the group. Yet it is critical to the effectiveness of the learning environment. There is an entire domain on group process in the MBI:TAC and TLC (See Chapter 19, Domain 6). Group process is relational in nature, and personal work done whilst in a group with others has the potential for normalising one's own experience. The pedagogy of the MBP teaching process is designed to maximise the way that the relational aspects of the group itself contribute to the work of communicating core teaching themes. The group process is thus proactively used to highlight common human patterns. Participant learning that emerges in this way tends to connect in ways that create enduring insights and behavioural changes. Didactic input from the teacher has its place, but unless it is skilfully integrated with the immediacy of felt experience it can easily be forgotten.

We have found in our teacher training processes that trainees tend to only be ready to build skills and awareness of how best to facilitate the group environment once they have built other core skills – such as becoming familiar with the curriculum of the programme, and guiding meditation practices. This is natural and understandable, and why training on how to work with group processes is usually situated in the latter stages of teacher training. At the same time, reflection using the TLC (in Chapter 19) is a useful way to bring the group process into your awareness right from the start of your training. It is important to understand how group processes are worked with in MBPs because:

- We are relational beings and connection with others in groups is an incredibly powerful catalyst for our learning (when the environment is conducive). Conversely, when the environment in a group is aversive or unsafe the learning process will be significantly compromised.
- We can use the group to help participants understand patterns of *universal vulnerability* that we, being human, all share, such as the stress reaction cycle, tendencies to ruminate etc.

- Some MBP groups are brought together with a *specific vulnerability* in mind (e.g. MBCT for depression, adapted MBPs for anxiety etc.). By meeting others with similar patterns of mind, participants can discover ways of shifting perspective about their specific vulnerability from one that is personal ('I always make a mess of things'), to one that is part of the broad, common spectrum of human experiences ('There are others here who feel like me; thoughts are just thoughts').
- As humans, we all suffer, and MBPs uncover this. This can help participants become more compassionate towards others and themselves, and more in touch with *common humanity*. Using the first-person plural when speaking of patterns or habits of mind helps this shift of perspective, e.g. 'So we can really give ourselves a hard time and put pressure on ourselves to be a certain way.' The group is thus intentionally and consistently referred to in order to learn about general patterns of mind (see Crane, 2017, Chapter 14, for more about personal and universal vulnerabilities and common humanity).
- As well as holding a sense of common humanity, it is important to hold the space in ways that allow for difference. This may be represented in the group by people from a range of backgrounds, gender identities, race, religions etc., and also by a range of ways of being in the group (outgoing, quiet, engaged, disengaged etc.). Within all this, the role the teacher takes is to create and maintain a learning container that allows people to show up as they are, and holds the potential for learning for all participants.
- It allows the teacher to explicitly support the group at different stages throughout the course. For example, strong group boundaries and safety need to be proactively established by the teacher in the early weeks of the course. Once the group and its norms are well established, the teacher's leadership style may become softer and less proactive.
- If the teacher embodies and relates to participants with the attitudinal qualities of mindfulness (e.g. curiosity, kindness, non-judgement, patience) this can encourage participants to explore these when relating to themselves and others during the MBP session. In the literature on group process this is also known as modelling or imitative behavior (Yalom & Leszcz, 2005).

THE INSIDE OUT GROUP (IOG) MODEL

The IOG model was developed within the context of the mindfulness training programmes at Bangor University (Griffith et al., 2019a). Although the model is simple, the understandings within it are not simplistic, and can take a while to embed into our learning and teaching practice. The IOG model is divided into five sections, the inner four happen inside the teaching space: 1) inside out embodiment, 2) reading the group, 3) holding the group, and 4) befriending the group; and the fifth section is the outer ring of the learning container, which represents the surrounding learning context influencing this particular MBP delivery. This outer ring describes conditions such as the social/cultural context of participants and teacher, venue, rationale for the group, the teacher's training, supervision, ethics and professional practice, the recruitment, orientation, and assessment of participants etc. Figure 13.1 offers a diagrammatic representation of the IOG model.

At the centre of the model, the embodiment of the teacher is represented by the permeable triangle, which has soft boundaries between the teacher and the three capacities of reading, holding, and befriending. In the IOG model, the teacher is embodied, and in

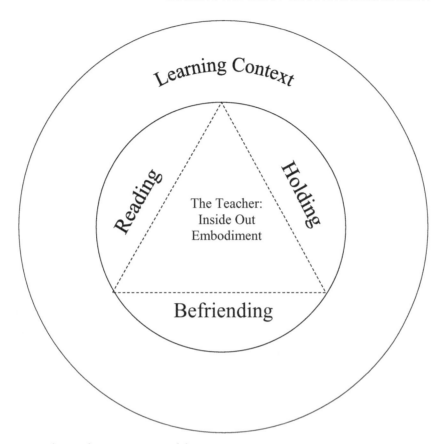

Figure 13.1 The Inside Out Group model

contact with these three capacities of group process whilst teaching. First, reading the group – whereby the teacher can viscerally sense or 'read' what is happening in the group and in their own being, and understand these in relation to theories of group process; second, holding the group – whereby the teacher establishes a learning container which is as safe as possible to enable participants to take risks and to learn; and third, befriending the group – the teacher coming alongside and befriending both participants and their own experience whilst teaching. The next sections explore two aspects of the IOG model: reading and holding the group. Befriending and embodiment are addressed in previous sections. The contextual influences within the learning container are covered in Part III of this book.

Reading the group

Reading the group relates to the teachers' capacity to understand and interpret what is happening in the group at any moment in time. Reading starts from the immediacy of connection with the felt sense of what is in the room. This connection is supported by the teacher's theoretical understandings of group process. Understanding theories allows the teacher to place the processes arising within the group into a wider context of understanding. The teacher needs to digest these theories in a way that releases them from consciously holding concepts during teaching. Once they are integrated as a coherent aspect of embodied practice, reading the group becomes part of the natural flow of awareness and responsivity to the moment.

Reading is grounded in how the teacher senses and 'reads' the room moment-by-moment. Through (outside) visual clues; such as noticing facial expressions and body language of participants and responding accordingly (for example, noticing if a participant who has talked for a while is keeping other participants interested, or if they have tuned out). Also, via internal sensory responses (inside), such as noticing if there is tension in the body which is reflective of what is happening in the teaching session. We recommend holding theory with a light touch, with awareness of the potential difficulties of trying to 'pin down' what is happening in the session to make it fit with theoretical understanding – this move into interpretation can be unhelpful if held too tightly.

How can I cultivate reading the group? Becoming familiar with some basic group development theories supports 'reading'. In Box 13.1 we summarise three particular theoretical frameworks that we recommend MBP teachers become familiar with.

Box 13.1 Three key theoretical frameworks on group process

1) Tuckman (1965) described four stages of group development: a) Forming, b) Storming, c) Norming, and d) Performing. This can be used as a map of how changes might evolve during the life of an MBP group. When a group first comes together (Forming), characteristically participants (and teacher) experience anxiety, and show a level of reserved-ness and dependence on the teacher. This is a time when teachers need to offer clear, firm boundaries to build a sense of containment and safety. This phase evolves when participants develop a sense of their place in the group, testing their interactions with the teacher and fellow participants (Storming). The next stage is Norming, when participants become used to their roles and establish group norms. Within an MBP this might be expressed by participants becoming familiar with the process of practice and inquiry. Performing follows when participants have formed bonds within the group and can work collaboratively. The group needs less teacher input, and participants support each other more independently in their discoveries of mindfulness practice, and show a deepening capacity for reflection. Tuckman added a fifth and final stage at a later date, called Adjourning (Tuckman & Jensen, 1977), which describes the ending of a group. In MBPs, this takes place when the programme finishes, the group dissolves and participants separate to take what they have learned into everyday life. Each group is different and may 'storm' in the first week and even have moments of 'performing' very early on. Some groups may never 'perform' or 'storm'. Different developmental stages may recycle several times in a nonlinear way. When the MBP teacher is able to identify normal processes at work within the group, such as storming, and view them as inherent, healthy and essential aspects of group development, it can have a positive impact on the confidence and capacity of the teacher, enabling more skilful responding to the needs of the participant/and group in the moment.

2) Berne's Group Imago (1963) theory highlights the importance for the group leader of acknowledging the multi-layered unconscious projections that each participant brings into the group. These are influenced by early family experiences and other personal

group histories. These unconscious projections influence the roles and interpersonal behaviors that get played out in the group. For example – someone who had a difficult relationship with their father may find it harder to connect with and trust a male teacher. Participants who have experienced societal oppression and marginalization may carry patterning and wounds that are activated in a group context. This is a complex area that highlights the hidden influences teeming under the surface of group process. Berne's group imago is a way of acknowledging and concretizing this, and describes the ways the group leader can support and make sense of the development of the group, without needing to know the detail of group members' backgrounds. In the context of MBPs, the group imago model underlines the importance of acknowledging the group within the process of participant orientation, assessment and preparation. It also supports the teacher to cultivate awareness and compassion for group and individual behaviors that arise, knowing their influence is often historical and may be unconscious.

3) Yalom and Leszcz (2005) have contributed extensively to the literature on group process in the context of psychotherapy. Particularly relevant to MBP teaching are the themes of 'universality' and 'imitative behavior'.

Universality: The movement from personal identification to recognition of universal human process is greatly facilitated by teaching that sensitively moves between hearing individual contributions, to supporting the group to connect to the wider learning that this points to.

Imitative behavior: The theme of 'imitative behavior' links to embodiment. How do teachers influence the group by modelling certain behaviors? If s/he is strongly embodied in the practice of mindfulness, this is likely to encourage participants to 'try on' mindfulness and acquire for themselves a chance to develop similar qualities of balance and stability. Modelling also happens between participants. They may see others in the group struggling with or resolving around similar challenges as they 'experiment' with practicing mindfulness and learn through seeing this in action.

Holding the group

The second capacity within the IOG model is holding the group. The two aspects of holding are: establishing a sense of safety in the group, which then enables participants to encounter new learning (Thornton, 2016). The holding process within the IOG model emphasizes the importance of the teacher including awareness of the group as an entity in its own right. Although the MBP teaching process itself is invitational, and responsibility lies with each person to engage in the way that is appropriate for them, the teacher does have a responsibility to create and maintain the conditions within which learning can take place. In the MBI:TAC domain 6 is 'holding the group learning environment' – a sense of creating a vessel, or a container for the learning.

Establishing safety

Participants need to feel sufficiently safe in a group in order to risk learning new skills (Palmer, 1998; Thornton, 2016). It is through a teacher's skilful holding that safety builds. MBP teachers need to help the group to form – and be aware of how 'holding' develops as the group matures. Holding is certainly most tangible at the start of the course when group forming is happening (Tuckman, 1965) – building trust through a warm welcome, well held boundaries, and safe connections. How can teachers establish safety in an MBP group?

- Ensure practical arrangements are clear and in place, such as the set up of the room, times and dates and any other practical arrangements.
- In the first session, establish group rules that all in the group are in agreement with, such as confidentiality, listening with respect etc.
- At the outset, participants are dependent on the teacher for direction about norms and expectations of behaviour. Participants are alert to authenticity, respect, compassion, and safety from the teacher, particularly in the first few MBP sessions, so it is important to embody these qualities.
- It is important at the early stages of the course to allow participants time to interact with each other, such as by asking them to talk about their experiences in pairs or threes before gathering the whole group. It is also helpful to encourage participants to move into new groups each time, so they have opportunities to connect with other people, not just those sat next to them. Small groups are facilitated a little differently when teaching online (Chapter 17).

Enable encounters with new learning

As the MBP group becomes established, the priority shifts from establishing safety to holding a process which enables participants to engage with the work they have come to do. If participants feel safe in the group, they will be more likely to take 'risks' alongside others and allow themselves to learn new ways of relating to themselves through mindfulness. How can teachers help participants encounter new learning?

- Regularly bring awareness to and visually scan around the group in order to stay in contact with the whole circle – not just to those who are talking, or those you are drawn to.
- Cultivate embodiment to help you to respond to what is arising, sensitively noticing the moments that require a particular intervention, or times when skillful holding involves no words at all, except perhaps a pause held kindly.
- Try to include everyone in the group, especially looking out for those who withdraw and become almost invisible in the group circle, and attempt to include them gently, even if they choose to stay on the sidelines or not speak in the wider group. Draw out the aspects of a participant's experience that others may identify with in ways that are inclusive; and support those who prefer not to speak into the group to participate non-verbally. 'Horizontal inquiry' is also useful (Chapter 9). Essentially, being alert to ways of including those who may feel at the margins, for 'the more 'at home' the margins feel, the more they can learn' (Lakey, 2010, p. 32).
- Be aware of individual participants and their impact on the group, taking steps to balance this if necessary. For example, if one participant dominates the group time, interventions to manage this can be utilised, such as regularly asking 'Is there anyone who hasn't spoken yet today who would like to share their experience?'
- A strong responsibility for each MBP teacher is to undertake training on non-discriminatory practice and unconscious bias, and make it an ongoing practice to proactively bring awareness to these processes in your reflective practice (see Magee, 2016, and Chapter 24).

14

The use of poems, stories, and images

Enough. These few words are enough.
If not these words, this breath.
If not this breath, this sitting here.

This opening to the life
We have refused
again and again
until now.
Until now.

                    David Whyte (1990)

This section outlines the intentions, rationales, and practical considerations for the use of poems, stories, and images in conveying course themes (which is particularly relevant to Domain 5 of the MBI:TAC). If you return your eyes to the poem above and read it aloud, perhaps slowly enough to *feel* the sense of the poem ... pause a moment ... what do you notice?

The poem may have stimulated thoughts, ideas, feelings, and/or emotions – or perhaps nothing in particular. The way a poem or story is recited, the context in which the poem is heard, including how the reader or listener is predisposed by culture or conditioning, all influence its impact. This is also true of any didactic input made by the teacher – but with stories and poems our sense of how it may be received is far less certain. Despite this uncertainty (or because of it) poems and stories can have an enormous impact on the learning process. In the interest of textural flow in this section the term 'poems and stories' will be used but it includes the other implicit teaching tools of images and visual aids. For example, the visual aid of a knotted shoelace being desperately tugged at can communicate volumes about our unhelpful tendency to rush to fix and make things worse!

Going back to the poem above, each reader of this page will have a sense of the breath, and of the words in a different way; each reader will have particular associations with 'opening to the life' ranging from memories to visual images. The poet's words stimulate our own very particular meaning, and through personal memory and association, we enter present-moment experiencing.

Poems and stories form a bridge between ideas and experience. Just as with the inquiry process, their use enables themes to emerge experientially. 'Opening to the life' conveys a treasure chest of themes including beginners mind, allowing, letting-be, trust, patience, non-striving, and acceptance. It conveys a meta-level theme that all of these attitudinal qualities are natural, and inherently appreciative. The inner wisdom that Saki Santorelli wrote of earlier in the book is drawn forth by skilful use of poems and stories. As with all the other aspects of MBP teaching, there are specific learning intentions, underpinning rationales, and practical considerations, including the intuitive and responsive reading of the group and context for the appropriateness of the use of poems and stories.

LEARNING INTENTIONS AND PRACTICAL CONSIDERATIONS

Poems and stories as introductions to session themes

In session 6 of MBCT, the story of 'John was on his way to school' can be used to introduce the concept of thoughts are not facts (Segal et al., 2013, p. 299). Poems can introduce session themes in a more subtle way so as to protect emergence of understanding and self-discovery. Such as in session 7 'Kindness' (Nye, 1998) can be a helpful poem as it speaks to the theme of the session.

Stimulating and enriching intentionality before and within practice

Sometimes reading a short poem, or fragments of a longer poem, as part of the set up for formal practice can seed and enrich individual and collective intentions in the room. For example, to seed the intention of being alive to striving and non-striving in the mindful movement practice – reading the first few lines of the prelude to 'The Dance' can be helpful (Dreamer, 2001). Subsequently, through the guidance of the movement practice short phrases from this poem can re-stimulate intentionality: for example, "perhaps moving into the harder edge of this stretch ... perhaps moving back a little to a softer edge ... perhaps we can simply let go and dance".

Introducing discussion and consolidating learning

Stories or poems can be used to introduce discussion and consolidate the theme of the session. For example the theme of allowing and letting-be is linked to working with difficulty in session 5, and Rumi's poem, 'The Guest House' (1995) is often used after the formal sitting meditation practice to stimulate dialogue about the problem with avoidance, and the opportunity raised by 'approach'. A good way of opening up this discussion is to ask after reading "What lines spoke to you in the poem/story?" However gentle the poem or story, their power lies in getting beneath the rational radar to the realm of values and emotions and so there is need for great sensitivity; reading the situation and the group may mean the poem is left out and a simple grounding practice substituted. Selection of poetry and stories is thus guided by our understanding of the group. For example, in some groups with participants who are currently experiencing strongly aversive experience or prone to be triggered, we may discern that 'The Guest House' poem may not be helpful with its invitation to meet experience at the door 'laughing'.

Marking transitions – especially beginnings and ends of practices or sessions

The transitions at the start of a session from what is often an active driven-doing mode to a more receptive being-mode can be eased with a brief poem, quote, or image. For example, at the start of session 1 the reflection on 'why have I chosen to do this course' is often supported by using an image of a lake and "A stone dropping ... zig-zagging ... down through the water". Or, at the end of a particularly emotional session 5 looking at changing our relationship to what is difficult in our lives, reading a more light-hearted poem such as Billy Collins' 'Another Reason Why I Don't Keep a Gun in the House' (2001) can be appropriate. The poem holds the theme but also responds to an awareness of the transition back into everyday life.

Responding to 'moments' in the group

There are times of heightened vulnerability or insight that will often benefit from introducing a short pause or grounding practice. Following this it can, at times, be helpful to recite a few lines from a poem – perhaps one recited earlier in the course – that addresses the vulnerability or insight in the room but in a way that feels more like a closure than a stirring up. The poem neatly communicates that the vulnerability is universal without having to say this explicitly.

Balancing the ethos in the group

Poems and stories can offer a helpful way to consciously rebalance group energies. For example, we might share an inspirational poem or an enlivening story when the group seems lifeless and under-motivated. Ideally, this is linked to the session theme but in some cases it may simply be a more general reminder of shared values and aspirations. Linking this to 'enactment' may mean inviting the group to walk or stroll around the room as the story is told or the poem recited. Depending on the teacher and the group one may even invite the pace and style of the walking to echo any feelings evoked. Conversely, if the group is becoming a little overly rational one may drop in a poem or story that evokes a deeper ethos: for example, 'The Peace of Wild Things' (Berry, 2013).

Additional considerations

It is not uncommon for a group to include one or more participants who are partially or fully *unable* to connect with metaphor. For this reason, it is important when guiding and when conveying course themes (Domains 4 and 5 – see Chapter 19) to offer sensitivity in this area, and include additional rational/concrete alternatives. These can be woven through the use of stories and poems in a discrete manner. If a participant is on the autistic spectrum and/or otherwise metaphor challenged, they can be forewarned and their possible confusion normalised by saying the images and metaphors may or may not be helpful before reading.

In some contexts such as corporate or business settings there may be institutional aversion to what are considered 'fluffy' training styles. The MBP teacher is required to find the language and approach most helpful to the context they are teaching in whilst staying internally true to their own style, curriculum, and approach. In terms of the use of stories and poems this may mean researching inspirational quotes and stories from the particular world one finds oneself in. For example, reading from the 'The 7 habits of highly effective people' (Covey, 1989), or quotes by well-known leaders of international companies. Finally, the main thing is to remain responsive to the class when deciding whether to use a poem or story. The teachers 'inside out' embodied awareness in the moment is an important guide to enabling creative engagement with the group (Griffith et al., 2019a).

15

Integrating the explicit and implicit curriculum

A significant proportion of an MBP session is spent engaging in formal meditation practice and inquiry. Alongside this there are the other elements – such as group exercises and didactic inputs. This section demonstrates how all these explicit curriculum elements are woven seamlessly together, and how the implicit, non-instrumental spirit of the teaching process is applied in MBP teaching. To illustrate this we offer sample narratives of three MBP sessions. We have chosen sessions 1, 5, and 8, to give a feel for the beginning, the middle, and the end of an MBP; and we offer a mixture of MBCT and MBSR examples. Throughout this section the MBI:TAC and TLC domains relevant to the explored teaching themes are indicated within the text (e.g. D6 is shorthand for Domain 6: holding the group container).

The respective curriculum guide for the MBP you are teaching is the best guide to the elements of each session. It is important when reading this section to remember that what follows are simply examples and are not absolutes: every group is different and every teacher has their own style. Our intention in presenting these examples is to convey a feel of the teaching process as a whole – how the teacher is continually making links between themes within and across sessions; how each element of the curriculum builds on the ones before, and lays the ground for what is coming. *How* we teach (the implicit/ non-instrumental) is as important – if not more so – than *what* we teach (the explicit/ instrumental). A key anchor point for your teaching process is intention – what do we want the participants to learn from the session? Stephen Covey's (1989) adage applies here too, how *do* we 'keep the *main thing* the *main thing*!'

SESSION 1: THE BEGINNING

This first session follows the engagement with participants through the orientation and assessment process, and is comprised of five main elements:

1 *Getting started – welcoming the group* – creating a safe, stimulating learning container
2 *The intentions and expectations reflective exercise* – why are we here?
3 *The raisin meditation* – why we don't use lychees!
4 *The body scan meditation and inquiry* – as described in Chapter 4
5 *Closing the session* – taking mindfulness home.

1. Getting started

The session starts before we begin to teach – even in the way we create the physical space. Does the tidiness of the room reflect care and attention to detail? Are all the things you need ready and organised (i.e. participant resources, session plan, raisins, mats, cushions). Do the participants have what they need to ease their entry into the space, such as parking/ travel directions, signs, information about toilets etc? (D1).

As the participants begin to arrive for the first session: what first impressions do you wish to convey about mindfulness and yourself as its ambassador? This is a big question which may generate many perspectives, mindfulness is not just about being polite, calm or friendly, but these qualities may help the participants settle. Therefore, as participants enter it is helpful to intentionally meet them with calm friendliness together with any other qualities that support the intention to make mindfulness seem ordinary and accessible. This group-gathering phase may take a while as people arrive into the space, some may be early, and some may arrive late and flustered. How do we best use this time? What issues are at stake? We may naturally be introverted or extroverted; it is important to be congruent in this early phase of the group process (D2, D3), and to allow our ways of welcoming fit our natural way of being. If we are new to teaching, we may be under the influence of stress and so prone to errors, such as sitting in complete silence or engaging in inappropriate babble! The main point is to bring some awareness to these important 'first brush strokes' on the canvas.

What issues are in play as we launch a new group? The circle of chairs is symbolic of harmony, inclusion and mutuality. If the circle is lopsided or uneven, or you are sitting on the floor cross-legged while everyone else is on a chair, it may convey the opposite (D6). Your eye and body language engagement can reflect the smooth inclusive flow of the circle such as taking time to scan the participants in the circle and make eye contact with each person ... or it could reflect the opposite, what would the impact be if you had your head down and were fiddling with papers? Our first few words may likewise convey awareness and openness, or the opposite. For example, if wishing to acknowledge any possible anxiety or uncertainty in the room it can be done in concordance with the theme of Session 1 (automatic pilot and the universal nature of habit patterns). It can be helpful to say with a smile, "Is anyone else feeling a bit anxious?" (D2, D3, D6), followed by inviting participants to tune into the feel of their experience in this moment. The emphasis here is on the ordinariness of mindfulness – a simple knowing of and giving space to what is here – in this particular moment as we arrive into this new space. We may then transition into linking this experience with a light touch reminder of what mindfulness is and what the intention of this course is – and within this honouring that participants have shown up for this time of investigation.

The next agenda item is usually the setting in place of group guidelines or 'ground rules' for participation; one way is to co-create aspects of this with the group by asking questions such as – what would support you to feel at ease here? We may offer reminders about important safety-building guidelines and the invitational nature of everything we do on the course. The important question here is: What can the teacher briefly remind the group about to help build the foundations of a safe, stimulating learning container? As ever, the way we engage with this topic is as important as its content (D2, D3, D6). Responsiveness to the feel of the room is more important than following any sequence in a curriculum guide. If forming the group and helping them to feel at ease and connected is the 'main thing' perhaps asking participants to speak with a partner during this setting up of group guidelines can be helpful. Or perhaps there has been a fullness of many words spoken and taking a deliberate pause to ground and connect feels important. The key question at this stage is: What is the main priority in this moment?

2. The intentions and expectations reflective exercise

Invite participants to engage in a short period of personal reflection on what brought them to the MBP course. One way of doing this is by using imagery of a pebble being dropped into a lake during the guided practice. The way this first brief practice is introduced can convey volumes about mindfulness (D2, D3, D4). After the solo reflection on 'what has brought me here?' invite them to turn to someone they have not spoken to yet and share what emerged. It is important to allow a simple approach to the discussion, perhaps not ringing a half time bell but rather simply inviting them to: "Both have a turn at speaking and I will ring a bell after four or five minutes". If you then walk around the circle after four minutes with an A4 card with 'two minutes' written in large felt tip you may embody a sense of care and safety without being too intrusive. If you wish to add to the themes of invitation and safety in order to reinforce the foundations of the learning container (D6) you may add to this instruction something like: "Remember to only share, at this stage, what seems ok to share ... and if you would rather not speak at all please let me know ... everything we do on this course is invitational" (D2). This exercise has content that is important because it introduces the importance of clear intention in mindfulness. Remember that the *process* used for the exercise may be equally important. The act of speaking in pairs is helpful as a means to set people at ease by facilitating connection at the start of the holding and normalising process of the group (D6). As facilitators of the group process, it is important that we hold these implicit intentions clearly whilst managing the explicit content about the importance of intentions (D2, D6). This reminder about invitation and sovereignty can be repeated when we invite participants to finish pair work and to share anything they wish to about their intentions and expectations into the whole group. It is important to normalise the choice to stay silent by saying upfront: "Remember it is absolutely fine to not say anything ... we will all have a chance to write something on this topic on a page in our private course handbooks".

Participants are then given an opportunity to share their intentions with the whole group – these can range from: to "manage anxiety" to "be more present" or to "be a better parent." When participants speak, the quality of our listening becomes the 'main thing', with perhaps a simple repeating of key words that emerge. It is important at this stage to keep things simple and safe by not asking for more detail or adding to anything they may say (D2). However, we can remember the various themes that emerge so we can refer back to them in a general broad-brush way. In this way, we may use some of the themes to highlight what mindfulness is and what it is not. Thus, if someone has said they want to "find calm" or "learn to relax" we can respectfully fold into a summary a few things about a mindful approach to finding calm or relaxation. This summary can be an ideal foundation for adding to the earlier definition of mindfulness, and it can be an ideal way to demonstrate to the group you have not only listened to everyone but have held and understood their meaning (D2, D3, D5).

As a by-product this activity could be used to remind the group about the ground rules – i.e. if any participant speaks across the group or speaks over anyone else this would be an ideal time to very gently ... and perhaps with humour ... remind them of the rules and why they are helpful. Some teachers invite participants to write a brief letter to themselves at this point outlining their intentions, which is then held safely and confidentially until the halfway review of the course in Session 5, or until the closing section of the course in Session 8.

3. The raisin meditation

First, why use a raisin and not chocolate or lychees? In order to introduce mindfulness as a skill anyone can bring into their everyday life, we choose a most ordinary object to explore via the five senses. Since sensing includes taste, we choose a simple object we can eat, as well as look at, touch, smell, and listen to. The humble raisin is good enough. If working with participants who have done this exercise before, it is especially important *not* to choose a different object such as strawberries, lychees or chocolate buttons, as this offers the opportunity to introduce a sense of 'beginners mind'.

The main intention for this first main mindfulness practice is to experientially demonstrate what mindfulness is and to begin to dispel any unhelpful associations or myths. A more implicit but important intention is to set the scene for how inquiry works (D5) and how the group will work together over the course (D6). Underpinning both is an intention to convey through embodiment the attitudinal foundations of mindfulness, and in so doing model 'kindness' and 'self-care' (D3). This further consolidates the work already done to create a safe and vibrant learning container. The specific curriculum intentions are to demonstrate the meaning and importance of 'paying attention in a particular way: on purpose, noticing judgement and in the present moment' (Kabat-Zinn, 2013), and the prevalence, power, problems, and advantages of auto pilot (D1). This first 'sensing' exercise is deliberately simple and straightforward. The concept of autopilot influences everything else that happens on the course, especially the body scan practice that immediately follows. Subsequent practical teaching considerations and arising inquiry themes are described in sufficient detail within Domain 5 of the full version of the MBI:TAC and within the MBSR and MBCT curriculum guides.

4. The body scan meditation and inquiry

The introduction to the body scan, intentions, safety issues, practical teaching considerations and inquiry themes are outlined in Chapter 4 and in the relevant curriculum guides. Linking this new long practice to all that has occurred previously in this session and the orientation provides an opportunity for consolidation and the enactment of important themes:

- The emphasis on kindness and self-care can be embodied and enacted in the way we help participants find a comfortable posture – e.g. personally offering blankets or cushions for the head and giving ample time to settle (D1, D3).
- Attention to equipment, room temperature, lighting etc., enacting what has been said about a balance between creating good conditions and meeting our experience just as it is (D1).
- The theme of invitation and choice rather than instruction can also be fully enacted in the setting up and in the guidance for finding a suitable 'anchor' for this practice – e.g. "finding an anchor that works for you in this moment – perhaps the feel of the breath or the sense of your hands resting on the ground" (D4).
- Tone, language and metaphor can all underscore the theme of mindfulness being an aspect of ordinary everyday life (D4).

- This is the first longer practice where participants (mostly) leave the safety of their chairs and the circle; in terms of the group process this offers a concrete opportunity to normalise difference and clearly *demonstrate* inclusion and acceptance of diversity (D6).
- An unhurried tidying of the room and recreation of the circle after the practice supports a sense of the group's mindful collective responsibility for the space and all that goes on in it (D1, D6).
- The transition from the body scan inquiry to the rest of the session is another opportunity to make implicit processes conscious – i.e. once back in the circle guiding a short 'pause' referring to 'transitions' and 'endings' (D3).

5. Closing the session

Consolidation is an important aspect of closing the session. If we wish to support the theme of trusting inner wisdom and self-empowerment of participants, this can be done by simply asking the group to call out some of the things they are "starting to notice" or "beginning to learn" about mindfulness. This can provide a grounded platform for clarification and other inputs so that the consolidation includes the main themes and learning outcomes of the session, whilst protecting the crucial experiential ethos (D2, D5).

Introducing home practice

It is vital to speak to the group about the rationales for home practice. First, this includes the more obvious rationale of skills training (as with learning a language or a musical instrument). Second, by practicing at home, participants begin to integrate mindfulness into their lives so it becomes more accessible and habitual. Third, research demonstrates a positive correlation between the amount of home practice engaged in and positive participant outcomes (e.g. Parsons et al., 2017; and Chapter 25).

It is helpful to bring the group into pairs at this point (remembering to encourage people to move to different pairs to facilitate group relations), to talk briefly about how they can fit the home practice into their lives ... specifically deciding the *time of day* and *place* to practice, and second, how they can remember to do it! It is then helpful to ask participants to look at their handbooks or handouts to explain how to record practice experience, and to know where to check the details of the set home practice. To underscore its importance, make sure you have allowed enough time in your schedule to introduce all three of the home practices (D1).

- *The body scan* – once a day for 6 of the next seven days. It is important to remind participants they do not have to achieve anything but just "do it and see what happens", and also that they do not need to enjoy it – although enjoyment is possible!
- *The routine activity – everyday mindfulness.* This practice links strongly to the theme of demystifying mindfulness; we can learn to pay attention 'on purpose, in a particular way' in everyday life at home and work. The idea of paying attention to some small, simple activity we do every day is introduced with a couple of examples. This can be linked to the experience of paying attention to the raisin – i.e. important learning can arise from simple everyday experience. One important practical consideration is to ensure no one is selecting a long or complex activity; it should not be done overly slowly; need not be done in any special way; and may take just a few minutes.

A clarifying example can be helpful, such as: "if you choose drying yourself after the morning shower" it could be "Just drying your toes or your hair"). Another common challenge is remembering! Share ideas from the group such as: phone reminders, post-it-notes, stickers on the bathroom mirrors etc. If it feels appropriate you might suggest they pair up and say what they plan to do, this means everyone leaves with a concrete plan in place.

- *Mindful eating*: the main thing to stress is to keep this light and simple. Thus, to decide to eat just one part of one meal mindfully when it is socially possible to do this. Or to just eat a sandwich in this way one day at work etc.

Ending the first session: Simply put, this first ending is highly significant. It is important to mark it with a quiet reflective moment or two – even if there is a time pressure. This may be accomplished by a poem or simply a short period of silence and bell. The poem 'Enough' by David Whyte (1990) in Chapter 14 can be a good one to read at this point in the course (D1, D3, D5).

SESSION 5 – 'THE MIDDLE'

Here we illustrate how the explicit curriculum elements come together with the implicit curriculum in Session 5. This typically has six main elements:

1 *Arrival and introduction to the session*: a brief practice and orientation to the theme of allowing/letting-be, recognising reactive patterns and learning to respond
2 *The sitting meditation practice and inquiry*
3 *Home practice review (including reporting back on stress reactivity in the week in MBSR)*
4 *Halfway review*: review learning and challenges so far
5 *Short practice for responding to everyday life situations*: the 3-step breathing space or S.T.O.P or Pause for responding to moments of everyday stress
6 *Closing the session*.

Overview of session 5

Sessions 4 and 5 mark the start of a new phase in the 8-week MBP course with an explicit focus for the first time on the particular difficulty underlying their participation in the course (i.e. stress in MBSR, depression in MBCT etc); and an examination of how to begin to work directly and explicitly with this suffering. The session 5 theme is about exploring the choice to recognise unhelpful (reactive) patterns, learning to approach rather than avoid, and responding to whatever arises – especially when it is unwanted or difficult. The skill being trained is how work with kindly awareness of the breath and body, rather than our usual habits of approaching difficulty by thinking about the problem and how to fix it, which can quickly tip into unhelpful rumination. Session 5 also marks the halfway point of the course, and teachers often invite engagement with a midway review.

Beneath the explicit curriculum elements, the implicit elements quietly do their work. For example, the rules, boundaries and 'tasks' of the group are now clear, and individuals will have tested the group to sense if they belong. So, whilst *storming* may occur in Session 5, there is often a sense of the group moving towards *performing* (Tuckman, 1965; Chapter 13). With this in mind the teaching approach implicitly encourages a movement towards this 'performing' phase (D6). The relational stance of the teacher (D2) is clearly and experientially understood as safe and affirming, creating a basis for appropriate challenge and transparency. The underlying attitudinal foundations are by now evidently embodied (D3) and their fundamental importance increasingly recognised.

1. Arrival and introduction to the session

By session 5, the pre-session moments can offer new and important opportunities. Thus, the teacher may prime informal conversations connected to the themes of the coming session. For example, asking, "we are about halfway through the course ... how have you noticed mindfulness starting to show up at work ... or at home?" With group process in mind (D6), the teacher may quietly prime an informal conversation such as this and then 'step back' a little; by this point in the course participants know the rules of the group and each other. Participants also know the patterns of the session so it is possible to simply invite the group, with a bell or words, into a brief and relatively unguided arriving practice: "Welcome, let's arrive together ... finding our feet on the floor and our body on the chair ... and perhaps using, sound or body sensations or perhaps, breath as an anchor". To further strengthen the group process, at the end of this it can be helpful to invite brief comments using horizontal inquiry (D5; Chapter 9) with no input from the teacher – i.e. "How was that practice ... perhaps just a single word or two?"

Following this, the introduction to the session's theme strikes a balance between saying too much and thus undermining experiential learning, and not saying enough, leaving the group less primed to engage with and recognise intended learning. The approach offered by MBCT achieves this balance by use of a story (Segal et al., 2013) which speaks to the value of *approach, allowing, and letting-be*. It can be fun to explore other ways to introduce the themes at the start of a class: telling stories, using a poem, or more action-based ways. For example, one could use a drama-based introduction: holding a pair of trainers on one's lap and easily untying the bow on one *but* finding the second shoelace going into a (pre-arranged) knot; the teacher can then tug and tug with puffs and groans until with exasperation asking the group: "What do I need to do? What can I do"? Someone in the group will (eventually) call out "Stop tugging" at which point the teacher stops, acting exhausted and after a few moments asks: "Ok, I've stopped but what do I need to do next, there is still this knot!" At this point the teacher is obviously *not looking* at the knot! Eventually someone in the group gets it and says, "Look at the knot". In this way the theme of the session of learning to first *stop and recognise* and then *look closely* at *the difficulty* is demonstrated experientially. In terms of Session 5 it is about *allowing* the knot to be there to enable us time to *look closely* into it and then subsequently, learn how we might begin to untie the knot or avoid making it in the first place. It is important to introduce the idea that perhaps the difficulty is not so much the knot itself, but how we react to it, making it more and more of a problem for us. This kind of introduction not only demonstrates the value of responding and allowing but it also points to the themes in sessions 6 and 7 – taking skilful action in our lives from a platform more clearly seeing (D5).

2. The sitting meditation practice and inquiry

Typically in MBSR the session starts with some standing yoga based mindful movement. In both MBSR and MBCT there is a 40–45-minute sitting practice which is a vehicle for participants to explore the session themes experientially, and the inquiry that follows aims to deepen and consolidate this experiential learning. The form, intentions and practical consideration of the sitting meditation are described in Part I, and there are programme specific structures to the practice which are presented in the curriculum guides. The important perspective being revisited here is how the sitting meditation links to, and extends, the main themes of session 5 such as: recognising aversion, allowing, letting-be, approach vs. avoidance, and responding vs. reacting. Thus, the teacher introduces and guides this practice (D4) with these themes in mind. In the inquiry the teacher also holds these themes in mind in readiness to recognise and respond to experiences that illustrate them (D5). To give an example, if a participant begins the inquiry by saying "How long was that practice?" the teacher is aware that beneath this question possibly lies a judgement about it being 'too long' ... and beneath this is an absence of *allowing and letting-be*. Because the teacher is aware of the importance of these themes they do not at first answer the question but inquire into whether the practice *felt* long or too short ... and how they experienced this (Layer 1 of inquiry process; Chapter 9). Having identified a felt sense of restlessness or impatience the teacher may inquire about how they related to these feelings of restlessness. For example, perhaps offering a little scaffolding to help the participant know what is being asked, saying, "Was it *very* difficult to feel these feelings or was it just *a little* annoying?" (Layer 2). The inquiry is aiming to help the participant realise that the difficult feelings they experienced arose from an *avoidance pattern;* from wanting a different experience to the one they were having. At an appropriate point the teacher may then open to the whole group and ask a Layer 3 inquiry question: "So, how often do we all want something that is not present or not want something that is present ... would anyone offer a recent example ... perhaps even in this session"?

Once the inquiry is finished, the theme of recognising and approaching difficulty and learning to respond is often consolidated by reading 'The Guest House' poem by Rumi (1995) – or part of Rilke's 'Letter to a Young Poet' (2012). These commonly stimulate a focused dialogue about the value of approach rather than avoidance, and also the perspective that this can be safe if we are mindful that the 'guests' are just that, guests who come and go like the weather. The way this discussion is guided needs to reflect the teachers reading of the group process (D6), and the vulnerability of the individuals present (D2). It often provides golden opportunities to model non-fixing and non-judging as questions and emotions are often strongly expressed. It can be at this point that divisions between the realists and idealists in the group surface, so a strong embodied presence is needed (D3). The poem can be a Pandora's Box and the lid needs to be replaced carefully with consolidating remarks about choice, timing, and the emphasis on allowing experience to be as it is in this moment rather than an emphasis on acceptance (which may fuel a sense of striving towards something). It is also important to convey that mindfulness supports creative engagement with experience – a wise response based on the conditions of the moment. At times this may be 'being with', 'stepping in close to the feel of things', and at others, it may involve acknowledging and stepping back to resource ourselves in other ways.

3. Home practice review

The home practice is then reviewed with similar background awareness of the session themes (D5). If the group process is borne in mind the teacher may structure this inquiry with pairs, triads or small group dialogue to further the movement towards behaviours conducive to performing (Tuckman, 1965). Group process can be further encouraged using horizontal inquiry (Chapter 9) by asking participants to briefly say what has been of significance or of interest over the last week. The performing stage of the group can be facilitated by the teacher beginning to 'get out of the way', and allow a more free-form conversation to arise (D6).

4. Halfway review

In MBSR this is an explicit element of session 5, whereas in MBCT the reviewing of learning so far may arise as part of the home practice review, or in the conversation arising from a poem such as 'The Guest House' (Rumi, 1995). The review offers participants and the teacher an opportunity to take stock, to reflect on learning, growth, or 'stuckness'. The learning intentions are to:

- help frame reflection on how one wishes to engage with the rest of the course
- consolidate in a very grounded way the attitudes, skills, and understandings fundamental to mindfulness
- encourage a sense of openness to the future and renewed commitment no matter what has happened up to this point.

The halfway review can be approached in many ways, but the principle of experience-based learning means a guided reflective practice is a helpful starting point. This helps participants more directly sense helpful ideas, perspectives, and personal challenges. The guidance needs to allow sufficient space for experiences to emerge and be *felt* whilst not being so spacious that participants disengage (D4). It can then be very helpful to invite paired discussion about this reflective practice before moving on to a whole-group sharing during which the teacher holds the learning intentions in mind. Awareness of group process informs both the process and content of the halfway review (D6). For example, the maturation into 'performing' can be aided by the teacher allowing a more relaxed approach in the wider group discussion. Some teachers also like to use the letters to 'self' – composed in session 1 – about their intentions and expectations as an additional reflective tool in the review.

Throughout this review phase, which may be a significant portion of the session, it can be helpful to invite pauses, and brief practice spaces to bring the group back to present moment connection. In the consolidating phase of this reflective exercise the group can be asked to share two or three words about what they sense to be most significant or interesting about going forward into the second half of the course. This can offer opportunities for the teacher to remind the group about what mindfulness really is and what it is not in a relatively non-didactic way! An outcome of this midway review can be a sense of a compass being reset to true north.

5. Short practice for responding to everyday life situations

The intention is to model in the class how a short practice, using a physical anchor, can enable a response rather than a reaction to a moment of stress or lowering mood. This can be the 3 Step Breathing Space, S.T.O.P. or Pause – as described in Part I. These short practices can be timetabled in, but they may also simply arise if the group or a participant seems to need grounding or stabilising. In such circumstances the tone, pace and guidance of the short practice can underline the way 'a response' is not the same as 'a fix'.

6. *Closing the session*

If the halfway review has not covered home practice, this can be an appropriate place and time to do it. It can be helpful to invite pairs to talk about any renewed plans for home practice and suggest each help the other to lightly troubleshoot them if helpful.

The main home practice tasks after session 5 are the sitting meditation practice and the integration of short practices such as the S.T.O.P and the regular breathing spaces throughout the coming week. Session 5 is often an emotional and energetic session and a clear, grounding closure is especially important. This can include a poem or story – perhaps one that leans towards themes of appreciation, gratitude, beauty, connection, or wholeness. In the final brief final sitting practice it can be helpful to bring in awareness of "our group" or similar appreciative sentiment.

SESSION 8 – THE END

We illustrate the final session with an exemplar of MBSR session 8 (although MBCT is very similar in terms of content and processes). There are two explicit elements linked to the theme of 'how to keep our mindfulness alive': first, reviewing what has been learnt, and second, consideration of how to take this learning forward. The aspects within this session vary a little according to the population and teacher preference but a typical session 8 will have the following five elements:

1 *Arriving and welcoming*: brief settling practice, acknowledgement of endings
2 *Body scan practice*: which could, segue into an unguided sitting meditation – with the possibility of some mindful movement at the start or end
3 *Looking back*: a reflective practice with dialogue
4 *Looking forward*: a reflective practice with dialogue
5 *Final sharing circle and closing the group*: a space for each participant and the teacher to speak; final closing ceremony or practice.

1. Arriving and welcoming

The ending of a course can evoke a range of strong emotions, both for the teacher and participants. Ensure you take time to prepare yourself, so that these 'inside' emotions are in awareness, and appropriately held as participants arrive (Griffith et al., 2019a; D3). The *performing* stage of the group in which participants feel relatively able to be transparent about their feelings is shifting into the *adjourning* stage in which there can be uncertainty and confusion (Tuckman, 1965). This understanding is helpful to bear to mind as we greet arriving participants. This informal greeting time can be an important opportunity for the teacher to normalise feelings, sometimes including transparency about one's own particular mix of emotions (D2, D3, D6). Also, in this ending stage of the group it is not unusual for some participants to arrive late or not arrive at all. During the short arriving practice, you can helpfully include words about "allowing or inviting space" for any feelings present and naming the fact of this being the last session. As ever, it is important not to pre-empt the experiential ethos by saying too much about the session, but it can be helpful to offer a few words about the themes of consolidating what has been learnt, and preparing for continuing mindfulness practice in the future.

2. Body scan practice

The theme 'looking back, looking forward' is operationalised by returning to the first ever practice the group experienced, the body scan. The light introduction to this practice with words such as, "so, after all these weeks we return full circle to the body scan, remembering what we discovered then about posture and comfort in setting up for this practice ... and settling in". The guidance (D4) can remind about the importance of forming a clear intention, and the teacher may offer a favourite poem from a previous week at the start of the body scan to help enrich and inform this intention. Part I details the basics about guiding this practice, but in session 8 the emphasis, as well as being spacious (more silence), can include qualities that have been mostly implicit up to this point, such as kindness, appreciation, gratitude, and self-compassion. An example is offered here to illustrate how such themes may be included in a practice: "Expanding out to sense both our feet ... as we breathe in ... as we breathe out ... perhaps noticing our feet at rest ... nowhere to go just now ... no need to help us balance ... climb stairs or stride along ... just resting ... perhaps inviting a sense of 'thank-you feet' ... as we breathe in ... as we breathe out". Later on, in a similar vein the guidance may point to the work of the back, "holding us up all day, carrying us around, now relatively at rest". Or, when visiting the hands, words such as,

sensing our hands in their warmth, or perhaps coolness ... perhaps tingling or pulse ... these hands that greet and sometimes offer care ... fingers that know how to type and test the ripeness of fruit ... these hands now relatively still and quiet ... *resting*, with the particular curl of fingers, as we breathe in ... as we breathe out (D4).

The inquiry following the body scan can helpfully consolidate themes that have been present over the whole of the course as well as the important theme of noticing *change*; exploring just how much has changed since the first body scan. The inquiry into home practice can be similarly responsive in consolidating previous learning and noticing how participants' practice has developed (D5). Sometimes, however, the teacher flows straight from the body scan into writing a letter to self (detailed below), followed by engagement with the reflective process on the learning from the course.

3. Looking back

When we were children, we sometimes left a party with a 'party bag', reminding us about the good time we had with our friends. Session 8 continues a little in this vein with a reflective practice that helps us connect with what has been helpful so it can be remembered and taken home. Ideally the process used will reflect the important implicit dimensions of experiential learning, the group process, and the invitational, open quality of mindfulness (D3, D6). Thus, the teacher may guide a reflection on participants' experience of the course. One possibility to aid this process is to display the flip chart sheets which were used to name each of the previous sessions. Others may make a flip chart 'ladder' on the floor comprised of these eight flip chart sheets and, with the help of the group standing around, ask what can be recalled about the main themes for each session. The guidance of this reflection itself aims to embody the qualities and attitudes of mindfulness (D2, D3, D4). An alternative would be to first invite participants to settle, find a helpful posture, and then recall first impressions of the room and group, and perhaps initial expectations and intentions. After this the main elements of session 1 are evoked, with sufficient space to allow these to be remembered and sensed, inviting participants to note body-felt or emotional responses as well as thoughts. In this way each session is evoked in turn, including the day of practice, with a meta-level refrain such as, "what stands out for me?", "what were the challenges and how did I begin to work with these?", "what was helpful?" If the guidance is too crowded the experiential aspect is limited, if too spacious minds tend to wander, diluting the experience. The implicit curriculum is present in the invitational, open and accepting language and tone, enshrined in words such as, "there may be nothing arising, and that is fine, perhaps just staying for a moment or two with the breath ... returning to the reflection when this feels appropriate" etc. Once completed, it can be very helpful to invite small groups of two or three to share together about what arose in the reflection (D6). This exchange can be a delight to sit back and witness. Then, the whole group can be invited to share some of their reflections – with reminders that it can be good to share challenges as well as delights. Whilst keeping in mind the time boundaries for this part of the session (D1) there can be opportunities for the group to move into discussion around important themes and occasionally for the teacher to offer helpful consolidating perspectives. At this *performing* and *adjourning* stage of the group process one of the main tasks of the teacher is to step back with a little less holding (D6). At an appropriate moment gather the group with an invitation to fall into a moment of silence and a short practice. It is good to remember how helpful it can be to get out of the chairs and stand up sometimes for these brief transitional practices; engaging in a standing meditation or mindful walking, or some other brief movement practice.

4. Looking forward

Session 8 is a game of two halves! Following a short practice participants can be invited to consider how best to keep up the positive momentum from the course and "keep their mindfulness alive". There are several ways to do this but, ideally, it is an experientially based reflective process followed by small and whole-group sharing. 'Looking back' has generated a shared pool of ideas about what has been helpful, including how to work with challenges, and this informs and enriches the 'looking forward' process. One helpful approach is to introduce this reflection as having two dimensions: firstly, there is a question about *what* combination of formal and informal practice seems possible, secondly, there is a question about *why* we might wish to take the trouble to do them. The first question is more rational, a question perhaps for the head to ponder, the second is more emotional and is perhaps best answered by the heart. The example here of guidance teacher might offer demonstrates to some extent how the implicit and explicit curriculum weave together: the teacher might invite the group to settle and "feel the ground" and "feel into a posture that supports gentle reflection ... awake and upright but comfortable". Then, invite participants to revisit the earlier 'looking back' reflections, noting the type of practices they felt most helpful, "was it the body scan or perhaps the mindful movement or one of the sitting practices ... and of course, how the shorter practices may have been helpful". Then, attention can be directed towards the more informal practices such as, "walking or daily tasks, journaling or sharing mindfulness stories with new friends, colleagues or family". It is important to value the informal ways that the learning will influence everyday life. Once again, the guidance allows sufficient space to support experiential responses whilst maintaining sufficient 'tempo' to support attentiveness (D4). The reflection can them move on to consider motivation, the *why* aspect of keeping mindfulness alive. One way to frame this is to gently and spaciously ask participants "what is it you value in this world ... perhaps, even what do you value *most* in this world?" and, "in what ways might mindful awareness serve this?" The guidance might remind participants that "perhaps nothing comes to mind right now and that this is ok ... it might simply be 'my health' or 'my well-being' .... how might mindfulness help my approach to what I value most?" The guidance then supports a return to simply sensing "the ground, the chair or cushion, the feet ... breathing" etc. Following this reflection, pairs or small group sharing can further strengthen the connections in the group, inviting participants to perhaps find someone they have not worked with so much during the course (D6). It can be helpful to briefly join some of these groupings – not to add anything except appreciation and to witness (D2). Then, the process can move to a whole-group sharing in which the teacher may just sit back to allow the group to 'perform'.

Towards the end of this process, it may be an appropriate to mention supportive resources such as books, drop-in sessions, future courses etc., and to point to a list of such resources on a website or in the handbook (D1). Some teachers favour enshrining whatever has arisen in this process by giving participants the opportunity to write a letter to their future self, describing 'what I want to remember over the coming weeks and months'. This is sealed, addressed and later posted to participants "at some point in the future". The teacher's role in this part of the process is to gently encourage and also to check for realistic intentions and goals.

This whole process can stir emotions connected to endings. Bringing this into conscious awareness is a helpful consolidation of crucial themes of approach vs avoidance, openness, awareness of change, etc. Suggesting a short grounding practice to mark the transition "into the last activity of this group" consolidates another crucial theme of 'responding vs reacting'. In this way the group can be invited to a brief settling practice.

5. Final sharing circle and closing the group

It is important to give this 'closing the group' section enough time which means holding effective time boundaries throughout the session (D1). The introduction to this closure helpfully reminds participants that although future ways to connect have been mentioned, this particular group will not meet again in this context. There are many ways to close the group. It may seem appropriate to simply encourage participants to "say a few words to mark the end". The teacher may offer an object to symbolise and sustain connection to the group and the learning within it (such as stones, shells, or certificates). Participants can be invited to pick up an object (which has been placed in the centre of the circle beforehand), and say a few words to the group whilst holding it in their hand. This communicates an implicit valuing of the participants efforts to show up and learn, and also a message that mindfulness is intrinsically linked to appreciation, generosity, and connection. The main principle underlying whatever process is used is clarity about the ending. For some this boundary, in itself, can be a very significant learning. Within and alongside clarity the teacher also demonstrates appropriate attitudinal foundations; modelling how kindness need not dilute clarity but augment it (D2, D3). The teacher's last words helpfully include a reminder from the start of the course about remembering confidentiality if 'chance meetings' happen in the street or other public places.

What follows after the end of the session can often be less tidy and organised: emotions, partings, and farewells. Some participants like to leave quickly, others linger. The teacher may also have a preferred habit around endings and at times it may be appropriate to be transparent about this whilst also taking care to communicate that such habits may change as we bring awareness to them. Finally, away from the group and the venue there are a number of things to attend to in order for the teacher to close the teaching process. Some of this involves purely practical activities such as cleaning blankets, and shredding or securely filing participant documents. Other activities include journaling about what has been learnt, what needs attention and deciding what to take to a final supervision session. Time to reflect is vital. The TLC in Chapter 19 is useful resource for structured reflection, and if possible dedicating time to engage in a reflective process with peers is hugely formative.

16
Orientation and assessment

It might seem strange that this section is placed at the end of the chapters on teaching rather than at the beginning! This is because both the implicit and the explicit curricula of the MBP are deeply relevant to the foundation for the MBP learning process. This section outlines the intentions and practical considerations relating to the first contact with participants, as they are assessed and orientated to an MBP course. As the adage goes, 'You never get a second chance to make a first impression'. In this section, the *assessment* process refers to assessing a participant's suitability for the course, and *orientation* refers to information you give participants.

There are important overarching principles to consider during assessment and orientation.

- *Embodiment*: the teacher, as the 'steward' (McCown et al., 2010) is an ambassador of mindfulness, what is said and done in this orientation and assessment phase matters, but *how* it is said and done matters perhaps more!
- *Safety*: If participating in an MBP is not helpful or safe at this moment, the assessment process needs to respectfully bring this to light.
- *Relationships*: This is the start of a relationship lasting over two months, so participants are keen to know and sense that they can belong and feel safe.
- *A good-enough fit*: The orientation/assessment process aims to check that participants know what is entailed, and have an opportunity to consider if the MBP course is what they want to do.
- *Equality, diversity and inclusion*: From considerations about facilities (access, toilets, lighting etc.), to the way the teacher holds difference and diversity, participants will feel more or less able to feel safe and engaged in the learning process.

TEACHER ROLE IN ASSESSMENT AND ORIENTATION

There are several ways to approach assessment and orientation, and how this is done will depend on the organisational context for the MBP, teacher preference, and participant vulnerability. Whichever approach is chosen, there are five key roles played by the MBP teacher:

1 *Assessor-protector*: It is necessary to *assess* if participants will be safe attending the particular MBP. This role may require specialised knowledge (if working with clinical populations or specific physical, psychological, or emotional vulnerabilities), and sensitivity to issues of inclusion. See section below for further detail.

2 *Cautioner*: In addition to not causing harm, the teacher needs to establish if attending the MBP will be helpful. This includes ensuring participants know how the course may impact on their life practically in terms of time commitment and home practice; and the emotional impact of practice (which can make things feel more intense, at least to begin with). Also, while there is an extensive evidence base about its effectiveness, communication that mindfulness training is not a 'cure all' magic potion is vital!

3 *Promoter-motivator*: It is important to encourage the seeds of curiosity and self-care that have brought the participants to an MBP, whilst being realistically frank about the challenges of the course. The assessment and orientation process is an important opportunity for participants to share their reasons for wishing to do the course. It can be helpful to invite a participant from a previous course to offer their experience of mindfulness practice at a group orientation session – this can be a grounded and authentic way to augment this motivator role.

4 *Informer*: At a practical level, information about the MBP can be given verbally and in written form. This includes the teacher giving clear information about costs, dates and times, venue location, parking, bus routes, what best to wear etc. It also involves communicating what a typical session will be like in terms of activity, group size, and expectations about participation. You can perhaps invite participation in a short experiential mindfulness practice.

   If there are any special considerations such as wanting to film sessions or include a trainee, these need to be clearly explained at the orientation stage. Also offer information about how MBPs have their effect, by presenting the evidence base and theory (Chapter 25). Ideally this is linked to the life issues the participant is presenting. At a group orientation session, asking participants to share their motivations and expectations for wanting to do the course can provide grounded material for informing them about what mindfulness is and what it is not.

5 *Connector*: Creating an *experience* of connection with participants, both as the group leader and individually, is vital in terms of establishing the seeds of a safe, vibrant learning container; and the seeds of confidence and courage to engage. It is important that the teacher is appropriately available for contact between sessions for any issues that arise in connection with the course.

Assessment – is the MBP suitable and safe for a particular participant?

Considerations for 'general public' groups

It is important to assess all participants who apply to your MBP course to ensure that it is suitable for them at this time, and remember to reflect on any participants you are unsure about with your supervisor. The participant's attitude, understanding of their own process, and willingness to work with their experiences and with the teacher, are all important factors in assessment of readiness to take a mindfulness course. Participants who are open-minded about what may happen, who are willing to discuss openly with the teacher if they have problems, and who will accept support (and/or leave the course) if necessary, may be able to take a course with a higher level of problems or illness than participants without these attributes. Participants who think mindfulness will magically solve all their difficulties are much less likely to do well.

With participants who are professionals interested in using or teaching mindfulness as part of their work, it is important to underline that the course is experiential, and that it is essential they embrace this aspect. It's also helpful to discuss beforehand how professionals will introduce themselves in the group. Otherwise, the sense of 'being observed' can inhibit other participants from sharing their experiences

During the application process, require that participants complete a form where they can confidentially share anything that may be useful for you to know, such as:

- History of mental health challenges, especially in the last few years – e.g. anxiety and depression
- Current medication
- Physical health challenges
- Recent difficult life events such as bereavement, divorce, job loss, or other major change
- Professional contact details for consensual checking of any participant safety issues (i.e. GP/Key Worker/Therapist/ etc.)
- Any history of trauma – it is important to explain the full breadth of what is meant by trauma with examples – see Chapter 23
- Why the participant wants to take a mindfulness course at present.

Suggested exclusion criteria for 'general public' groups

These notes offer a broad-brush stroke on the topic of safety and appropriateness. It is usually possible to use inclusive language when considering 'exclusion criteria'! For example, several of the suggested exclusion criteria may apply now but not in future months in which case the person can be told: "This is not a good time for you to do the course, it is better to wait and do it later when ...." Or, if there are criteria that are not time specific they may be informed about "More suitable approaches for the challenges you have" or "It may be helpful to explore x y or z before embarking on this type of course". The 'exclusion criteria' listed below are subject to judgement, experience of teacher, and available support. Questions/concerns about any of the categories listed below merit careful consideration in supervision:

- *Active or recent physical addiction to alcohol or drugs*: If participants are currently physically dependent on drugs or alcohol, they are very unlikely to be able to undertake an MBP; as their awareness and ability to stay in the present are negatively affected their lives may also be too chaotic to make a regular commitment. Participants who are psychologically but not physically dependent on substances, and who meet other criteria for taking a course (e.g. well-motivated to change, some insight) may be able to engage with mindfulness training, and to work with their reactive use of substances, as would participants dealing with ruminative thinking, anxiety or stress. Mindfulness-Based Relapse Prevention (MBRP) has been specifically developed for people who are working with misuse of substances.
- *Suicidality*: This is a dangerous vulnerability for new meditators, so people who are feeling suicidal should be asked to wait and take a course when things are better for

them. A comprehensive source of perspective and information on assessment and orientation for this specific issue can be found in Chapters 5 and 6 of Mindfulness-Based Cognitive Therapy with People at Risk of Suicide (Williams et al., 2017). It is important to note that although MBCT adapted for suicidality is the course a participant with this vulnerability should be signposted to – it is not uncommon to find such vulnerability in general-population groups. If, or when, this crops up midway through an MBP it is an issue for immediate supervision.

- *Physical illness making attendance difficult*: MBSR and MBCT are generally used with participants with chronic problems or illnesses or mental health challenges. Periods of acute illness (or sometimes an acute episode of an existing condition), when people are dealing with high levels of stress, and can be getting used to dealing with a new and different way of being, are generally not good times to engage in the intensity of an MBP training process. For people with ongoing physical limitations, it is important to check in with them about support and adjustments which will make the course accessible.

- *Life crises*: Participants who have had a recent bereavement, divorce, etc., are usually advised to wait until things are more settled before taking an MBP. Pre-existing mindfulness practice is very helpful in dealing with strong, raw feelings of grief, shock and anger, but these are often too overwhelming for participants to learn how to meditate while dealing with them. This is an area where there is some flexibility depending on the individual, the support around them, the existing resources they have, and the experience/confidence of the teacher.

- *Social anxiety which would make attending a group difficult*: Also consider if the social anxiety of one participant would be disruptive for the rest of the group (in which case suggest a 1-to-1 MBP).

- *Active psychosis/schizophrenia*: Participants who are out of contact with what is considered usual reality, are unlikely to be helped by mindfulness meditation offered in the form of a structured 8-session MBP, and may be harmed. There is a small amount of evidence (Britton, 2019) that meditation has triggered psychotic episodes in some individuals, and although this may not be true of mindfulness meditation, with its emphasis on grounding in physical sensations and other bodily senses, it would make sense to aim for safety here. There is some mindfulness for psychosis research and practice which offers guidance on careful tailoring for this group (Chadwick, 2014).

- *Post-traumatic stress disorder*: This important issue is covered in more detail in Chapter 23, and it is important to familiarise yourself with current literature in this area (e.g. Hopwood & Schutte, 2017). In brief this area needs individually tailored assessment and orientation. The key considerations are the level of awareness the individual has of the trauma and the ways it is impacting in the present. If they are in a relatively stable place in their life; have done some personal work on the issues, ideally with the support of a therapist; and these are coupled with an understanding of how re-triggering might show up and how they might take care of themselves when this happens, then engagement with an MBP that is taught in a trauma sensitive way (as all MBPs should be!) could be an ideal next step. The teacher and the participants can have a conversation in advance of the sorts of choices the individual can make during the sessions and within the home practice; and they can stay in touch with each other through the 8-weeks to monitor things.

- *Participants with current psychological challenges*: MBCT was originally developed for people who are vulnerable to depression but in remission whilst taking the course. Comprehensive coverage on assessing for this population may be found in Segal et al (2013, pp. 94–108) and Crane (2017, pp. 103–105). There is research and practice on offering MBCT to people with current episode anxiety and depression, and residual, chronic and treatment resistant depression which you should familiarise yourself with if working with these populations (e.g. Strauss et al., 2014; Cladder-Micus et al., 2018). It is important to familiarise yourself with the ways that depression may manifest – especially in a non-clinical context – and to know why and how it may make attending an MBP problematic or harmful. From such understanding, the conversation about other options including attending an MBP in a clinical rather than a general public context, or waiting for a better time, may be helpful and compassionate.

  It is essential that participants understand what the course entails, and are given (and give themselves) full permission to step out of the course if they are finding it counterproductive (though be aware that this may reinforce negative self-image). It's most important that they are fully supported, either by the MBP teacher, or by their own therapist; the former needs to understand the nature of their difficulties, and the latter needs to understand the experiential, and potentially challenging nature of learning about awareness and acceptance in an MBP. Whilst preparing participants to expect that the learning process will bring them close to the difficulties they are experiencing, it is also helpful to prime them to recognise that this is the very work they may need to do – learning how to relate in new ways to difficult thoughts, emotions and sensations.

Ensure you have training in and experience of the particular problems/conditions that participants are experiencing, and an understanding of how these interface with the practice of mindfulness and working in a group. If you don't have this training/experience, work alongside someone who does. Listen carefully to your own concerns about participants, as well as assessing their motivation and understanding, and make your own judgement alongside your supervisor on whether they have enough support, and you have enough knowledge, time, and confidence to work with them.

Other considerations

Participants with learning disabilities

There is a growing evidence base showing that mindfulness training can been helpful for participants with learning disabilities (Chapman et al, 2013). If you are thinking of working with this population, read the good practice guidelines for teaching mindfulness with people with learning disabilities (Griffith et al., 2019b). Practices need to be simplified and carefully tailored, and also seek specialist training and advice if contemplating working with this population.

Participants with asthma or other breathing problems

Although alternative anchors to the breath for attention are offered as standard good practice – the general emphasis on use of the breath in MBPs can leave a participant with breathing difficulties feeling disadvantaged. Thus, it is important to talk this over in the pre-course interview or orientation. In addition, it is important to mention that use of an inhaler, as and when necessary, in the class is completely ok.

Practical considerations for combining assessment and orientation

The range of possible ways to assess and orientate participants are briefly described below-beginning with the most thorough approach, to lighter touch options. The choice around this depends on the participant group, organisational context and experience of the teacher. Any group offered in a clinical context will need a thorough assessment (Williams et al., 2017), whereas perhaps a lighter touch approach is enough if you are an experienced teacher teaching a general public class.

1 *Individual assessment plus a group orientation session*: This is the most resource heavy approach with a one-to-one assessment process (phone or online) followed by a group orientation session. This enables a more accurate and detailed assessment, and the start of a personal connection between the participant and the teacher. Because the assessment process is separated out here, the orientation session can be more clearly dedicated to enabling the group forming process to begin.

2 *Individual assessment with no group orientation session*: This method of having one-to-one sessions with each participant prior the MBP achieves a high degree of safety and relational connection between teacher and potential participant, although the participant has to make a commitment to the whole course before actually meeting the group or experiencing the venue.

3 *Group orientation session with an integrated individual assessment process*: In this approach, potential participants may make contact with the teacher after seeing the course advertised. The initial contact may include the teacher emailing more information about the course along with an invitation to complete a self-assessment questionnaire. If the teacher feels that there is a need to contact the individual based on their responses to the questionnaire (perhaps they report a recent difficult life event, or are on medication for depression), then this is arranged and helps to determine if the course is suitable for that person. If assessing in this way, at the group orientation session, it is important to make reference to safety and possible reasons not to do the course "at this time" or "in this format", and potential participants should be offered an opportunity to book a one-to-one meeting before deciding whether to commit to the MBP. The majority of people attending the orientation will not require a meeting like this, so this approach is more time efficient and avoids repetitive meetings with each potential participant, whilst maintaining a relatively high degree of safety.

SUMMARY

For many would-be participants the assessment process and/or orientation will be their first contact with mindfulness and a mindfulness community. The quality of this initial contact is therefore highly significant. There is important *content* to be communicated, primarily revolving around safety and the ethics of 'do no harm'. At the same time, assessment and orientation provide opportunities to communicate, via embodiment, equally significant foundations for learning. Thus, without explicitly mentioning anything about openness, trust, honesty, non-judgement, acceptance and so forth we endeavour to invite these supportive attitudes tangibly 'in the room'. Without saying very much about mindfulness being about self-empowerment and compassion we act in ways that plant the seeds of this understanding. We 'walk the talk' and the participants begin to 'catch' mindfulness! In addition, assessment and orientation provide opportunities for important contracting that help prevent difficult situations arising in later sessions of the course. A good example of this is contracting around the inquiry process, so that participants can be forewarned about the possibility of the teacher asking them to stop unravelling a narrative and focus once again on their immediate experience, "Not because we are not interested in you, or your story, we are, but because in this learning context it is helpful to come back to the direct experience". If this piece of contracting is clearly done before the course starts it is so much easier to step in and direct in a less obviously directive manner. Contracting also facilitates forming a vibrant whilst safe learning container, collectively discussing and agreeing guidelines about respect for others in the group, confidentiality, giving advice, punctuality, leaving the teaching space, managing upsets etc. The orientation is an opportunity to make things clear so that when inevitable awkward glitches arise in the sessions, they can be handled by *reminding* participants about what had been agreed and discussed rather than having to adopt authoritarian methods. Comprehensive information about the content and rationales of pre-course assessment and orientation may also be found in the various curriculum guides (i.e. Crane, 2017, pp. 103–105; Kabat-Zinn et al., 2021; Segal et al., 2013, Chapter 6). Thorough preparations and the way we go about creating them are crucial for creating safe, enjoyable and effective learning.

17

Teaching mindfulness-based programmes online

Our world is changing fast, with new challenges and new technologies. In March 2020, the trend towards delivery of MBPs online was accelerated due to the coronavirus pandemic. Online MBPs may have some limitations as a teaching context but also offer important new opportunities, such as increased accessibility – including to under-represented groups, and reducing the carbon footprint from people physically travelling to meet.

In this section, 'online' teaching refers to teaching to a group 'live': i.e. that you log in at the same time to have regular (usually weekly) sessions together, akin to what would happen in a face-to-face course. Sharing pre-recorded courses, or videos of practices may be useful in certain contexts, but this is not what is addressed here. There are a range of digital platforms for online teaching that offer similar functions such as ways of 'seeing' the whole group or individual participants when they are speaking; enabling breakout rooms for dyads and small group work; screen sharing for using whiteboards and presentations; and engaging in live written communication ('chat') between individuals or with the teacher. In this section, online teaching considerations are structured and explored within the six domains of the MBI:TAC. Throughout the text the MBI:TAC domains being referred to are cited in brackets (i.e. D2 refers to Domain 2 Relational Skills).

DOMAIN 1: COVERAGE, PACING AND ORGANISATION OF THE SESSION (INCLUDING PRE-COURSE AND ORIENTATION CONSIDERATIONS)

Coverage and pacing

The content of the curriculum does not need to significantly alter, and nor does the 'pacing' of the main session elements. However, extra time in addition to the core time frames outlined in curriculum guides needs to be factored in for each session. For example, the orientation session requires perhaps an extra 20 minutes to help participants familiarise themselves with the online platform and to troubleshoot technical issues. Also opening the online 'room' 15 minutes before each session and encouraging participants to join early allows them to meet and greet each other before class, and pick up on any technical problems.

Another difference with online delivery is that the inquiry process may take more time to allow for small group work in triads/dyads and for 'pop-corning' (see horizontal inquiry, Chapter 9) to foster engagement prior to the whole-group inquiry. More time is also beneficial for short, whole-group connecting activities at the start of the course, such as a brief go-round where participants might be invited to say one or two words about how they are feeling. Other aspects though may take less time – e.g. getting into and out from small group work can be very much quicker as there is no physical movement of chairs etc.

Choice of the online platform

The choice of software may simply be personal preference, but some commissioning organisations specify digital platforms that meet their particular security and confidentiality requirements. Ideally the platform should enable breakout rooms for triad, dyad and small group work. All this needs checking as part of the basic 'organisation' for the course.

Confidentiality

There are many additional considerations when teaching online. First, ensure that anyone who is not signed up for the sessions cannot enter the online meeting. From the first point of contact, participants need to be informed about the way confidentiality and privacy will be ensured. It is important to establish a ground rule that participants do not record sessions or take screen shots, and to reassure them that the teacher will not be recording the sessions (unless recording is happening for training, assessment or research purposes, when there is clear governance to protect the process). We recommend that any recordings of sessions that have participants in them are not shared with participants due to security considerations. Furthermore, confidentiality cannot be preserved if other members of the household can see or hear what is going on within the class. Individuals who share households with others therefore need to participate from a room with a closed door. If this is not possible then headphones with a noise cancelling microphone is required. These issues need to be addressed during the orientation session.

Assessment and orientation

In addition to the usual preparation processes for teaching 'in-person' courses (Chapter 16), online teaching requires a slightly different emphasis. The opportunity that assessment affords for one-to-one 'meeting' and 'connecting' with prospective participants is particularly significant. As well as ensuring all of the usual safety functions, this first contact lays the ground for the relational context (D2), and the learning container (D6), both crucial for effective teaching. Setting up individual meetings with each participant prior to the start of an online course is highly recommended. This enables some principles of trauma sensitivity to be set in place with a particular emphasis on the invitational nature of the learning process, and the encouragement to make self-care choices and to connect with the teacher if they are experiencing any challenges in relation to taking the course. Consider the need for 'informal' connecting time during assessments, in addition to its necessary content. This also gives a time to check participants' ability to commit to and benefit from an online course.

If conducting an orientation in a group rather than individually, the session may include building connection between participants as well as with the teacher(s). It can be helpful in forming connections, to share with participants the geographical location from where the teacher is teaching, and for participants to share their location also.

Small group work (particularly in early sessions) is even more significant in the online teaching context because the group does not have the informal connection involved in arriving and being in a physical space together. Note that as the breakout rooms are 'blind' to the teacher, it is safer to organise triads or tetrads rather than dyads in the initial stages. This will limit the possibility of a participant finding themselves on their own with a partner who may become difficult or inappropriate. Once the group has formed and is more fully known to the teacher, safe use of dyads becomes possible. An extra safety net is provided by reminding all participants that they have the option to contact the teacher ('the host') from the breakout rooms using the 'chat' function, and that they can leave the breakout room at any point to return to the main 'room'.

This first meeting gives an opportunity to check that participants feel safe enough to have their cameras on during the sessions, so the teacher can see everyone for safety reasons, and to facilitate connections across the group. Speak about and normalise how it can sometimes seem as if you are not looking directly at the person when speaking to them due to the camera location.

Teach participants how to use the technology

At the assessment, check participants' internet connection, to ensure they have adequate bandwidth for the video function, and their ability to use the digital platform. Ensure that participants are connecting from a computer, laptop or tablet that is resting on a hard surface (not a handheld device). Ensure a ground rule is in place that all other windows (i.e. e-mail, social media), phones and other devices are turned off. At the orientation, rehearse the various essential functions such as 'mute/unmute' 'camera on/off', 'hide self-view', 'chat', 'joining and leaving' the 'breakout rooms' (or equivalent). This can be fun and serve the function of connecting. For example, you could ask the group to all unmute their microphones to 'popcorn' (participants making a comment to the group when they are ready, rather than calling on each participant in turn) on a question like: "Where is your favourite place in the world?" Seek agreement on basic ground rules such as: having their camera on at all times (unless poor internet connection makes this impossible); muting the microphone when not speaking; raising your hand and unmuting when speaking; renaming yourself with the name you want to be known by; not to use the chat function or your keyboard during the session unless explicitly invited to by the teacher; logging back on immediately if you drop out of the meeting. It is preferable not to do too much digital training at this stage ... just the essentials! Give the participants a phone number for sending messages should their internet fail completely. Participants may also need to consider negotiating with those with whom they share their living space to request that bandwidth is prioritised for the session.

Organising personal equipment and space

A 'kit' list can be sent with the e-mail accepting the person onto the course after the assessment meeting, including reminders of agreements negotiated at the orientation session about online etiquette; a clean non-slip mat for floor work; blankets for warmth,; a cushion for head and/or hands to rest onto; straight-back chair; good front facing lighting; pad of paper for notes; and some coloured pens. Not all these will be needed every session, but it is helpful to have them ready. Lastly, at the orientation it is helpful to speak about space for the lying down postures.

Be prepared

Make a document for each session with the specific small group instructions ready to 'cut-and-paste' into the digital broadcast/announcements function and other helpful instructions that can be pasted onto the 'share' screen to make tasks in the session as clear as possible. Set up materials you plan to use through 'share screen' in advance, and close unnecessary screens.

Hybrid online/ face-to-face courses

Consider the possibility that some situations and contexts might allow a mixture of in-person and online meetings. For example, where geographic isolation is a main reason for online teaching it might be possible for the day of practice to be in-person. Other formats may also be possible such as an in-person initial day covering sessions 1 and 2, followed by an online week-by-week continuation.

Making reasonable adjustments/accommodations to ensure the course is as accessible and inclusive as possible is a key thread that runs through all the above points. However, it must be acknowledged, the online option may not be suitable for everyone

DOMAIN 2: RELATIONAL SKILLS

Online groups who have met physically – even just once – usually have a natural entry to connection and empathy with each other. However, it is also striking how connection, empathy and community building can happen at depth in well held online spaces.

Prioritise connection

More time and attention is needed to build empathy and connection in the online space. These lie at the heart of Domain 2 and profoundly influence the other domains. Replicate the informal before and after session meeting time by signing in 15 minutes before the session starts and allowing all the microphones to be on. Take a lead in creating an ethos of informal light socializing ... perhaps recalling ordinary non-confidential details such as which location they live or the name of their cat! At the end of each session, consider saying 'goodbye' individually, using their name. If a participant leaves the session during the session, it is essential to follow-up on this, just as one would in an in-person course. The online teacher needs to be proactive in making themselves available for individual connection. As one would in an in-person course, encourage participants to seek contact outside the formal sessions.

Appearances

In an online context, good lighting on the face is important to facilitate connection. To avoid unhelpful shadows, ensure the lighting is 'from the front' and ideally from more than one source. In addition, relational connection is better without the use of a 'virtual background' but this means *neutralising* the space seen by participants of any political or religious biases (i.e. images, icons, posters etc). What is in view influences the connection, so consider what it says about who you are!

Many online digital platforms offer a way to hide 'self-view' and this can be very helpful in replicating the in-person group situation. Being able to see yourself whilst teaching has some benefits in terms of personal feedback (for example noticing how we may be fidgeting or frowning inappropriately), but, mostly it can unhelpfully absorb attention and detract from connection and presence.

Ease

Connection is facilitated by being at ease with the online context and its technology. If technology stress does occur, take time to model mindful awareness of this. Don't let technical issues get in the way of connection with yourself and the group!

Assistant or co-teacher

We recommend having an assistant or co-teacher, so there is someone available to take care of the technical side while you teach. Specifically, they can take responsibility for monitoring the chat, for setting up the breakouts, for giving feedback to the teacher if there are any issues arising, and for keeping alert to individuals within the group. If anyone is visibly distressed, they can arrange to 'step out' with them into a breakout room. A co-teacher can also assist if someone has dropped out of the room because of problems with the internet connection. If the teacher's internet connection is troublesome or fails, the co-teacher can take the reins.

Use of PowerPoint and other slides

Be aware of the tendency to lose a sense of interpersonal connection with the group during a presentation online. Consider using no more than two slides at a time.

DOMAIN 3: EMBODYING MINDFULNESS

Become familiar with the technology

When technical issues or other challenges related to the online platform arise – as they will – it is important to allow exactly the same response as in an in-person context (i.e. pause, recognise, breathe, fold the issue into the session and normalise it). Familiarise yourself with the platform by practicing online guiding, inquiring and didactic teaching with peers. Embodiment can also be disrupted by the challenges of using a microphone when leading movement or body scan practices, and/or by having to reposition the camera or microphone. Consider using a wireless headset.

How do I look?

Embodiment has a relational or contextual dimension which means staying connected to the group as well as to ourselves. In this respect, it can be helpful to experiment with sometimes hiding 'self-view'. Sensing our connection with the group can be further supported by using the 'gallery view' whilst guiding and facilitating inquiry – rather than 'speaker view'. Dressing how you would normally dress for teaching is also important.

Pause, connect with the ground

This is all part of the usual attention we give to personal practice before and after a teaching session. Having checked the technology, resources, and teaching space, leave enough time to settle and connect before the 'meet and greet'. Another consideration is to remember to ground oneself whilst the small group 'breakout rooms' are underway. This is another reason to prepare cut-and-paste ready instructions on your desktop, enabling maximum opportunity in these 'off-duty' periods to touch in with your experience. Looking away from the screen for these periods (if you have co-teacher to hold the space), can also foster groundedness.

Pesky interruptions

A factor that can very quickly erode embodiment is unforeseen interruptions, especially noise from your own teaching space during the session. We may well be teaching from a room in our home rather than a dedicated teaching studio. We can quickly mute our own microphone if the noise is momentary, and/or be explicit about the interruption, folding it into our teaching, but it can leave us unbalanced. Therefore, it is good to do what we can to limit such interruptions including switching off non-essential devices. Participants will be alert to how you handle things. No one will remember a small technical hitch or interruption – they happen all the time – but they are likely to note *how* you handled it. Approach these as part of your practice, and as an opportunity to implicitly embody the attitudinal foundations of mindfulness.

DOMAIN 4: GUIDING MINDFULNESS PRACTICES

Maintaining connection while guiding practices

An important aspect of guiding practices is aliveness and responsiveness to what is happening in the group and environment. It is important therefore, to ask participants to leave their video on at all times. It is helpful to mute all participants during a guided practice (they can of course unmute themselves should they need to) as this prevents auditory feedback.

Guiding floor-based practices

Guiding the body scan and mindful movement online presents practical challenges. For the teacher this includes, how to position yourself to be visible by the group, and, how to stay in touch with the participants who will most probably not be in view! For the body scan, it may be preferable to lead from a chair. In mindful movement, standing back far enough for your whole body to be visible is facilitated by having a wireless headset, and by asking the participants to switch to 'speaker view'.

Use inclusive and normalising language

Participants are likely to have sounds and other interruptions coming from their home environment, even if they have been strongly encouraged to create good conditions for practice. As with an in-person group, interruptions are helpfully acknowledged and normalised, creating an alive sense of what is actually happening. However, in an online group, with muted microphones, sounds are not shared. So, it can be helpful to weave into the guidance regular, more general references to "Any unwanted sounds ... from inside or outside ... and noticing any impact these are having on us." In addition, occasional guidance for other possible interruptions such as pets or children arriving to check out what is going on!

Acknowledge the screen

A main, alive experience that participants will be having as they go into and come out of formal practices is the screen. It can be helpful to bring this into the guidance (e.g. "letting go of the screen and the images of our group in front of us ... and either looking down or gently closing the eyelids"; or, "As we transition out from this practice, perhaps opening our eyes and connecting once again with the screen in front of us ... and the live group here with us").

Teacher to lead mindfulness practices with eyes open or half open

This is important because many other cues which can be picked up during an in-person class are not available (for example, the sound of a participant leaving the room, a participant crying, being restless, or sensing a shift in atmosphere/energy of the group). If the teacher usually undertakes personal mindfulness practice with eyes closed, their own practice will need to incorporate meditating with eyes open or eyes half open in order to build up confidence and ease with this way of guiding.

DOMAIN 5: CONVEYING COURSE THEMES THROUGH INTERACTIVE DIALOGUE AND DIDACTIC TEACHING

Visual connection

Effective inquiry requires the teacher to be as fully connected to the participants as possible. So, as well as ensuring a good sound connection it is helpful to be able to pick up body language (e.g. the use of hand gestures). For this reason, it can be helpful at the orientation session to invite participants to angle their video camera so as to show more than just their head and shoulders. Because inquiry is 'relational' it is also helpful if your own video captures your arms and hands (e.g. so when mirroring a gesture made by a participant this is visible to them).

Rehearsing the basics

At the orientation and perhaps again at the start of session 1, rehearse horizontal inquiry, with all microphones unmuted using a simple, light topic such as "If you knew me you'd know that ...". As part of this, rehearse clearly raising a hand just before you call out. Then rehearse vertical inquiry by saying for example: "And now please everyone mute your microphones ... so, would anyone like to say a little more about what you've just shared? Just raise a hand and unmute your microphone when you are ready to share".

Encouraging involvement

It can be easier to hide in an online group made up of tiny head and shoulder images in little rectangles. It can be helpful to explicitly mention the challenge of online inquiry at the start of the course, mentioning directly how, for some, the screen may quite naturally lead to a sense of feeling less actively involved in the inquiry process. Because of this, a slightly different approach to inquiry may be required. Whilst doing our best to protect the invitational ethos of inquiry, we may consider:

- Increased use of small groups, triads and (once the group has 'formed' dyads) as a preliminary to whole-group inquiry;
- At times be more direct about asking participants to join in by saying, for example, "Would those who have not yet spoken in this session feel ok to say a little about your practice";
- 'Harvesting' input from the group through the use of the chat function or whiteboard.

Fully utilising the software

The digital platform you are using may well have functions for collecting simple feedback such as 'polling', 'chat' or typing on a pre-prepared word document through 'share screen'. These can be used a little like horizontal (or popcorn) inquiry, gathering a lot of simple responses. A more direct and connected way of using the screen for horizontal inquiry might be to invite a "thumbs up, thumbs down, or thumbs horizontal" in response to a question such as "How did you get on with the new movement practice?" One might play with using the chat function to elicit a "one or two word" response to an exercise or a practice.

Use of small groups, triads and dyads after inquiry

As mentioned above, dyads are best avoided until there is a clear sense of trust between all members of the group and/or the teacher has confidence that all participants will adhere to the basic ground rules established at the orientation. What can be usefully included though is the judicious use of the 'broadcast' function. This allows instant messages to be sent to the screens of those in the breakout rooms. The teacher can send successive instructions to keep the participants on track. For example, participants may start with the instruction to "Just talk a little about your experience of the practice"; then after a few minutes the broadcasted message can pop up saying "Now, check in together about any sensations or emotions you noticed during that practice" and a few minutes later, "Was there anything shared or different?" The first time the breakout rooms are used it is important to say that "Silence may happen and that is ok" and, "You can always contact me (the teacher) using the 'chat function' if for example you find yourself alone or feel confused about what you are doing or uncomfortable for any reason." With some online platforms the teacher (the 'host') can enter the breakout room when appropriate.

Modifications for group exercises

Some exercises need adaptation when offered online. There are multiple creative opportunities. Box 17.1 offers two examples of adaptations.

Box 17.1 Modifications for teaching online

Session 7 MBSR – changing seats practice

Given individuals will typically be alone in a room, the teacher can invite participants to sit, stand or lie down somewhere else in the room or move their existing seat to face towards another direction, like a wall, window or door.

Session 8: Writing letter to self

Options include:

- A handwritten letter inserted into a paper diary at the chosen future date (3–6 months on)
- Using the future me website www.futureme.org
- Inviting the participants to journal.

DOMAIN 6: HOLDING THE GROUP LEARNING CONTAINER

This domain needs careful consideration when teaching online. When creating the learning container, establishing safety is key. When building the learning container, a helpful question might be: what is needed to help this online group 'form', 'norm', 'storm' and 'perform?' (Tuckman, 1965; Chapter 13).

Forming

Aspects of forming such as safety and a sense of belonging in an online environment will require more time and different activities then for in-person groups. In an in-person group, the act of talking together about ground rules and confidentiality can create a sense of shared safety and belonging that is harder to create online. Participants may feel safer individually because they are in their own space, but in terms of 'forming' it is important to build a sense of *shared* safety and belonging. This is one good reason to consider not having an overly large group for an online MBP. We recommend (certainly when in the early stages of teaching) that the course is not bigger than the number of participants that can be seen on one screen; this is another reason for encouraging suitable equipment for an online course.

It can help to give time at the start of each session to have a 'go-round' where everyone is invited to say their name and "perhaps one or two words" about how they are (we sometimes call this an internal weather report). In an already time constrained curriculum this can seem inefficient unless the value and power of the group is sufficiently remembered. Forming can be also be facilitated by the informal meet and greet time before each session as described above. The meet and greet time has no private or paired conversations and so the teacher may need to be active in getting things going. It can also help 'forming' to facilitate a session ending where each participant can "with one or two words, say goodbye". One possibility is to ask the whole group to unmute and call out their farewells, good wishes to the rest of the group as they sign out. Also, consider pausing at intervals throughout each session to invite the group to "take each other in ... glancing around the screen ... sensing we are all in this moment together ... appreciating each other and this shared experience of being here."

Storming

The possibility of passive storming may be more likely in an online format (i.e. simply absenting oneself either physically or verbally), rather than being openly critical or testing. It can be helpful to be more proactive in inviting between-session contact with participants to encourage the expression of doubts and concerns about content, process, or the group. Then, whilst ensuring no slippage of confidentiality, generalised references to themes or concerns can be non-judgementally brought into subsequent sessions. Using the advantages of the online context can also help. For example, a polling function could be used, say in session 4 to vote on "The most difficult aspect of practising at home with voting choices of: a/ time b/ interruptions c/ the teacher's voice d/ being told you should do it"! Remember though that sometimes the civility of an in-person group can be lost. So periodically reminding the group that respect is part of the ground rules and is just as important within an online setting as it is in-person.

Norming

Norming happens as the group gets familiar with the online context, rules, patterns, and activities of a typical session. It can be encouraged by making the context, rules, and activities clear. This can include writing these into a pre-session friendly e-mail and taking time to repeat them explicitly. Taking care to use participants' names when interacting is also very helpful. Facilitating an online forum through which participants can connect between sessions can be helpful. However, this entails commitment and work by the teacher, to carefully monitor the content to ensure that the clearly negotiated ground rules are maintained.

Performing

This is facilitated by a 'timely' stepping back from the foreground of teaching and facilitating the group to work together on a common 'task', using small or half-groups in the breakout rooms. Thus, for example in session 7, having worked in pairs on discussing nourishing lifestyle choices, the small groups could be tasked with pooling strategies about how to make individual ideas "more workable, possible and sustainable". Similarly, later on in the course, in the meet-and-greet phase before and after the session, the teacher's task may be to step back and allow more peer-to-peer interactions. Some factors in the online context help this domain. For example, the way participants' home ground is visible can create a subtle intimacy. An occasional bored child may arrive and hang on the neck of a participant, or their cat may peer into the screen! Care must be taken not to assume we, as teachers, have permission to comment on background visuals but, often the participants lives are much more clearly in view than in an in-person group. A different kind of intimacy can be a strong feature of online group teaching.

Adjourning

At the end of the course it can be symbolic (and fun) to take out open hands with palms facing the camera to the side edges of the screen which gives the appearance of hands touching each other making the group container visible before it dissolves.

SUMMARY

Whilst there is huge value in teaching in-person, there are many reasons why this may not be possible, and the question then becomes, not shall I teach online but, 'How do I best teach online?' Mindfulness is about living with awareness and flourishing, as best we can, in the context we are actually in. Learning to flourish and help others flourish through an online platform becomes a gift when the option of an in-person course is closed. The challenge is to work with that gift skilfully to create safe learning spaces.

Part III

Resourcing ourselves as mindfulness teachers

INTRODUCTION

So far in this book we have explored what happens within the MBP teaching space itself. Here in Part III, we present nine chapters, written by members of CMRP's training team and close colleagues, on a range of important themes surrounding MBP delivery. The common thread between these chapters is that they address areas that are vital to engage in as part of your mindfulness teaching practice journey. There is a lot of surrounding study and practice that supports and nourishes the actual work in the teaching space. As the field has become more established, it has become clearer what the key resourcing ingredients within a pathway towards being an MBP teacher are. We aim to describe the main aspects of each ingredient and then to signpost you to further reading.

Rebecca Crane first offers an overview of the territory of how we resource ourselves as MBP teachers; Gemma Griffith, Rebecca Crane, Karunavira, and Lynn Koerbel present the TLC, which offers a structure for reflecting on your MBP teaching; Bridgette O'Neil examines how we can engage with and support our personal mindfulness practice; Alison Evans writes about how mindfulness supervision is a key support to our MBP teaching practice; Pamela Duckerin explores reflective practice and how we apply this to an ongoing exploration of professional issues and ethics; Eluned Gold presents the theory and practice of offering MBPs in ways that are trauma sensitive; Bethan Roberts and Rebecca Crane examine the social context within which MBP teaching is situated; Gemma Griffith and Karunavira write about how science and theory informs MBP teaching; and finally, Rebecca Crane and Heledd Griffiths discuss how to skilfully engage with the process of implementing MBPs.

18

How do we resource and support ourselves as MBP teachers?

An overview

Rebecca Crane

Being an MBP teacher is both a very ordinary and a very extraordinary role. The ordinariness is that we are engaged in a core exploration of the everydayness of being human – what is the water I swim in? The extraordinariness is that through the practice of mindfulness, we deliberately inquire into the veil of habits and perceptions that are layered on top of the immediacy of experience, and thus we proactively engage with the undercurrents that drive our lives. The very tool we have for this job is our own being – our own capacity to show up as an embodied authentic human. Vulnerability and exposure are part of the job description. The process of becoming an MBP teacher takes us on a journey that can involve significant shifts in identity. It comes with the satisfaction and challenge of being a whole life engagement. It is not just a job we do in our working hours; it is a way of being that we embed into the fabric of our lives. How do we support and resource ourselves through the years as we engage with this work? This chapter aims to:

- Examine intention as the ground for our teaching practice
- Reflect on the conditions that support the development of skills, qualities, and knowledge for MBP teaching practice
- Present the practicalities that need to be in place to start teaching.

CONNECTING WITH YOUR INTENTION

What is your motivation for engaging in this work? Being an MBP teacher is not a very clear route to career prospects, a company car, or a pension! The engagement is a calling – an inner pull towards work that has deep meaning to us. Connecting with this inspiration and motivation is so important. The work is a direct expression of love for what we deeply care about, and of our compassion and concern for the suffering we connect with in the world. Mary Oliver (1992) in her poem 'The Summer Day' passionately challenges us with the piercing inquiry: 'What is it you plan to do with your one wild and precious life?'

I invite you now to pause; to let the book rest on your knees; to feel your body with the breath moving within; and ask yourself: "What is my heart wish in relation to my work? What are my core motivations? Where is my energy – my joy?" Offer yourself a period of time to sit quietly with this inquiry – and periodically remember to come back to it during reflective practice. We can lose touch with our intentionality in the fullness of everyday life, and with this we lose touch with our motivation for engaging wisely and sanely with what matters. But our intentions are very forgiving, we can always return to them, and they are not fixed – they evolve as we evolve. This is a place to keep inquiring into – to keep discerning the layers of motivation that bring us to this work. Our intention connects us with a natural movement towards love, compassion, truth, awakening, and aliveness. Our intention has both big expressions – the love we have for other beings and for the natural world, our deep wish for ease and peace in ourselves and the world; and then there are the smaller everyday moment-by-moment intentions – the way we wish to connect with our friend, the aspiration we have for the teaching space we are holding today, and so forth. Returning to connection with these core intentions can help keep a skilful engagement with our work alive. Beyond our intention, there are three core elements needed to be a mindfulness teacher – we need skills, we need particular personal qualities, and we need knowledge.

DEVELOPMENT OF THE SKILLS, QUALITIES, AND KNOWLEDGE NEEDED FOR MBP TEACHING

This book is dedicated to exploring the skills, qualities, and knowledge needed for MBP teaching. Parts I and II have a particular focus on the teaching skills and qualities needed within the MBP sessions themselves. Part III focuses on the surrounding reflection, study and practice that resources us to show up in the teaching space in ways that are optimally effective. Here, I offer some brief reflections on our development process as MBP teachers in these areas.

Developing our skills

In our development work on the MBI:TAC we were particularly keen to explore both *what* skills are needed, and *how* these skills evolve and develop over time. There were two broad areas of inquiry. First, we identified the domains or areas of the teaching process – we ultimately arrived at six key domains of teaching. Second, we identified a methodology for discriminating levels of competence within each of these six domains. It is this second area that is helpful here in understanding *how* skills develop. For the MBI:TAC framework to discriminate levels of competence, we drew on the work of Dreyfus and Dreyfus (1986) who created a model of skill acquisition, which offers a developmental approach to learning new skills. We were also informed by an adaptation of this work for skills development in clinical psychology trainees by Sharpless and Barber (2009). This work appealed to us for a number of reasons. Dreyfus and Dreyfus (1986) examined the common patterns by which people develop skills. They looked at people who had invested deeply in their skills such as grandmaster chess players, professional musicians, and airline pilots – expertise that involve hours of dedicated practice to become skilled. MBP teaching falls into this category – it is a complex craft. Dreyfus and Dreyfus (1986) discovered that across all these areas there are common patterns to skill development: the development of skills is a lifelong endeavour with subtle, predictable shifts occurring throughout development; and key to these shifts is the increased role of intuitive decision making as the need to follow rules drops away. As the individual becomes more proficient in the skill, they become more embodied and intuitive. Dreyfus and Dreyfus (1986) stated that skills are gained through experience, instruction, and imitation, and importantly, our learning needs evolve at each stage of development. We find this an encouraging model – it states that competence does naturally develop over time provided the right conditions are in place. Essentially, we need to put ourselves in the way of learning and it will happen!

This model makes clear that at the early stages of teacher training (within CMRP's structure, this is the 'Teaching 1' module on our Masters programme, and 'Teacher Training Level 1' within our Teacher Training Pathway), trainee teachers need structure and clear frameworks within which they can develop the core (explicit curriculum) skills of guiding practices and facilitating inquiry. We emphasise the embodied qualities of the teacher from the beginning by ensuring that our trainees have their own personal meditation practice, and attend annual meditation retreats (as per the good practice guidelines, see BAMBA, 2019). However, we also recognise that it is at a later stage in training, once trainees are familiar with the basic structures of the teaching process (i.e. the explicit curriculum addressed in Part I), that they will have enough attentional capacity to more fully discover how to teach from an embodied intuitive place (i.e. the implicit curriculum addressed in Part II). Outside of the formal teacher-training sessions, we encourage our trainees to proactively practice their teaching skills (because it is only through practising skills that they develop). In the early stages of learning how to teach, this needs to be in contexts that are safe and accessible for both participants and trainee. The first forays into teaching are often short sessions delivered to peers or colleagues, or teaching some curriculum elements whilst working as an apprentice to an experienced teacher.

Remember also that the skills we need as MBP teachers go beyond the teaching space. The chapters that follow point to the various areas that we need to focus on. One skill area that we can easily forget is all the practical work that is involved in simply getting an MBP course up and running. Skills such as how to market courses, how to build networks, management, leadership and administrative skills, skills in navigating through the structures and systems of mainstream institutions – and so on. There is much that will push us to the edges of our comfort zones! See Figure 18.1 for a mind map that outlines some key practical pointers for preparing to teach an MBP (and see also Chapter 26 on implementation). The relationship with your supervisor is one of the central pillars that is supportive when navigating these process (Chapter 21).

Developing the qualities needed for MBP teaching

What are the personal qualities needed to manifest MBP teaching skills? In Part II we wrote in some depth about embodiment. Here we will move into this territory again but from the angle of how we navigate the inevitable vulnerability that embodied practice brings us close to. Cindy Cooper, one of our much-loved teachers in CMRP who died in 2017, used to say "Teach from your wobbles". She wasn't speaking about some theoretical ideal – she knew the experience of engaging in this work from the felt experience of the vulnerability of pain and illness. The expression of vulnerability is different for each of us (though there are also some remarkably predictable expressions of this), but we all know the vulnerability of being human. A very classic vulnerability for many of us is the fear of not being skilled or good enough. I wrote about my experience of this in an article which has proved popular amongst our trainees because it speaks to shared but often unspoken themes of shame, vulnerability, and exposure (Crane, 2014). At the same time, of course, we want to be skilled. You are reading this book because you care about becoming the best vehicle possible for this teaching. This drive is very wholesome. And it is also important to rest lightly with the need to be skilled, because the whole basis for authentic embodied practice is the importance of showing up as we are – imperfect, vulnerable humans. In the end this is what is of most service to our participants – it is a place of connection with our human qualities. It offers to our participants the opportunity to be alongside a guide who combines intentionality, skill, and knowledge with a deep willingness to be

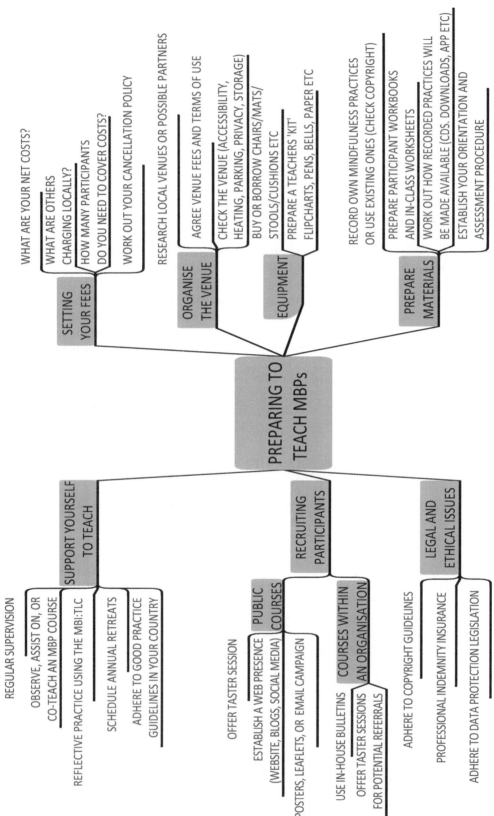

Figure 18.1 Mind map – Preparing to teach MBPs

ordinary, authentic, and congruent. We are not helping our participants or ourselves if we reach out towards some ideal of how we would like ourselves to be. This is not a path of comfort – it involves allowing ourselves to be open to whatever shows up – heartbreak, disappointment, set back, as well as joy, connection, and meaning.

There are many paradoxes that these themes throw up. How do we honour our values whilst working within an outcome-driven health service, for example? Our mindfulness practice is a resource in this. Awareness is vast and has the capacity to hold all that arises – including the paradoxes and seeming contradictions. Mindfulness practice is a training in discernment about where it is skilful to place our attention moment-by-moment. It also allows us to hold complexity, bigger issues and contradictions in a spacious and responsive way (see also Chapters 24 and 26).

Developing knowledge for MBP teaching

Having touched on how we can support ourselves to develop the skills and qualities we need as MBP teachers, we turn now to the development of underpinning knowledge. In the following chapters you will find sections that address some of the key areas of knowledge that are needed by MBP teachers – the theoretical and empirical underpinnings, how we orient towards social context etc. Here we will touch not on the *content* of these issues but on the *process* by which we approach our development in this area.

There are different phases to this development process. While in training, MBP teachers need to immerse themselves in a focused process of knowledge acquisition. The training structure helps keep the focus on which aspects of this territory to engage in. There is a responsibility to keep engaging with the development of our understanding beyond training. It is important that this is not a burden – but rather that it is an ongoing alive engagement with themes that are relevant, stimulating, and resourcing. Allow it to be inquiry rather than duty led, and to be stimulated by themes that are arising in your teaching practice. Give space to nourish yourself with some reflection provoking input. Bring themes arising from this to supervision and peer reflections. For example, you may have a participant who is highly anxious and is struggling to engage with home practice. Alongside bringing this to supervision, this could be a trigger to research the literature on offering MBPs to people who experience anxiety. Allocate some time each week to reading, listening to teachings and reflecting to support your development.

It is through our reflective practice that we can stay connected to our intention; discern what we need to support our learning at different stages in the journey; be willing to push the edges of what it is possible to open to; be intuitive and trust the process of our unfolding; allow room for vulnerability, humanity, shame, and imperfection. Reflective practice is also a check on ourselves: it will help us to discern when we should not be teaching: maybe there is a lot of turbulence in your life, maybe your health is compromised, maybe the inspiration feels lacking, and time is needed to pause, regroup, heal, and invest in your wellbeing and learning. There is huge wisdom in taking quiet fallow time.

SUMMARY

A number of organisations have developed Good Practice Guidelines and ethical frameworks (e.g. BAMBA in the UK, Mindfulness Teachers Association Ireland, the European Associations of Mindfulness-Based Approaches, and the International Mindfulness Integrity Network). These are essentially an outline of the conditions needed to support initial training and ongoing learning and adherence to good practice and ethics. It is important to become familiar with the guidelines in your country.

At the heart of the conditions needed to support your learning is your own personal mindfulness practice. As MBP teachers we engage in a deep dive into our own interiority, exploring how to bring the learning from this interior journey into the communities and contexts we live within. This movement asks a lot of us. Building the skills, knowledge, and qualities we need to offer mindfulness-based programmes takes time and requires particular conditions, including:

- Maintaining a daily personal practice (allowing this to be creative and playful rather than a duty!), and an annual teacher-led mindfulness meditation retreat.
- Having regular mindfulness supervision
- Engaging in an ongoing process of reflective practice. Use the TLC (Chapter 19) to support your reflections
- Recording yourself teaching – watch, reflect, learn, and then delete!
- Allowing room for vulnerability, humanity, shame, and imperfection
- Becoming part of and creating communities that support your personal practice, and your teaching practice
- Keep reconnecting to intention
- Knowing when not to teach
- Allowing this journey to be a lifetime of exploration. Finding a trusted therapist or counsellor at certain points can be an important way to support ourselves, and to build self-awareness and the capacity to attune.

The Mindfulness-Based Interventions
Teaching and Learning Companion (MBI:TLC)

*Gemma Griffith, Rebecca Crane,
Karunavira, and Lynn Koerbel*

The purpose of the MBI:TLC (we use the shorthand 'TLC' in this book) is to support the reflective practice of MBP teachers. It is designed to be helpful for teachers at all stages, from those just starting their teacher training to those who have been teaching for years. Reflective practice is essential to teaching MBPs with integrity; it gives space to see what we are doing well, and to explore the inevitable 'edges' that arise when teaching.

This companion reflective guide is based upon the Mindfulness-Based Interventions: Teaching Assessment Criteria (MBI:TAC: Crane et al., 2018) which offers a map of teaching skills and is used worldwide to assess mindfulness-based programmes (MBP) teachers. The TLC is also available to download and print, so you can use it multiple times in your ongoing reflective practice (www.routledge.com/9780367330798).

WHAT IS REFLECTIVE PRACTICE?

Being an MBP teacher asks a lot of us on a deeply personal level, and skilful engagement with reflective practice is key to our development. Effective reflection requires an element of critical thinking – it is a combination of analysis and questioning within an open reflective approach, which encompasses engagement with our whole system – body, emotions, and cognition.

Developing reflective skills is a learning process in itself. It is important that it includes and engages with our personal mindfulness practice, our teaching practice, our everyday life, the values we hold, our social conditioning and so forth. The development of critical reflective skills is key to enabling learning in an MBP context, and helps ensure that MBP teachers are part of a culture of reflective practice and self-assessment which continues beyond formal training. In this way the ethics and integrity of the field is held largely at a grassroots level.

There are some key features to reflection:

- It encourages us to look at issues from different perspectives, which helps us to understand and scrutinise our own values, assumptions, biases and perspectives.
- It results in learning – through changing ideas and our understanding of the situation, it may lead to shedding of outworn attitudes, ideas, or behaviours. Reflection is thus part of our evolution as people and MBP teachers.
- It is an active process of learning and is more than thinking or thoughtful action.

- It recognises that teaching MBPs is not without dilemmas, challenges and issues.
- It is not a linear process, but a cyclical one where reflection leads to the development of new ideas which are then used to plan our next stages of learning.

As MBP teachers we are trained in facilitating inquiry. The inquiry process (Chapter 9), with its three layers of friendly and curious engagement with the immediacy of experience, our relationship to experience, and the wider implications of what we are noticing, is a beautiful and effective system of reflection (Segal et al., 2013). The aspiration we hold for our participants (and ourselves!) is that this way of inquiring into experience becomes a natural default way of engaging with our lives.

WHY WAS THE TLC DEVELOPED?

Over the years, fellow teacher trainers have often spoken about how they use the MBI:TAC for reflective purposes, either personally, with peers, or with trainees. To understand a bit more about how the MBI:TAC is used, in 2018, we conducted an international survey among 79 international MBP trainers and supervisors. We were surprised to find that 95% of respondents already used the MBI:TAC with their trainees to support reflective process, and 85% used it as a tool to reflect on their own practice (Russell, 2018). Those who used it for reflection had adapted the MBI:TAC idiosyncratically in order to use it for this purpose, e.g., "I used it with more emphasis on how to grow rather than rate ... more focus on process involved."

Because the MBI:TAC is a necessarily complex and in-depth assessment tool, it was reported to be intimidating for new trainee teachers, partly because "It can be overwhelming in its level of detail" also, "The word 'assessment' ... immediately creates an impression of evaluation or measurement" which some trainers felt could put trainees in 'fear' mode and thus be unhelpful to the learning process. In addition, as with learning any new skill, the path to becoming an MBP teacher often includes phases of self-doubt. Some respondents wanted a way of using the MBI:TAC that represented these moments:

The MBI:TAC is written in a very aspirational way. Is there any room in there to describe relating with oneself in the midst of the rough, darker, wobbly, lost, reactive energies that arise during teaching?

There was therefore a call to explore ways to adapt the MBI:TAC explicitly for use as a reflective aid, one that would meet the call to "highlight areas of strengths and learning and development needs". The TLC thus answers the need for a reflective practice tool for MBP teachers at all levels of experience.

HOW CAN THE TLC SUPPORT MY DEVELOPMENT AS AN MBP TEACHER?

- It offers a structure for reflective engagement with personal process and skill development as an MBP teacher
- It serves as a gentle introduction or stepping stone to the MBI:TAC, without the 'threat' of an assessment, as it maps onto the MBI:TAC (with the same six domains and key features).
- It offers practical guidance to support ongoing development. At the end of each domain, there are pointers to practices and resources.

- There is a section towards the end of this chapter which enables you to reflect on a particular teaching incident – which can be used in combination with the TLC or separately as the need arises. Challenging or uncomfortable teaching moments can offer rich learning if we use them to enable a deeper reflection.
- The TLC encourages you to also reflect on your strengths – this may help to counteract tendencies to be overly critical and to build confidence and understanding about how to further develop.

The TLC is designed to be a companion throughout training and beyond. It supports a self-reflective process around your teaching skills that comes from your internal sense of your own process as a teacher – the 'inside out' feel of things. The TLC may serve as a basis for discussions with peers or your supervisor. It can be used many times over, with the invitation to treat the self-reflection as part of your mindfulness practice – noticing when criticism or praise arises, and being aware of any bodily or emotional responses as you reflect. Remember, that while we naturally aspire to be as skilful as possible in our teaching, it is also important to allow ourselves to be where we are from moment to moment. Using the TLC we can play with holding the natural (and wholesome) wish to be a 'good' MBP teacher with kindly awareness, rather than being driven by it.

The TLC can act as a 'stepping- stone' to greater familiarity with MBP teaching skills, without the focus on assessment inherent in the MBI:TAC. As you engage with the TLC over time, you may wish to fine-tune reflections beyond the suggestions given in this document. When arriving at that stage, you can turn to the full MBI:TAC, which gives more details on each domain (see mbitac.bangor.ac.uk). A printable version of the TLC is available online (www.routledge.com/9780367330798), enabling you to use the tool creatively by jotting notes on it as you reflect.

HOW TO USE THE TLC

It may be useful to ground yourself before engaging with the TLC using a short meditation practice. This may be particularly important for those of us who have natural tendencies to judge and strive. This is about your internal process of being a teacher; an 'inside out' feel of things, rather than a way of judging or comparing yourself to others.

Notice when the mind gets caught in concepts – e.g. "I'm no good at embodiment", and subsequent proliferations on particular themes e.g. "I shouldn't be teaching at all if I can't embody the practice". If this happens, take a pause and invite yourself to move from thinking to directly sensing in the body. What impact does getting caught up in thought have on the direct *here and now* experience? For example, if a memory arises of a mistake made during teaching, this may be accompanied with a sinking sensation in the chest, or a fizzy feeling in the abdomen. All of this is rich information and can be used to help reflection and journaling.

Notice if thoughts move into more of a narrow judging mode when reflecting upon your teaching – given the human mind, judgement is almost inevitable, and this can often feel unpleasant. Hold any such judgements as lightly as you can, and integrate mindful pauses, with the option to step away from the process and return later. Be open to noticing and reflecting on moments of excellent or effective teaching also, and to hold these positive judgements equally lightly. Finally, remember that everyone who engages in the work of becoming an MBP teacher has been through similar questions and doubts (including the authors of this work!). You could even step away from the TLC and come back when ready, or, if your mind is drawn to a particular teaching incident as a result of using the TLC, you could turn to the Atkins and Murphy (1993) model to help you reflect upon this (a 'how to' guide for reflecting on particular instances of challenge while teaching is located at the end of this chapter).

The MBI:TAC maps the teaching process into six domains of teaching skills/ capacities, which is mirrored in the TLC. Each section covers one domain, with brief descriptions of the key features within it. You are invited to complete a table which facilitates reflection on your teaching strengths and areas for development in each domain by ticking the box that feels most closely aligned with the stage you are currently at – which range from 'Yes I definitely do this' to 'I've never even thought about this key feature before'. This usage is why the downloadable version of the tool will be helpful.

Choose the category that feels most honest and accurate in this moment, the one that intuitively feels most closely aligned. Remember that the process of learning is one of ongoing development, everyone has to start somewhere, and there is no right or wrong response. The intention of the TLC is to enable you to pause and self-reflect, to support your practice and development as an MBP teacher.

There is space under each table which is divided into two sections. Under 'strengths' the invitation is to reflect upon areas of teaching strengths in that domain. Always find something positive to write, even though this can sometimes feel challenging. Under 'areas for development' the invitation is to reflect upon skills that would be helpful to cultivate. At the end of each domain, there are some practical pointers to cultivate your skills further.

We recommend keeping a journal as an aid to this developmental process. If specific teaching points or questions arise as you complete the tables (e.g. from big questions like "How do I know if I'm embodied?" to small practical points such as "I need to ensure the chairs are set up before participants arrive"), write these down to aid deeper reflection with yourself, peers, or with your mindfulness supervisor. Also notice when you are unsure about what to write and acknowledge that this is ok; in fact, use this uncertainty itself to point towards deeper self-reflection. Invite awareness of the process itself as part of this reflective practice, noticing how it is to self-reflect in this way – holding any judgement or self-criticism that may arise with kindly awareness. Remember that your writing is for your eyes only, so allow yourself to be free and unencumbered.

KEY TO THE CATEGORIES

Below are descriptions of the categories: hold them lightly; there isn't a right or wrong here – you are capturing aspects of your subjective experience in this moment. You may well feel that you fall in between them, in which case indicate that on the table by ticking in between the categories. Use the process freely and intuitively to support your reflective process, learning, and development.

Yes, definitely

This category represents being aware of this as a key feature of MBP teaching; it is present *consistently* while you are teaching; you have confidence in your capacities in this key feature, although there may be still some fine-tuning to be explored.

Yes, sometimes

This represents an awareness of the key feature, and of it being present regularly while teaching, but it can be *inconsistent*; or this key feature is present in your practice consistently, but there is a reflective sense that it could be improved substantially.

Yes, but rarely

You apply this key feature less than half of the time, or are very inconsistent or unconfident with it, or it may be an 'edge' being worked with. You recognise the process of becoming familiar with it and learning to cultivate it within MBP teaching.

No, not yet

You are aware of this feature as part of MBP teaching, but you have not applied it when teaching MBPs just yet and you would like to work on doing so.

Not sure

This category is for when a key feature is unfamiliar to you, perhaps not thought about before; you do not know whether you include this when teaching MBPs yet, or, you have not yet had the opportunity to put this key feature into practice.

DOMAIN 1: COVERAGE, PACING AND ORGANISATION OF SESSION CURRICULUM

Key features

1. Adherence to curriculum

Your teaching adheres closely with the MBP curriculum guide for the course being taught (e.g., Kabat-Zinn et al., 2021; Segal et al., 2013).

2. Responsiveness

There is an appropriate dynamic balance between the session plan being used and the needs of the moment e.g., if working with difficulty emerges as a strong theme from the group in session 1, you are able to incorporate this appropriately without losing the particular intention of session 1; if the dialogue is particularly fruitful you are able to give it the space it needs and dynamically rework the timings for the rest of the session in ways that are coherent and complete.

3. Appropriate inclusion of themes and content

You stay close to the core themes of the session and do so safely (e.g., it is inappropriate to encourage proactively directing attention to difficult intense sensations in early sessions).

4. Organisation

All materials are organised and at hand. You have a session plan and have prepared the room or online space before the participants arrive.

5. Pacing

The rhythm and flow of your teaching gives space for participants to understand and reflect on the themes. Sessions are not rushed, nor unhelpfully slow.

Table 19.1 Domain 1: Coverage, pacing, and organisation of session curriculum

	Key Features of Domain 1	Yes, definitely	Yes, sometimes	Yes, but rarely	No, not yet	Not sure
1	Do I adhere to the chosen curriculum?					
2	Am I able to balance flexibility and responsivity to the needs of the class while covering the curriculum?					
3	Am I able to appropriately introduce course themes and context – and be flexible around these when needed?					
4	Am I well organised for class (e.g., timetable, all materials to hand, the room)					
5	Is my teaching appropriately paced? e.g., I allow space for participant learning, without stagnating around a particular issue?					

Strengths:

Areas for development:

Tips and resources for Domain 1: Coverage, pacing, curriculum

Your familiarity with and understanding of the curriculum lies at the heart of this domain. It is important to not only understand which practices and themes go where in the curriculum (i.e. mindfully eating a raisin is session 1), but also the *rationale* and *intention* of the practice. Developing this as deep embedded knowledge will guide decisions when teaching and will free you to be responsive to the needs of the group.

To further develop:

- At the early stages of training, anchor your learning into a single established MBP curriculum and focus on this, rather than trying to figure out several curriculums at once which can be confusing. If you know one curriculum very well, it is then much easier to understand the overlaps and differences between it and other MBP curriculums you may encounter.
- Become very familiar with your chosen MBP curriculum by reading the relevant guide and key texts multiple times, and exploring it with peers and your supervisor. Explore study strategies that work for you (mind maps, lists, drawings etc). Perhaps seek volunteer opportunities as an assistant on an MBP course to deepen familiarity and knowledge.
- Reflect on how the elements of the curriculum, session by session, support each other, for example, what learnings that arise from the body scan that are later useful when bringing awareness to difficulty? How does the sitting practice link into making skilful life choices in session 7?
- Reflect upon what themes participants will hopefully engage with and learn in each session – this will help connection with the rationale and intention of what is being taught. Also investigate the common themes that often emerge in each session (e.g., session 2, sleepiness and finding time to practice are common participant experiences). Perhaps write this down from your knowledge right now as a mini-exploration, in order to identify gaps in your understanding of the curriculum.

DOMAIN 2: RELATIONAL SKILLS

Key features

1. Authenticity

You teach in a way that is aligned with who you are, congruent and open in your relationships with participants. Responses to individuals or the group arise from a responsiveness to the moment, rather than a cognitive focus on what 'should' be happening.

2. Connection and acceptance

You 'tune into' what a participant is saying, both in terms of content and emotional tone, with the ability to reflect this back, meeting the participant where they are in the moment, fostering a sense of acceptance of yourself and the participant.

3. Compassion and warmth

You convey authentic warmth and compassion towards participants. This manifests through relating with attentiveness, encouragement, and compassion in difficult moments, and being a 'fellow-human' who is interconnected with the experiences of the participants.

4. Curiosity and respect

You encourage participants to actively explore their own experience rather than relying on your expertise as the teacher, with a consistent message of encouraging them to participate in their own way, and with deep respect for participant's vulnerabilities and boundaries. You convey genuine curiosity about participants' experiences as they unfold.

5. Mutuality

You communicate a sense of shared exploration, of co-journeying with participants, emphasising the human vulnerabilities we all share.

Table 19.2 Domain 2: Relational skills

	Key Features of Domain 2	Yes, definitely	Yes, sometimes	Yes, but rarely	No, not yet	Not sure
1	Do I relate to participants in an authentic way?					
2	Can I 'tune into' the participant's world, and convey an accurate and empathic understanding of this?					
3	Do I give participants my full attention when they speak, and relate in a warm and compassionate manner?					
4	Am I able to be genuinely curious about participants experiences, and respect individual vulnerabilities and processes?					
5	Do I foster a sense of shared exploration among participants, of which I am a part?					

Strengths:

Areas for development:

Tips and resources: Domain 2: Relational skills

In this domain, much relies on your natural relational abilities and we all have strengths and edges in regard to how we relate to others. To further develop:

- How you relate to others with warmth, curiosity, and compassion can be developed through an intention to cultivate these qualities through a committed mindfulness practice. This process manifests in as many different ways as there are people. It is however, reported by most people who have developed a regular practice that this helps them to be of better service to others. It becomes clear that we are not meditating primarily for our own benefit, but that our practice supports and deepens our connections with others. We are intimately interconnected with all beings. Personal meditation retreats are important in supporting deepening of your mindfulness practice. Perhaps consider attending an 'Insight Dialogue' retreat (Kramer, 2007) which cultivates mindful awareness in the context of relationship.
- When reflecting on how we relate to others, it is helpful to have an intention to proactively bring to light our biases and blind spots. How do we respond when we feel some resistance or fear about certain participants, or they hold views we don't agree with? Read 'Societal themes' (Chapter 24) and the suggested resources for further exploration of this theme.
- In using the TLC, you may notice thoughts popping-up about where your 'edges' might be. Note them, perhaps write them down, and bring them to your next supervision session. It is critical we deepen understanding of our own patterns in relationships, as we will meet participants who challenge us. Supervision is a particularly important place to bring the personal vulnerabilities and tender edges that arise relationally in the teaching process. It may be that regular coaching or therapy is a supportive adjunct. Challenges in relationship with participants are a natural part of becoming an MBP teacher. The process of bringing our edges to light is an uncomfortable one, but one that can be both personally rewarding, and will ultimately be of benefit to our participants (and ourselves and our families!). The reflective article on the vulnerability of being an MBP teacher by Crane (2014) may be a useful read.
- It is good practice to pause before you teach. Once you have set up the room, see if it is possible to meditate for 5–10 minutes before your participants arrive. This will help to ground in the present moment, building connection with yourself as the ground from which we connect with others. It can also be a helpful practice to pause regularly during teaching with a simple intention to reconnect with the people before us (this is especially helpful when teaching MBPs online).

    It is important to build awareness and skills in offering teaching in ways that are sensitive to those in the group who have experienced trauma. This is a relational skill that is vital to ensuring safe practice (Chapter 23).

DOMAIN 3: EMBODYING MINDFULNESS

Key features

1. Present moment focus

You are grounded and steady in the body (but not stiff) whilst teaching, which is also manifested in the rhythm and pitch of your speech, so that your physical manifestation of mindfulness is 'sensed' by participants.

2. Present moment responsiveness

You are mindfully responsive to what is emerging internally within (thoughts, emotions, physical sensations etc), and externally in the teaching space (curriculum issues, participants, group processes etc). This includes how you respond to the group moment-by-moment. You guide the session with a steady intention.

3. Conveying steadiness alongside alertness

There may be inner reactivity arising within whilst teaching (particularly during challenging moments), while fully acknowledging this, you are able to convey steadiness alongside alertness and vitality. You convey stability and vitality within discomfort – opening to and allowing moments of wobble, vulnerability, and uncertainty; being responsive rather than reactive.

4. Attitudinal qualities

You convey the attitudinal foundations of non-judging (developing a stance of friendly witnessing to participants and personal experience), patience (working with the present moment, allowing things to emerge in their own time), non-striving (allowing things to be as they are, not trying to fix), and allowing (modelling a kindly presence towards self, others, and experience).

5. Natural presence of the teacher

You teach through your own unique, authentic, natural style of being, and inhabit your own personhood. There is no sense of putting on a 'persona' of what a mindful person 'should' do as you teach, rather, teaching naturally from who you are and from your own practice.

Table 19.3 Domain 3: Embodying mindfulness

	Key Features of Domain 3	Yes, definitely	Yes, sometimes	Yes, but rarely	No, not yet	Not sure
1	Am I grounded and steady in my body when I teach, with a present moment focus?					
2	Am I responsive to internal and external experience when teaching?					
3	Am I able to remain steady and alert through challenging teaching moments, and teach from a place of connected groundedness?					
4	Do I convey the attitudes of allowing, non-striving, non-judging, and patience while teaching?					
5	Do I feel that I teach authentically from 'myself'?					

Strengths:

Areas for development:

Tips and resources: Domain 3: Embodying mindfulness

Embodiment is not really possible to grasp conceptually – it needs to be 'felt'. So, if this domain feels challenging, it is because it *is* challenging, and takes time to grow into. Embodiment of the practice of mindfulness is at the heart of MBP teaching, and manifests uniquely in each person, yet we somehow 'know it' when we see and sense it in others. It is not really a 'competence' or a skill, but is more akin to a capacity that will naturally emerge as you embed the practice of mindfulness congruently into your way of being.

- The main way to cultivate embodied mindfulness is (guess what!) from your ongoing engagement with and exploration of personal mindfulness practice and the teachings within which these practices are embedded. As you practice and inquire into practice, a lived and felt sense of what embodiment feels like grows, and this will naturally be present as you teach. In particular when developing embodiment, shifting your practice to more body-based practices such as the body scan and mindful movement can be helpful. Also exploring the use of the body in relation to observing thoughts and emotions arising and ceasing during sitting meditations can be particularly supportive.
- When exploring embodiment, it can be common for trainees to focus on how they *convey* embodiment to others; we encourage dropping notions of what you might look like from the outside. Embodiment crucially involves congruence, so the ground for embodiment is your own connection to the immediacy of experience as teaching is happening. This includes a particular emphasis on visceral sensory experience and being attuned to thoughts, emotions, and what is going on in the wider teaching space. Trust that developing awareness of inner processes along with extending awareness into the teaching space, will naturally lead to deeper embodiment. It is an emergent process that arises from the cultivation of mindfulness practice; and is not one that can be systematically taught.
- Actively question embodiment and bring this into the forefront of your exploration of teaching MBPs. What does it mean to you? How do you sense when you are embodied? How do you sense when you are not? What helps ground you in your body as you teach? What do you do if you lose contact with your direct experience and go into conceptual doing-mode as you teach? By bringing these questions into reflective awareness (perhaps with the support of your mindfulness supervisor), you can deepen your understanding of embodiment.

DOMAIN 4: GUIDING MINDFULNESS PRACTICES

Key features

1. Language is precise, yet conveys spaciousness

In each practice these three elements are present:

a. Clarity about which aspects of experience participants should direct their attention to.

b. Guidance about how to work skilfully with the process of mind wandering (with emphasis on this being a natural process), such as how to note this natural movement and bring the mind back with kindness. Offering silent spaces within practices to allow participants to engage with the guidance. Giving clear invitations to modify the guidance offered if it does not suit them.

c. Naming what attitudinal qualities to evoke (e.g., inviting non-striving, trust, curiosity).

2. Making the key learning for each mindfulness practice available to participants

You are aware of the core intentions of each mindfulness practice and ensure that this learning is clear to participants both through implicit and explicit teaching processes.

3. The specific elements to consider when guiding each practice are clear

For example, in the body scan, always start with grounding in the whole body before exploring specific body parts, name different experiences (e.g., sensations may be quite intense, or there may be no sensation); and attending throughout to safety and trauma-sensitivity considerations.

There is a helpful summary of these specific elements in the MBI:TAC (Crane et al., 2018).

Table 19.4 Domain 4: Guiding mindfulness practices

	Key Features of Domain 4	Yes, definitely	Yes, sometimes	Yes, but rarely	No, not yet	Not sure
1	Do I give clear guidance on attention, mind wandering, and attitudinal qualities within each mindfulness practice?					
2	Am I aware of what the core intentions are of each practice, and convey these to participants when guiding?					
3	Do I address the elements that need consideration while guiding practices?					

Strengths:

Areas for development:

Tips and resources: Domain 4: Guiding mindfulness practices

- Listen to a range of audio recordings of guided meditations by different MBP teachers as part of your personal mindfulness practice: this illustrates how different teachers cover the same elements in various ways. Be aware that some older recordings may have been made before the field became aware of the importance of trauma-sensitive language. Some people find that transcribing audio recordings helps them become familiar with the material. As you develop and become familiar with the material to be covered in each practice, your natural, unique guiding voice emerges. Don't worry if at first it feels like your guidance is using other people's words, this is perfectly natural and will fade with time as the intentions and elements for each practice are internalised. Increasingly guide from your own lived experience of practice.

- When first learning, it can be helpful to guide practices with a few brief notes in view. Hold an intention to let go of the notes once the basic structure of the practice has been learnt, so that more of your attention can be given to the immediacy of the moment. Letting go of notes can feel anxiety provoking at first, but will pay immediate dividends, and allows a fuller connection to your own practice while guiding. No-one will expect a 'perfect' guided practice when learning (indeed such a thing does not exist!). We strongly discourage reading full 'scripts' of guided practices, even in the early stages. A few key pointer notes suffice when first learning to guide – but very quickly let go of these, and prioritise guiding from a connection to your own process.

- Make yourself familiar with the intention behind each practice – What is the main learning available within each practice? How are these made clear in the guidance? How does each practice connect to the theme of that teaching session?

- It can be helpful to audio record practices, then meditate to your own recorded guided practice a few times. Then delete it and re-record. This is a good way to pick up what works well, and where you might develop.

- As the main elements of a practice become increasingly internalised, play with emphasising your experiential engagement with the practice *as* you guide. This means that the guidance arises from an embodied connection to moment-by-moment experience. For example, if loud drilling begins outside your teaching space, then you can offer guidance around how participants can work with this sound; if you sense yourself or participants becoming restless, offer guidance around this etc. It may also be helpful to journal about this experience to attend to the meta-learning that is occurring. How did it feel to allow awareness to be both inside and outside? Over time guidance will become more intuitive, more 'in-the-moment', whilst still staying within the form of the practice.

- Keep practicing! As with any skill, it develops over time.

DOMAIN 5: CONVEYING COURSE THEMES THROUGH INQUIRY AND DIDACTIC TEACHING

Key features

1. Experiential focus

You support participants to connect to their direct experience (particularly emphasising sensations in the body) and encourage awareness of the different elements of present moment experience (thoughts, sensations, emotions). You bring participants back to the immediacy of direct experience if they start to become abstract or conceptual, and use open questions to explore experience, with a non-fixing orientation.

2. Use all 'three layers' of inquiry

Use all layers in a way that is non-linear, emergent and with a light touch.

> **Layer 1:** *Direct experience of participants.* E.g., ask questions such as "What did you notice?" "What was that sensation like?" "Were there any thoughts related to that?"

> **Layer 2**: *How participants relate to their direct experience.* You inquire into the inner relationship the participant had or has with a particular experience e.g., "How did you feel when the mind wandered?" "How does that sensation of restlessness feel now you have named it?" "How did you work with impatience in that practice?"

> **Layer 3:** *Linking what participants say to the theme of the programme or to wider life, when appropriate.* You encourage participants to make links themselves, by allowing them to see how their mind gets caught. You can do this by inviting links between practice and wider life, e.g., "Does striving show up elsewhere in your life?" Note that it is better to allow learning to arise from participants then shoehorn a point in because we think we 'should'. Some dialogues will just cover layers 1 and 2, and that is fine.

3. Conveying learning themes

This key feature includes many elements – it describes how you may draw on a range of teaching strategies to enable learning. In different moments you will offer didactic teaching, psychoeducation, links to theory, experiential engagement; stories, poems, and metaphors. You use a range of teaching aids (flip chart, post it notes, drawing materials, etc).

4. Fluency

This covers your capacity to teach in a way that is fluid and intuitive, and arises from your knowledge of key themes.

5. Effective teaching

This key feature is about whether your teaching effectively enables participant learning. E.g., How engaged are the participants in the sessions? Do you sense that participants are integrating the learning material into their personal process?

Table 19.5 Domain 5: Conveying course themes through inquiry and didactic teaching

	Key Features of Domain 5	Yes, definitely	Yes, sometimes	Yes, but rarely	No, not yet	Not sure
1	Do I skilfully bring participants back to direct experience during dialogues, and generally keep them on track?					
2	Am I aware of the three layers of inquiry, and do I navigate between them as appropriate when teaching?					
3	Do I teach the course themes in ways that enable effective experientially engaged learning?					
4	Do I feel confident in my knowledge/understanding of the themes of the program? Am I able to convey these fluently?					
5	Is my teaching effective – does it enable participant learning to happen?					

Strengths:

Areas for development:

Tips and resources: Domain 5: Conveying course themes through inquiry and didactic teaching

The key to improving skills in this domain depends on you first developing *knowledge* of the curriculum themes, and then developing the *teaching skills* to enable creative communication of these themes to participants (i.e. enabling a learning context in which themes emerge from participant experience). This domain is about both 'how' themes are conveyed, and also the 'intention' behind the themes conveyed. Particular areas of focus include:

It is important to have a clear grasp of the theoretical underpinnings of MBPs in order to be able to speak to them with authority and accuracy. Go through the MBP curriculum and identify what aspects you feel confident with, and which you require more knowledge of. Once this is known, learning can be tailored to enhance any missing theoretical knowledge (e.g., stress-reaction cycle, negative bias, neuroscientific evidence etc).

For many, inquiry is often the most challenging aspect of MBP teaching to learn, so if this is true for you too, you are in good company. Trust that learning will naturally emerge over time and with experience if the necessary conditions are created for this to happen.

When working with inquiry, remember that our hardwired relationship to experience (the pull towards pleasant, aversion towards unpleasant, and indifference towards neutral), is at the root of the reactivity that leads to distress/suffering/emotional pain etc. It is important therefore to investigate this in your own experience and bring it to the fore within the inquiry.

Make recordings of yourself facilitating inquiry and share these recordings in supervision. It is helpful to reflect with an experienced teacher on both the process (your 'way of being' during the inquiry), and the content (the choice points that emerged and how you responded to them).

Reflect on which aspects of your teaching invite participant engagement and which aspects are less effective, and if there is a way to creatively change delivery to enhance participant engagement and thus the effectiveness of your teaching.

DOMAIN 6: HOLDING THE GROUP LEARNING ENVIRONMENT

Key features

1. Creating a secure learning container

You create an environment that enables participants to feel safe with clear group boundaries and ground rules, such as confidentiality, time keeping etc.

2. Group development

You work with core group development processes in ways that enhance the learning potential, including skilfully managing beginnings and endings of the group, and dynamics within the group. This includes working with challenging participants in a way that support the whole group.

3. Personal to universal processes

You use the group context to highlight the universal nature of human tendencies/ patterns, and raise awareness of the interrelatedness of personal and universal stories. For example, during inquiry when one participant speaks of the distracted mind, you use the language of 'we' and 'our' e.g., "We all have minds that wander" thus drawing from individual experiences to make wider teaching points. You include the whole group in your awareness, even whilst engaging with one participant.

4. Leadership style

Your authority as a teacher is drawn from having 'walked the walk' in your own practice; and you can confidently communicate a sense of co-journeying with participants.

Table 19.6 Domain 6: Holding the group learning environment

	Key Features of Domain 6	Yes, definitely	Yes, sometimes	Yes, but rarely	No, not yet	Not sure
1	Do I maintain a safe and effective container for learning throughout the course?					
2	Am I aware of key group development processes and apply these when teaching?					
3	Do I use individual contributions to draw the groups attention to universal processes?					
4	Is my leadership style authoritative yet non-hierarchal?					

Strengths:

Areas for development:

Tips and resources: Domain 6: Holding the group-learning environment

Learning about how to use the 'group' to facilitate optimal learning in MBPs can easily be overlooked, especially when first learning how to teach the 'nuts and bolts' of MBPs (i.e. the explicit curriculum). However, it may be that group process work becomes more salient the more experienced you get. Learning about group process theories, and applying them while teaching is key to developing these skills.

- Establishing safety: reflect on how a feeling of safety and an invitational atmosphere is cultivated amongst participants; what are the actions and attitudes of the teacher that support this environment, without ever naming the space as "safe"? Remember this is particularly important to establish in the early stages of the course. It is also important to offer opportunities for participants to connect with each other in sessions, so pair and small group work are vital. For example, after some practices, invite participants to move into pairs or threes to discuss their experience before moving into the wider group, which also facilitates key features 2 and 3.
- How do you already bring universality into the course? Remember that mentioning universality frequently, and in a light touch way can help participants consolidate learning. Are there ways in which this could be further developed?
- Remember that although there is a universality to the experience of being human, participants in the group will not be experiencing the same things. We all come with history, conditioning, and life experiences which lead to particular areas of confidence and vulnerability. Creating safe spaces involves being aware of how to include the margins, and a commitment to engaging in a personal process of learning about unconscious bias.
- If not already, become familiar with key group development theories as described in Griffith et al. (2019a) and use them to facilitate working with the group. Also see McCown's (2016) work on stewardship of the group.

HOW TO REFLECT ON A CHALLENGING TEACHING EXPERIENCE

The TLC is designed as an aid to reflect on your current teaching skills and learning development – but what about those times when we wish to reflect upon a particular teaching experience, especially one that we found difficult or unpleasant? We particularly recommend the model by Atkins and Murphy (1993) to engage in this type of reflective practice. This model was originally designed to be used to support reflection on a professional incident that was challenging, and it is also well suited to the MBP teaching context. This model can be used in conjunction with aspects of the TLC but does not quite map on exactly, although some principles from it may be useful when reflecting on core skills. This section can be used separately for those times when it may be helpful to take some time to digest and learn from an uncomfortable or challenging teaching experience.

Hold the model lightly as a structure within which to engage in deeper reflective practice on themes that are emerging in your personal process or from a particular teaching moment. Reflecting in this way on challenging or uncomfortable teaching incidents does require us to engage with our vulnerabilities and perhaps also our habit patterns, including how we can so often 'get in the way of ourselves' when teaching. Bring kindness and presence to your process. Below is the description of the model (Figure 19.1), followed by a worked example of how I (GG) have used this model to reflect on a challenging teaching experience.

Awareness

Begin with this 'awareness' stage of the model, and notice your experience of the event as you begin to reflect – with the emphasis on the emotions, thoughts, and body sensations that occurred at the time, or while you are reflecting on the experience. What was the experience, and how did it impact on your emotions?

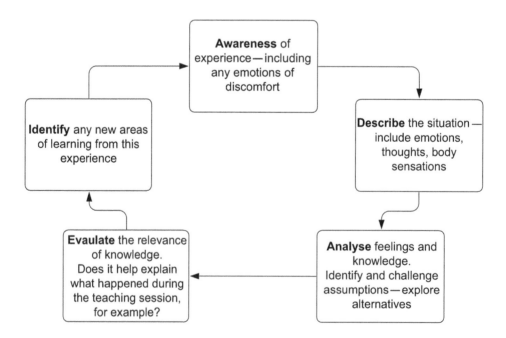

Figure 19.1 Atkins and Murphy's (1993) model of reflective practice, adapted for MBP teachers

Example: A participant was talking a lot during session 1 of an MBSR course. He went into rather detailed stories about his workplace several times, this took time away from the focus of the session, and I started to feel uncomfortable about how much time he was taking up in the group. I also noticed my mind wander, my thoughts were engaged with 'how can I get this person on track, or to finish this story quickly' I worried about the impact on others in the group. I felt my stomach and jaw start to clench and underneath that, a kind of sense of resignation 'oh well I'll have to let him get to the end of his story'. I was anxious and unsure about what might be the right thing to do during the session. Right now, as I reflect, I have a feeling of uncertainty and am not feeling very confident, and underneath that, a fairly stable 'ok-ness' with feeling these unpleasant feelings.

Describe

This is where the practical, background details are described – what were the key events? What did you do? What did other people do?

Example: It was session 1, so the group is at an early forming stage with group norms not yet established. The participant was male, in a mostly female group. He said he was going through a difficult time at work and described this is some detail during first go-round, and again during the inquiry after the body scan. I saw that he was going into 'story' mode as soon as he started talking and tried to find a space where I could ask him about how that is manifesting in his body, but couldn't find an appropriate place without feeling I was interrupting. Later on he also came back to this issue – and then other participants started sharing stories about the workplace for about five mins or so before I could get them back on track. I could see some other participants look bored when he was talking. I started to feel a bit resigned when he started talking in detail (part of my habit pattern- akin to a kind of 'freeze' mode), which was unpleasant to experience. As soon as I could bring him back into experiential mode after his story, I did, careful to validate his experience at the same time.

Analyse

In this stage, we analyse any assumptions we may have made about the event – are they actually true, or simply our perceptions?

Example: As teacher, I have a sense of expectations for how I want the class to go and a curriculum to cover – participants wouldn't be aware of this. They may not have shared my anxiety about this person talking so much about a work situation, and indeed, some joined in so it was engaging for some. I thought I saw other participants look bored, but I don't know what they might have been feeling. I also think perhaps he is trying to establish his place in the group and working out norms of the group by testing them unconsciously, and that this is thus a normal part of group process – but this too may or may not be true. This also taps into a habit pattern of mine – I find it challenging to be assertive or to intervene – I feel much more comfortable letting someone run with a story (even if it not helpful for the group) and then bring them back on track when they naturally pause.

Evaluate

How was the analysis you did in step 3 useful – how does it explain what happened or your discomfort about it? What steps could you take to work with this challenge?

Example: This habit pattern of preferring not to intervene directly is known to me, and is not easy to face as it means coming out of my comfort zone and becoming more directive as a teacher. Maybe I need to do this in this case or perhaps not, I do still wonder if it may be too early in the course to take direct action towards him as an individual, and think I largely did the 'right' thing, but do have a question about whether it would have been helpful to be more directive. At the same time, he may be finding his place in the group and, as the group norms become established, be less inclined to describe his situation at work as time goes on.

Identify

This is where you can identify any learning that has arisen from this reflective process. What will you do in future situations if something similar arises?

Example: In the short term with this class – I intend to frequently ask to hear from people who have not spoken yet to encourage others in the class to contribute, and to keep a close eye on whether this participant's contributions become problematic for others in the group – it is too early to tell right now. In future courses – I think I will emphasise listening in the 'group contracting' in session 1, and also pre-empt participants going into story mode by saying to the group something like 'I may re-direct you back to exploring your here and now experiences, so if I do this to you at any point, know that it is not personal, but it is to help us explore mindfulness together.' I also need to explore my habit patterns around this both within the teaching space and in everyday life – but not quite sure how yet, I'll take this theme to my mindfulness supervisor at our next session.

SUMMARY

- The TLC is a tool which enables you to reflect upon, and develop specific teaching skills.
- The Atkins and Murphy (1993) model is a useful basis from which to reflect on challenging teaching experiences.
- You may notice from the example that the reflective process brings up as many questions as it answers, and the point of reflection is not to find specific answers, but is a process in its own right, and helps us to deepen our engagement with our teaching practice.

20
Developing your personal practice

Bridgette O'Neill

This chapter explores the role of ongoing personal practice as an essential resource for mindfulness-based teachers. It begins with a focus on why a personal mindfulness practice is important in teaching mindfulness, seeing it as central to the quality of presence of the teacher, to the teacher's wellbeing and that of participants, and to enable an awareness of broader contextual influences on the teaching space. The chapter also examines what we mean by personal practice and considers the different forms it can take. Common paradoxes and pitfalls of practicing mindfulness are explored, including those that can lead us to give up. The chapter ends by considering practical ways to invest in mindfulness practice in daily life and through retreats.

WHAT DO WE MEAN BY MINDFULNESS PRACTICE?

Mindfulness, as it is used within MBPs, is multi-faceted and cannot be easily defined. Various definitions have been offered in order that we can study and operationalise it within MBPs. Feldman and Kuyken (2019) devote the first chapter of their book to exploring different definitions of mindfulness, and an ongoing exploration of different definitions is recommended for teachers of MBPs. One of the most widely known definitions offered by Kabat-Zinn (2003) is that mindfulness is the awareness that arises from paying attention on purpose, in the present moment and non-judgmentally to things as they are. This awareness involves 'a way of being in a wise and purposeful relationship with one's experience both inwardly and outwardly' (Kabat-Zinn, 2015, p. 9).

   This way of being is a natural human capacity that can emerge in certain conditions. We also have tendencies towards automatic reactivity that cloud our awareness, and can cause us and others trouble. Therefore, rather than wait for particular conditions to come together for mindfulness to naturally arise, training and commitment are needed to bring mindfulness into our everyday lives or, in other words, to live our lives from this orientation in a more sustained way. This training and commitment are what we call mindfulness practice, and this involves working with the three core elements contained within Kabat-Zinn's (2003) definition, and clearly described by Shapiro et al. (2006) in their intention, attention, and attitude model (see Chapter 3 for details of this model).

WHY IS PERSONAL PRACTICE IMPORTANT FOR TEACHERS OF MINDFULNESS-BASED PROGRAMMES?

Mindfulness-based programmes and embodiment

Mindfulness-based programmes rest on the experiential engagement of participants and teachers in systematic and sustained formal and informal mindfulness meditation exercises (Crane, 2017). This engagement is not just during MBP sessions but also involves practicing meditation at home most days. This is what makes a programme 'mindfulness-based'.

The original development of MBSR was rooted in Jon Kabat-Zinn's personal experiential engagement with mindfulness practice within the Buddhist tradition. He drew together his learnings from personal engagement with practice, with contemporary understandings from his scientific training (Kabat-Zinn, 2013). His ongoing personal meditation practice was a central factor in developing MBSR, and he has always been clear that mindfulness teaching is sharing a way of being that emerges from 'one's own practice and the never-ending learning curve it entails' (Kabat-Zinn, 2010, p. xviii).

Segal et al. (2013) described their decision to commit to a personal mindfulness practice as a turning point in the development of MBCT. Through their visits to Jon Kabat-Zinn's Center for Mindfulness and their observation of MBSR teaching, they describe a growing clarity that mindfulness enables a more compassionate way of relating to experience. A way that can only really be known 'from the inside' of ongoing personal practice and that participants learn both through their own mindfulness practice, and from the ways in which mindfulness practice is expressed in the teacher's way of being in the teaching space – also known as embodiment.

Embodiment is considered central to the quality of mindfulness teaching and is one of the six domains in the MBI:TAC (Crane et al., 2018). It concerns the quality of the teacher's presence; how able they are to notice and be responsive to present moment experience within their own mind and body, within the group and the broader environment; and their capacity to meet this experience with the core attitudinal foundations of mindfulness practice: non-judging, patience, beginner's mind, trust, non-striving, acceptance, and letting go. There is practice-based evidence that the teacher's level of engagement in personal practice is directly linked to their embodiment of mindfulness within their teaching; because of this, ongoing personal practice is an essential resource.

Knowing the territory

Mindfulness practice is concerned with what it is to be human and therefore the teaching of MBPs requires the teacher to be engaged with this exploration themselves in order to support others with their exploration. It can be likened to being a guide on a journey within the territory of human experience with some knowledge of how to explore safely, some maps of the territory, and familiarity from prior explorations of different landscapes. The guide is still exploring the territory along with their fellow travellers. Conceptual knowledge of contemporary and ancient understandings of what causes struggles and what leads to wellbeing provide maps for this exploration (Chapter 25). Personal practice enables teachers to increase experiential understanding through direct familiarity with the territory. The ability to guide others in this exploration will depend on the degree to which the teacher is willing to explore this territory through their personal experience with the practices. As Kabat-Zinn states in the Mindful Nation report (2015) 'exquisite intimacy with one's own mind states is essential' (p. 10).

Mindfulness is a natural capacity of being human, an open, interested, friendly, and wise state of awareness. However, we can easily become disconnected from this natural capacity. From an evolutionary perspective, we have basic survival tendencies that protect us from immediate danger and propel us to meet our survival needs. Biological reactivity in the face of threat is automatic and cannot be avoided; our individual learning histories and assumptions from our cultures shape our threat and drive systems (Gilbert & Choden, 2013; Hanson, 2009). Without conscious awareness, we can add to the strength and duration of reactivity. These automatic reactive processes can have harmful impacts on others and ourselves (e.g. Britton, 2016; McGonigal, 2013). Through regular mindfulness meditation, we can intentionally train our ability to be with our experience, as it is, to recognise reactive processes at play, and to relate to them wisely without adding more struggle. This is an ongoing process and requires a commitment to ongoing practice.

In her reflective account, Rebecca Crane (2014) describes how coming to consciously know aspects of our own experience that are shared by many others, for example feelings of fraudulence, informs our understanding of universal human processes. Our willingness to work with our own particular struggles through personal practice connects us to the struggles of people coming to our courses. Our awareness of the nature of these struggles and how we can relate to them wisely through mindfulness practice supports not only our own wellbeing but also the quality of our mindfulness teaching. The same is true of our joys and delights.

Good practice guidelines

In the UK, good practice guidelines for teaching MBPs have been developed by the British Association of Mindfulness-Based Approaches (BAMBA, 2019), who represent the leading UK teacher training organisations. These guidelines require in-depth personal experience of the mindfulness practices taught in the MBP during training, and there is an ongoing requirement of daily formal and informal practice and participation in annual teacher-led meditation retreats.

Protective awareness, wellbeing and the ethics of mindfulness teaching

Drawing on traditional metaphors, Feldman and Kuyken (2019) describe four interconnected dimensions of mindfulness: simple awareness, protective awareness, investigative awareness, and awareness that reframes perception and views. A traditional image used for protective awareness is that of a gatekeeper at the entrance to a town. The gatekeeper sees who is approaching and decides who to admit and who to refuse entry to, based on whether they will bring benefit or harm. This image can keep us connected to a clear intention towards our own and others' wellbeing in our personal mindfulness practice and our mindfulness teaching.

Mindfulness is inherently ethical. As Feldman and Kuyken state: 'It is a path of understanding and a way of being and acting rooted in non-harming and beneficence. If it is not rooted in this intentionality then it is not mindfulness' (2019, p. 209). Personal practice is an essential ingredient in supporting teachers to create an ethical space within their life and so within the teaching space (McCown, 2013), and for taking personal responsibility for the integrity of the process through their embodied teaching (Crane, 2017).

We have both the potential to relate to our experience with wise friendly awareness, and also to be carried unaware into automatic and powerful patterns of reactivity. This is true in all areas of our life including when we teach mindfulness. In fact, as we step into a leadership role as an MBP teacher, reactive mental processes (such as our beliefs about not measuring up, our need to be right, to be liked, to be funny, to be certain and know the answers, to not make mistakes etc) may be strongly triggered. Without conscious awareness, these patterns will affect the teacher's ability to create an ethical space. They are also likely to cause suffering for the teacher and, when they drive behaviour, potentially for their participants' too (through unhelpful interactions, and a reduced likelihood that participants will feel able to mindfully meet their own experiences). Our ongoing personal mindfulness practice in the moment of teaching and in our formal practice offers an essential 'gatekeeping' resource for self-regulation and continued learning, for our own wellbeing and for the wellbeing of our participants. In a sense, it helps us to get out of our own and others' way.

As well as supporting the teacher to work helpfully with their inner experience including their responses to themselves, individuals and the group, personal practice also supports the teacher to recognise and work skilfully with group processes. Griffith et al. (2019a), in their model of working with group process within MBP teaching, locate the teacher's inside out embodiment of mindfulness at the centre. There is also growing recognition of the need to bring social and contextual influences through unconscious bias and structural inequalities into awareness (Chapter 24). Alongside training and supervision, personal practice is an essential resource in becoming aware of how our own particular experiences have shaped our thinking and behaviour in relation to gender, culture, class, race, our relationship to the environment, and power relations. It can help to notice how we might work more skilfully with these aspects within MBP teaching to minimise the risk of harm and support wellbeing (Crane, 2017; Magee, 2019).

Mindfulness teaching requires taking personal responsibility for the integrity of the teaching process, working sensitively with inherent human vulnerabilities (including the teachers own), minimising the risk of harm, and maximising the benefits. However, this work is not about being perfect: inevitably, we will get caught in reactivity and unawareness; there will be ruptures within the group process. What matters is our commitment to meeting these experiences with mindfulness for the benefit of our own and others' wellbeing. Personal practice is an essential ingredient in this process, along with ongoing training and supervision.

Paradoxes and pitfalls of mindfulness practice

It is helpful to consider common challenges involved in practicing mindfulness as they can often lead us into reactivity and discouragement. Having a map of common challenges is likely to enable us to recognise them when they arise and to meet them with friendly interest and a commitment to our learning and wellbeing (Wellings, 2016).

Shapiro et al. (2018) described four paradoxes within mindfulness that can be confusing and challenging to navigate: acceptance vs change; effort vs non-striving; escape vs engagement; and self-focus vs non-self. These can be held within our practice as an invitation to deepen our understanding of the nature of being human with our competing needs, motivations, and automatic tendencies.

Through practice, we can begin to see our understandable desire for things to be a certain way (i.e. not have unpleasant experience), and how resisting what is already here simply adds further struggle. We can come to value acceptance as a key attitude that can enable change. However, our uniquely human capacity to imagine how we would like our experience to be and to aim towards it is powerful. We are likely to repeatedly see how we create ideals to measure our experience against in multiple subtle ways. We can easily believe that our formal practice should be more settled, or less sleepy, or that we should not be feeling a certain way in our daily life.

Our tendency to measure experience against some desired state is known in cognitive science as discrepancy-based monitoring (Williams, 2008), or simply wanting something else to be happening! It can lead us to feel discouraged and even give up on our mindfulness practice. Seeing this in operation and coming back to mindfulness practice as a moment-by-moment orientation, rather than a training aimed at achieving some desired state can help us navigate this human tendency to want to 'get' somewhere. It can be very helpful to know that certain challenging experiences are part of the territory of mindfulness practice, that we are likely to encounter them at some point, and that we don't have to see them as personal failures. These include sleepiness, boredom, restlessness, worry, craving, wanting to hang onto pleasant experiences, resisting and wanting to get rid of unpleasant experiences, and doubting ourselves or the practice. These can all be met with mindfulness. The present moment is all we have, and we can meet all experience in this present moment with conscious friendly awareness – *including* our resistance and ideas about success and failure.

A similar dynamic can be explored in relation to effort. Mindfulness practice requires a commitment to create helpful conditions, and discipline to work with our experience in a particular way. However, we can find ourselves moving between being lost in our streams of thought, or caught in goal orientation, and 'over-efforting' in a way that creates stress, and is likely to lead to discouragement and a sense of failure. Recognising when either we are under or over-efforting, exploring what kind of effort is required, and how it can be balanced and sustained, is likely to be another dynamic to be explored in practice.

Our tendency to move away from the unpleasant and towards the pleasant can also lead us into a pitfall of using practice simply to develop calm, and to avoid connecting with internal and external challenges. Avoidance will leave us vulnerable to being driven by unprocessed needs and feelings (*Tricycle*, 2011), which can cause ourselves and others harm and disconnect us from our values. Mindfulness practice supports fuller, non-reactive, caring engagement with life, which in turn supports skilful action. In our practice, we discover where it may be wise to step back from the immediacy of difficult experience, which enables us to build more stability before returning to explore the area again. This stepping towards and stepping back from, guided by our intentions and our direct sense of experience, is likely to be another live dynamic in practice especially when we are in the midst of difficulties or in relation to challenging past experience (Treleaven, 2018; Chapter 23).

A discomfort with mindfulness practice can be that it feels self-indulgent. However, the exploration of our particular human experience in our mindfulness practice not only develops greater self-awareness, leading us to cause less trouble for others and ourselves, but also a greater appreciation and sense of connection to what it is to be human more generally. As we become more familiar with the flow of our experience, our sense of ourselves can both expand and loosen and this can make us more available and sensitive to others.

HOW WE CAN KEEP OUR PRACTICE ALIVE

We can find ourselves in autopilot in practice just as in any other area of our lives, and we can fall into reactive unconscious struggles in our relationship to practice. One of the most common obstacles is to view it as another chore on the 'to do' list. So how can we keep our practice alive?

A journey of discovery

Seeing practice as an ongoing journey of discovering more about the landscape of being human can be a support to sustaining and continually refreshing practice. We can pause periodically to ask 'what am I learning?' Regular journaling and study can support this reflective process as well as giving yourself the freedom to focus on what is important to you rather than trying to get 'good' at practice. If you see practice as relevant to the whole of your life, you can investigate whatever is pertinent for you right now, whether that is finding balance between rest and work, public speaking, relationship to money, communication with colleagues, your tendencies in groups, engagement in social action or any other area of energy and interest.

Support from others

Having others to talk to about practice is likely to be very helpful; this may be a supervisor or a practice mentor with whom you focus entirely on your personal practice rather than your teaching practice. Being part of a community of mindfulness meditation practitioners is also likely to be supportive. Many of us find that practicing with others provides a sustaining energy. You could find out if there are any groups of people practicing together in your area and if not, you could perhaps consider establishing a practice group.

Retreats

Periods of more intensive practice in the form of teacher-led mindfulness meditation retreats are a good practice requirement for mindfulness-based teachers (e.g. BAMBA, 2019). The retreat environment offers an opportunity to let go of everyday demands and give yourself over to practice. With longer periods of practice within a supportive environment, a stability and sensitivity of attention and awareness can develop in relation to a range of mind states, enabling a depth and clarity of learning from direct experience. Many people talk about the retreat 'all day' in an MBP course as a turning point in their personal practice. There is evidence that longer retreats of three days or more increase participants' mindfulness and compassion (Khoury et al., 2017).

An increasing number of retreats tailored for people training to teach or teaching MBPs are now available. These retreats offer input around key psychological frameworks from both Buddhist teaching, and contemporary theories and science. As well as deepening practice, these retreats can lead to a greater integration of conceptual and experiential learning and increased confidence in and embodiment of mindfulness in the MBP teaching space. Although the teaching of MBPs is generally not directly considered while on retreat, there is some emerging evidence to suggest that retreat experience can be a turning point in people's experience of teaching (English, 2019; Place, 2019).

Deepening and refreshing practice through structured courses

Finding structured ways to broaden and deepen one's personal practice and understanding is important. Two helpful areas of ongoing professional development include compassion focused trainings and interpersonal mindfulness. There are a number of mainstream compassion-based courses now including Mindful Self-Compassion (Neff & Germer, 2018), Compassion Cultivation Training (Jinpa, 2016) and Mindfulness-Based Compassionate Living (van den Brink et al., 2018). The Interpersonal Mindfulness Programme (Kramer et al., 2008) is also a course designed to be taken after an initial MBP. These courses offer additional ways to broaden our practice within our relationships with ourselves, our struggles, and with other people.

SUMMARY

- A programme cannot be said to be mindfulness *based* if the teacher is not engaging personally in mindfulness practices. The teachers' level of engagement in personal mindfulness practice is thought to directly link to their capacity to embody mindfulness within their teaching
- Personal practice supports the teacher's self-awareness as well as awareness of the group and broader social influences within the teaching space. This awareness supports ethical practice.
- Practicing mindfulness involves working purposefully with intention, attitude and attention in our moment-to-moment experience, creating conditions for greater awareness and wiser responding. Personal practice includes formal practice, brief practices in everyday life, informal practice and contemplative inquiry and reflection.
- Common paradoxes and pitfalls of mindfulness practice can be obstacles to sustaining practice. Recognising and coming to understand these challenges can help us to work with them skilfully.
- Autopilot and driven-doing mode can creep into our relationship to practice. We can refresh and keep our practice alive through an ongoing learning orientation, being in connection with others, retreats and follow on courses.

RESOURCES

Shapiro, S., Siegel, R., & Neff, K. D. (2018). Paradoxes of mindfulness. *Mindfulness, 9*(6), 1693–1701. doi:10.1007/s12671-018-0957-5
Wellings, N. (2016). *Why can't I meditate? How to get your mindfulness practice on track.* Piatkus.

Online resources and self-help books

There is a huge range of online resources available to support personal practice. Bangor University (www.bangor.ac.uk/mindfulness/audio/index.php.en; Centre for Mindfulness Research and Practice, n.d.) and the Oxford Mindfulness Centre (https://mbctapp. oxfordmindfulness.org/practices/mbct/; Oxford Mindfulness Centre, n.d.) offer guided practice audios on their websites The developers of MBSR and MBCT have published self-help books that come with audios and their teaching is available online. Dharma Seed (https://dharmaseed.org/) offers a wealth of online talks. Sangha Live (https://sangha. live/) offer online talks and courses.

21
Mindfulness-based supervision

Alison Evans

A regular space that is contracted between supervisor and supervisee, which enables reflection on the supervisee's mindfulness teaching practice and how this interfaces with their personal mindfulness practice and their life. The process is dedicated to developing and deepening the growth, understanding, integrity, safety and effectiveness of the supervisee's application of mindfulness, both personally and in their working life.

Cindy Cooper and Jody Mardula, 2011, as cited by BAMBA, 2019

Mindfulness-Based Supervision (MBS) is key to supporting MBP teachers' learning and development, and for the emergent field of MBPs to maintain standards and integrity. This chapter aims to share CMRPs knowledge and experience of MBS. These understandings have been developed though ongoing delivery of training for supervisors, engagement with experienced mindfulness-based supervisors, collaborative dialogue, and empirical research.

AIMS OF CHAPTER

1 To clarify why supervision is important for MBP teachers
2 To introduce an updated framework of MBS, and briefly describe its different components
3 To explore how you as a supervisee might engage in and productively use MBS
4 To identify what to look for when choosing your supervisor

WHY IS SUPERVISION IMPORTANT FOR MBP TEACHERS?

The relationship with your supervisor is one of the central pillars that supports you in navigating the experience and process of becoming an MBP teacher. What makes MBS central to the process of teacher development? It is a place for supporting the integrity of your teaching in several ways:

- developing your MBP teaching skills, underpinning qualities and understandings, reflective skills and confidence
- building capacities to more fully inhabit your own humanity with all its inherent vulnerabilities

- reflecting and dialoguing about ethical issues that arise through teaching
- it gives a place for another to have a critical view of our teaching, and challenge where needed.

I reflected when writing this piece about what makes supervision a central pillar. In my early days of teaching MBPs there were fewer opportunities for training. Some of my fundamental early learning came through supervision. I was fortunate to receive frequent, skilful supervision from a wide range of experienced teachers, in the context of research trials, which included review of recordings of my teaching. Through supervision, I processed and was able to find the links between what the MBCT manual described (Segal et al., 2013), the needs of the participants in my courses, my personal mindfulness practice, and how the teaching comes through my unique personhood. Supervision facilitated this in a way that enabled me to find my authenticity. I started to move out of agenda, theory, and wanting to get it right – into connection with my whole being, and into something alive and engaged. Without supervision, I believe I would not have made these transitions. This process continues. I continue to engage with personal supervision as I move into new areas of work, meet new situations, and revisit familiar experiences with the potential for fresh eyes. I find a passion and delight in working in this way with my supervisor. It is alive, engaged, nourishing, stimulating and challenging.

In those early emergent years, we knew that MBS was important, but we had not done the work of articulating what it is. As training became more organised and structured, it became clear to us that it is a vital ingredient within the range of inputs that support teacher growth. This stimulated us to put work into understanding what happens within MBS. This in turn spurred me to study MBS as my major doctorate project, culminating in a thesis: Supervisors' and Supervisees' Perspectives of Mindfulness-Based Supervision: A Grounded Theory Study (Evans, 2019). This qualitative research underlined that MBS is both an essential part of learning to be an MBP teacher and ongoing professional development, which in turn contributes to the delivery of high-quality MBPs and integrity of the field.

A MINDFULNESS-BASED SUPERVISION FRAMEWORK

The framework in Figure 21.1 provides an update to the framework first described in our article *A Framework for Supervision for Mindfulness-Based Teachers: a Space for Embodied Mutual Inquiry* (Evans et al., 2015). This framework visually communicates the training, experience, attitudes and skills required of a mindfulness-based supervisor. It is intended as a guide for both supervisor and supervisee to the process of engaging in supervision. It assumes that MBP teachers continue to develop throughout their lives, with the MBS process evolving to meet these developmental phases.

The container of mindfulness: The framework's outer circle

This outer circle represents the container of mindfulness, which holds the entire supervision process, imbuing it with the characteristics of mindfulness. The framework proposes four areas that are important basic aspects of holding the container for MBS. The supervisor and supervisee experientially engage with these together supported by their personal mindfulness practice. You may find that part of how you learn about these qualities is through sensing them embodied in your supervisor.

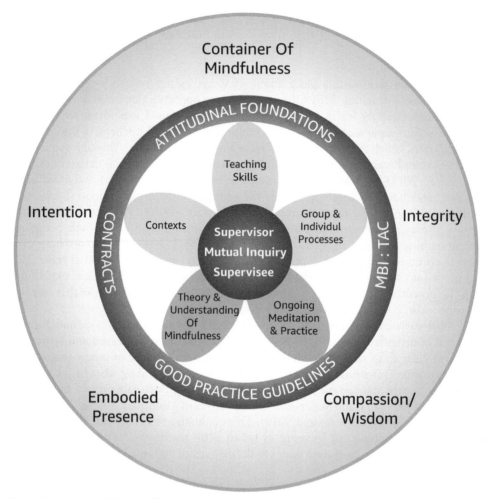

Figure 21.1 A model for mindfulness-based supervision for MBP teachers

Intention

This relates to the power and importance of a clear sense of motivation, purpose, vision and directionality to the practice of mindfulness and the process of MBS. Your supervisor will support you to reconnect with intention as issues arise within the process. This is done on a micro level of clarifying the intentionality of curriculum elements and of choice point moments in the teaching process; and on a macro level of supporting you to connect (and reconnect) with various layers of intentions for engaging in this work.

Embodied presence

The supervisor carries mindfulness to the supervisee through their way of being. In Van Aalderen et al.'s (2014) research on the role of the teacher in mindfulness-based approaches; the embodiment of the method by the teacher was one of four key factors that mattered most to both participant and teacher. MBS is a relational process, which mirrors these mindful qualities and thus supports the supervisee to bring them into their own being and process. The supervisor brings their experience to the process but there is an emphasis on humanity rather than expertise. Meeting in this way is helped if the supervisee and supervisor can allow their whole being into the space – including the tender vulnerable aspects of experience.

Integrity

This is the importance of staying true to the underlying philosophy and practice of mindfulness, and to underpinning theories of the MBPs (drawn from contemporary understandings and contemplative traditions). Integrity within the supervision process includes ensuring that both the supervision itself and the supervisee's teaching practice is held within a code of professional ethics (Baer 2015; BAMBA, 2019), and that the embodied ethics of mindfulness practice are integrated throughout (Grossman, 2015). This includes keeping the supervisee's course participants at the forefront of the process in terms of protecting them from potential harm. Your supervisor will thus explicitly encourage you to reflect on your ethical stance, your fidelity to the programme and so on.

Compassion and wisdom

Sometimes your supervisor will encourage you to engage in open reflective practice on a theme, and in other moments, you will notice that they are more directive, questioning and challenging. The welfare of the participants in supervisee's courses is paramount. The supervisor takes responsibility to protect their safety and the integrity of the work, with the firm clarity of wisdom that accompanies compassion. It can be difficult to balance challenge with compassion. It requires trust and openness within the relationship that builds over time.

Holding the integrity: The framework's inner ring or 'belt'

The inner ring sets the standards that hold the supervision process, and in turn holds the ethics and integrity of MBPs. Here I highlight four guiding touchstones:

Attitudinal foundations

These are the qualities that underpin mindfulness practice, MBP teaching and MBS. Both supervisor and supervisee have an intention to bring these qualities into their interactions with each other, so the supervisee can in turn live and embody them within their life and the teaching space.

Contracts

Contracts are mutually agreed arrangements made between supervisor and supervisee which serve to clarify business arrangements (dates, times, payment, confidentiality, etc.), and how you will work together, including intentions, boundaries and adherence to good practice. These contracts are an important part of setting up the supervision process well from the beginning. It is essential to make time for an initial session to begin to get to know each other, and talk through these arrangements, and the expectations and boundaries of supervision. As a supervisee this is a key moment for you to outline what your needs are. An important part of supervision is periodically re-visiting, reviewing and adjusting these agreed arrangements and intentions, as you and your work shifts and changes.

Good practice guidelines

These are clear statements of what training, practice and ongoing learning is important for MBP teachers, supervisors, and trainers (BAMBA, 2019). These guidelines may be referred to and form part of the dialogue within supervision. For example, you may discuss with your supervisor what training steps are most important for you next, or the challenges you have in attending an annual retreat.

Mindfulness-Based Interventions: Teaching and Learning Companion (MBI:TLC)

The TLC presented in Chapter 19 is highly relevant within the supervisory relationship. It is explicitly designed to support reflective practice through encouraging systematic self-reflection focused on each of the six domains. Once supervisees are sufficiently experienced and a relationship of trust has been built, the version of the tool that is designed for assessment – the MBI:TAC – may be used to enable direct in-the-moment reflection. Later, this may be extended to include the supervisor reviewing levels of competence in any of the six domains by viewing videos of the supervisee's teaching.

The content of supervision: The framework's 'petals'

These are the issues that you as a supervisee choose to bring to supervision; areas you wish to investigate and reflect on. Your supervisor may also bring in areas of focus. Not every petal needs to feature in each supervision session, but every so often, you may step back and see if there are areas you neglect. In practice, we discover that everything is connected. For example, as you explore how to teach a body scan, you may reflect on your own experience and practice with the body scan, then you may consider particular aspects of the population you are teaching that impact on how you might guide the practice, and then you may review the intentions of the practice and the theoretical underpinnings.

We encourage you to refer to other sections in this book to bring your awareness to the aspects of teaching that you may inquire into and reflect on within supervision. In summary the five petals are:

Teaching skills

The specifics of what teaching skills are explored in supervision will depend on your development stage. In the first stages of teaching, conversations will focus on the explicit curriculum, such as preliminaries needed before beginning to run a course, details of the appropriate curriculum, what to teach, how to lead practices, making practice recordings, compiling handouts, and timing issues. Later there will be more space for nuanced conversation on the implicit curriculum, such as ways of conveying teaching themes, refining inquiry skills, and managing moments of challenge. Space can be given to reviewing recordings of your teaching together with your supervisor. These explorations may point to further training and practice to support ongoing cultivation of qualities, knowledge and teaching skills.

Contexts

A useful focus for supervision is the match between the programme form (e.g. MBSR, MBCT), with a particular population (e.g., people with cancer, children, people with addictions), within a particular context (e.g. hospital, workplace). When choosing a supervisor, seek one who is experienced with the programme form you are delivering. The supervisor will ideally also have experience of the context and population that you are working in and with, but this may not always be possible. If it is not, there may need to be discussion about how you receive guidance on these areas. These contextual issues affect the teaching process enormously and figure strongly in supervision inquiries. There is often a tension between meeting the needs of the context and population, while also adhering to the integrity of the programme form. Another important aspect of context is the cultural and social context: this will include awareness of how the programme is situated within the community or organisation; and of potential dynamics related to power, oppression, social exclusion etc. Supervision is an important context within which to examine and heighten awareness of equality, diversity and inclusion and the implications for how the programme or the teaching process might be adapted (Chapter 24). Recognising and working with our unconscious bias usefully forms part of supervision.

Group and individual processes

Many supervisees usefully bring specific moments that have arisen in their teaching that relate to the learning and developmental processes of individuals and the group, along with group dynamics, the teaching process and the issues that come up during the course. If you are co-teaching, supervision is a place to reflect on this relationship.

Theory and understanding of mindfulness

Understanding why things are taught and done the way they are in MBPs includes a broader and deeper understanding of the different epistemologies: contemplative teaching/practice and contemporary western empiricism/culture (Crane, 2017; Feldman & Kuyken, 2019), and how they come together as underpinning principles for MBPs. This understanding of theory is both a conceptual and an embodied knowing which develops over time.

Ongoing meditation and practice

Essential to authentic MBS and MBP teaching is the understanding that arises from personal formal and informal mindfulness practice (Chapter 20). There are many ways that practice can support the supervision session. The following are a few examples:

- A short, silent 'pause' at the beginning of the session to ground, notice and be with what is here.
- The supervisee might guide a practice and inquire of their supervisor, who can then give feedback.
- You may ask your supervisor to guide a particular practice and do an inquiry around it – to demonstrate the practice.
- Whenever either of you are faced with uncertainty or difficulty, you can pause, ground and breathe, either implicitly taking your attention more to internal process or explicitly naming and taking a mindful pause.
- A short, silent moment or two at the end of the session can give space to settle and digest.

Space between the petals

Bringing practice directly into MBS also acts as powerful reminder that space is an essential part of life – easily forgotten in the midst of a busy life. Mindful pauses help both supervisor and supervisee to reconnect with the immediacy of felt experience and their intention. See Box 21.1 for an example of a pause within MBS. This example builds upon the ideas already discussed about navigating our inevitable vulnerability of being human and how we can 'teach from our wobbles' rather than trying to getting rid of them or hide them.

Box 21.1 Pausing within supervision

Last week I arrived at my phone supervision out of breath and emotionally overwrought. I'd just come from a highly emotional counselling session which had run overtime and left me in an agitated state. Because I was late, I wanted to make up for lost time and leapt right into the agenda of our supervision session, which I had just located on my laptop. But my supervisor invited me to pause, telling me (in a kind way) that she could feel my agitation through the phone, into her own body. I was lightly guided in a short mindfulness practice – stopping, feeling our feet on the ground and our breath, then opening to whatever was here in experience, and letting it settle without having to do anything with it. After a short pause time, I could see how affected I had been by the experience and by the rushing. I saw how vital it was to be aware of the agitation, to make space for it, to allow it to settle, and to relate to it in a new way. This allowed me to approach supervision with clarity, and without having the hidden agitation inadvertently hijack the process. As we discussed this further, I was surprised to see how my supervisor had been affected by my unacknowledged agitation, just as my participants might be affected. I saw how important it is to be human with my participants, rather than a know-it-all expert who is beyond being disturbed.

The centre circle – the heart of supervision

In MBS, connection between you and your supervisor is made and strengthened through mutual inquiry: a moment-by-moment inquiry into both supervisee and supervisor experience (see Figure 21.2). The attentional field includes: your internal experience (vertical lines); the experience between them (horizontal lines); the overall bigger picture (the circle) which includes an understanding of mindfulness and its foundations; the issue brought to supervision; the supervisee's work and context; and the supervisory relationship.

From this embodied groundedness, you as a supervisee can be supported to explore experience through inquiry, beginning by bringing to mind what happened, and then inquiring into the layers of experience related to this using a similar framework to when inquiring within the MBP teaching space. The supervisor is employing and thus modelling the same inquiry process that you will use with your participants (Chapter 9). Supervision thus brings the 'then and there' into the 'here and now', much as happens in the MBP inquiry process. When we bring to mind past experience, it becomes present within us in this moment – often along with its accompanying physical sensations, emotions and thoughts. The supervisor facilitates a moment-by-moment exploration of what is arising around the supervision issue through relational inquiry. Any learning that comes from the mutual inquiry can then be woven back into your MBP teaching.

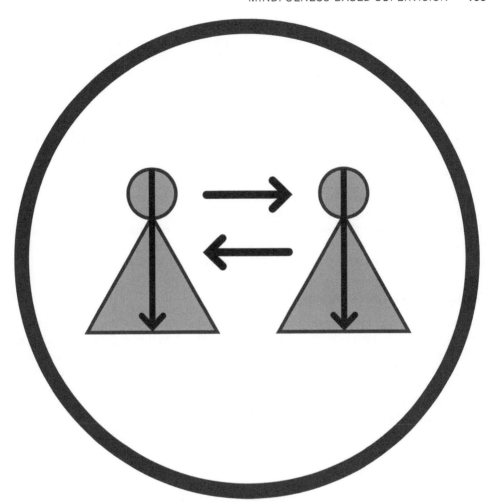

Figure 21.2 The flow of attention in the supervisory relationship

HOW MIGHT YOU ENGAGE WITH MINDFULNESS-BASED SUPERVISION?

Understanding what MBS is

Understanding more about the nature of MBS through reflecting on the framework presented above can help you to engage productively with supervision.

Engage in reflective process

Reflecting on supervision before and after the session can be immensely helpful to the process and for your learning. Prior to supervision you could spend some time contemplating what you wish to take to supervision: What is alive for you in relation to the different petals in the framework, or in relation to the TLC? Maybe there are immediate themes such as challenging relationships within the teaching space or concerns about safety. Sometimes, there is nothing that immediately jumps out. Therefore, you may look at the framework of the TLC, and see if there are aspects that you never take to supervision. Whilst there is a strong encouragement to arrive into supervision with questions, themes for exploration and particular experiences to explore, it is also important to connect to the moment and discover what is most alive. Your supervisor may also have things that they wish to bring in.

Many supervisees make a few notes during supervision – sometimes just some key words/pointers. It can be helpful to have some time shortly after supervision to further reflect and make notes on the supervision dialogue. It may be that themes have come up for further reflection of investigation within your practice, or that you wish to find out more about. Let supervision feed into and out from your life and teaching, not stand as an island.

Live teaching

Increasingly, supervisees take live teaching to supervision. This might be through video/audio clips, or by guiding practices/inquiry within the supervision session. It can feel very daunting to be 'seen' in this way. It is also an excellent way of getting specific feedback on your teaching. You do not need to give your supervisor huge amounts of teaching to view – short clips of 10–15 minutes will be enough for an in-depth exploration.

Giving feedback/reviewing supervision

Your supervisor may formally review the process and experience of engaging together in supervision with you periodically, or more informally ask you how things are going and if there is anything you would like to change. Sometimes reviewing gets missed in the fullness of supervision. It is though important to take time to stop and reflect whether you are getting what you need from supervision and whether there is anything that could be different. It can be hard to ask for what we need, and we do not always know, but it is important to be an engaged part of shaping what happens within your supervision. Supervisors cannot always know either, so welcome hearing from you.

Getting yourself ready

In several places in the framework – embodiment of mindfulness has been highlighted. You might find Figure 21.1 helpful in preparing yourself for the supervision session by reminding yourself of the different elements you can bring in. Can you give yourself as optimal conditions as possible to be present in your body and with the emerging moments of dialogue? Perhaps this means taking a few moments before supervision to pause, turn email off, get a glass of water, go to the bathroom, arrange your physical space, choose your seat, or if you go to your supervisor perhaps arrive a little early and take short walk or sit a moment.

At several points in this book, we have spoken about the vulnerability of being human and an MBP teacher. Coming into an intimate and sometimes intense dialogue really requires a willingness to 'show up'. A good dose of kindness and compassion towards oneself is needed, as we allow the felt experience of vulnerability of reflecting on personal process to be known. Perhaps asking yourself: 'How can I best support myself to feel safe within the container of my supervision process?'

Frequency of supervision

Good practice guidelines for teachers (BAMBA, 2019), recommend that an inexperienced teacher have a minimum of three hours supervision over the period of an MBP, and experienced teachers have supervision monthly during teaching periods. When you are new to teaching or teaching a new programme there is often a need for an increased amount of supervision. There are often so many aspects of teaching that you wish to bring to supervision. As supervision is about an embodied dialogue, agenda items cannot be rushed – something is missed if we do. For more experienced teachers once a month can be a useful gauge. Many teachers choose to have supervision in an ongoing way, regardless of whether they are actively teaching at the time – finding that there are ongoing themes within their own practice to explore.

WHAT TO LOOK FOR IN A SUPERVISOR

MBS is a complex process, requiring considerable experience, training, and skills as set out in the good practice guidelines for supervisors (BAMBA, 2019). It is critical that your supervisor meets these guidelines. MBS requires the supervisor to have a strong foundation of MBP teaching experience, professional integrity and ethics, consistency, reliability, supervisory competence, positive intentionality, safety, and kindness. All these arise from years of engagement with mindfulness, teaching practice, and study. Another aspect is connecting with a supervisor who is experienced and knowledgeable with the type of MBP that you are teaching and the population that you work with. Therefore, you need to investigate who is a good match for you. You need to find a supervisor with whom you have a relational fit. This can be hard to ascertain initially, so may at times mean changing supervisors. This becomes a topic for the supervision itself as the motivation and intentions behind a desire to change are reflected upon and held within the supportive attitudinal foundations of the supervision process. As identified in the framework, so much of the process of the inquiry within MBS rests on a trusting and secure relationship, which creates the container within which you can explore tender and challenging issues. It takes time to build this.

Finally, we need different things from supervision at different stages in our teaching and development. There is benefit in a long-standing supervisory relationship, and some wisdom over time in connecting with different supervisors at different stages in our journey. For example, if you are teaching a new programme you may need to shift to a supervisor with more experience of that curriculum. Or you may have reached a place of comfort with your supervisor and feel it may be helpful to see what it may be like to be with somebody who may see different things in you and challenge you in different ways. Open and honest communication is needed in making these decisions to ensure endings and shifts that support growth. It is ok to say you wish to change supervisor and explain why.

SUMMARY

- A framework is presented to describe the nature of MBS: a process that is mindfulness infused and draws on the theories and pedagogies of MBPs.
- MBS is core to how an MBP teacher aligns to integrity and appropriate ethical practice.
- MBS supports a variety of functions including skills learning and embodiment, ethical and professional issues, and your wellbeing as an MBP teacher.
- Embodied relational inquiry is at the core of MBS.
- As a supervisee, you are an active participant in the process, so can enhance supervision through understanding what MBS is and finding ways to engage effectively and proactively.

RESOURCES

Evans, A., Griffith, G.M., Crane, R.S., & Samson, S.A. (2021). Using the Mindfulness-based interventions: Teaching Assessment Criteria (MBI:TAC) in supervision. *Global Advances in Health
and Medicine, 10*, 1–6. https://doi.org/10.1177/2164956121989949.

Evans, A., Crane, R., Cooper, L., Mardula, J., Wilks, J., Surawy, C., Kenny, M., Kuyken, W. (2014).
A framework for supervision for mindfulness-based teachers: A space for embodied mutual
inquiry. *Mindfulness, 6*(3), 572–581. doi:10.1007/s12671-014-0292-4

For updates to the framework, finding a supervisor and other information about
supervision visit: www.mindfulness-supervision.org.uk/.

22
Professional practice

Pamela Duckerin

Teaching mindfulness is a great privilege, providing the opportunity to connect with the full range of human experience. With this comes the call to make ethical commitments to meet each participant in our teaching and learning communities with as much sensitivity as possible.

Rhonda Magee (2016, p. 244)

In her conference keynote address at a CMRP conference, Christina Feldman offered a reminder that mindfulness has a narrative, and encouraged us to recognise that we are all part of its unfolding: "All that we are now is the result of all that we were. All that we will be tomorrow is the result of what we are now" (Feldman, 2016). This applies to the development of mindfulness from its traditional beginnings right up to today. Christina challenges us to place what we do under the microscope, to question how we engage, and to reflect on the ethical values that are informing our process, and about both the perils and the possibilities of this work. "What is important to retain and what is important to relinquish in the service of enabling this practice to transform at both individual and societal levels?" (Feldman, 2016).

Box 22.1 Definition of ethical practice and professionalism

Definitions

- Ethical practice
  - o Ethics are the moral principles and values that govern our behaviour – they are our understanding of what is right and wrong. They help us navigate dilemmas that we ... encounter, particularly ones that challenge our values – so that we can figure out how best to respond (Feldman & Kuyken, 2019, p. 203)

- Professionalism
  - o A professional is one who applies the knowledge, skills and values of a chosen profession.

Professional integrity: the professional who consistently and willingly practices within the good practice guidelines of a chosen profession.

In the context of the developing field of MBPs, where do we look for guidance around professional issues and ethical practice? In the absence of formal regulatory bodies, how do we ensure as teachers of MBPs that we grow the necessary skills, knowledge and attitudes to practice with integrity? As MBPs become more widely available, how can we protect the interests of the public who attend our courses? In this chapter, we offer a framework that invites reflection on these professional ethical practice issues.

STRUCTURING OUR REFLECTIONS

The intention of this chapter is not to provide a set of instructions or answers, but to encourage an awareness of the terrain of professional practice, and to consider the strategies we need to employ in order to work ethically and safely. Here is a reflective space to consider the nuances, tensions, and the unfolding nature of this topic. This is a lifelong exploration, which can be studied from a micro-perspective (within our own personal/teaching practice), from a wider perspective (e.g., looking at an MBP in a specific context), and from the perspective of the professional field (such as the work of the British Association for Mindfulness-Based Approaches [BAMBA, 2019]). It is likely that what feels most pertinent at any given time will change, influenced by the developmental stage of the teacher, and in response to particular themes within and around the mindfulness-based field.

We approach this using the framework in Figure 22.1, which outlines three dimensions that contribute to an ethical response in any moment within our teaching practice – the teacher, the mindfulness-based teaching context, and the wider context. We explore each

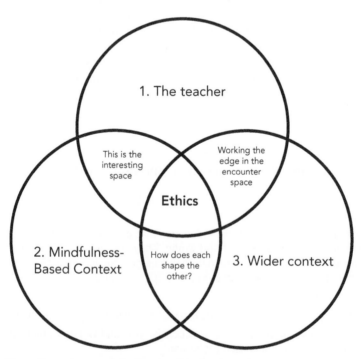

Figure 22.1 Three dimensions contributing to ethical outcomes

dimension, inviting you to be curious about the encounter spaces, noticing how each dimension shapes and is shaped by the others.

The teacher

We are all influenced by our underlying beliefs and values. However, we are often not aware of the profound way they influence our work as MBP teachers. 'It has always felt to me that MBSR is at its healthiest and best when the responsibility to ensure its integrity, quality and standards of practice is being carried by each MBSR instructor him or herself' (Kabat-Zinn, 2011, p. 295). Palmer, an educator, wrote:

> The most practical thing we can achieve in any kind of work is insight into what is happening inside of us as we do it. The more familiar we are with our inner terrain, the more surefooted our teaching- and living- becomes.
>
> (2007, p. 5)

Personal mindfulness practice is central to the development of self-awareness (Chapter 20). It enables us to gain insight and understanding and allows deep reflection on our social and cultural background (Chapter 24). Through mindfulness practice, the teacher is embarking on a personal journey of connecting with their own inner authenticity, integrating the qualities of mindfulness practice into their being, and learning to teach from this embodied place (Crane & Reid, 2016). This embodiment of mindfulness is key to enabling us to authentically inhabit, from the inside out, the ethical dimension that is called for moment-by-moment. As Feldman and Kuyken (2019) wrote:

> We often sense ethics quite intuitively; we have a sense of the right response. Ethics can spark a sense of discomfort or unease which may alert us to some misalignment ... at these moments we know something is not quite right and our embodiment can help us recognise this unease.
>
> (p. 205)

Reflecting on your life journey

Pausing now to map your own journey by specifically reflecting on your personal values and beliefs, and how they contribute to your ethical framework. You could visualise (and perhaps draw) your life as a river. How have the tributaries coming into your 'life stream' contributed to your motivation and intentionality for undertaking the work of mindfulness-based teaching? This exploration may bring you into greater contact with your own narrative, which requires gentle sensitivity around moments of personal history, trauma and vulnerabilities.

o What has influenced and shaped your values and current ethical standpoint? (e.g. early experiences, culture, race, gender identity, education/training, family, career/profession institutions, spiritual beliefs, particular people, life events etc)

o How would you define/depict these key influences?

A model which may support an inner process of exploration in this context is the Johari window (Luft & Ingham, 1955). This model represents our personal space as it is experienced by ourselves and also by others (e.g., feelings, experiences, views, attitudes,

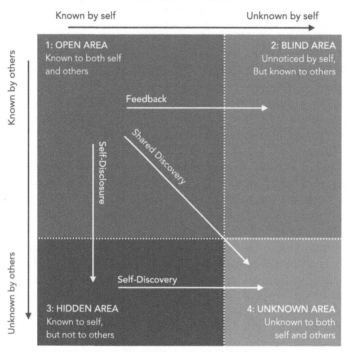

Figure 22.2 The Johari Window

skills, intentions, and motivations). It offers a self-reflection tool that we can use to further our understanding of our personal process (see Figure 22.2).

This framework can help us to map ways in which we might increase the size of the 'open self' area by reducing the size of the blind, hidden, and 'unknown self' area, through processes such as feedback, self-discovery, shared discovery, and self-disclosure. MBP teaching is all about *shared discovery*: a mutual exploration between the teacher and participants of how it is to be a consciously engaged human. Through personal reflection on our teaching practice, and in dialogue with peers and through supervision, there is the opportunity for *self-disclosure* and *self-discovery*. There will be moments in supervision and with discernment within the teaching when we choose to *self-disclose*. In the teaching space this is in the service of building a sense of common humanity and mutuality and reducing the tendency to idealise the teacher.

Reflecting on who I am as teacher
- What life events, challenges, people, and learning have shaped my ethical standpoint?
- How do my values 'show up' in my teaching practice?
- How do my conditioning, culture, gender, race, class etc influence my teaching practice?
- How do I work with my vulnerabilities and sensitivities?
- How can I open to oversights, blind spots, and biases?
- What do I want and not want others to know about my personhood and teaching practice?
- How do I meet ethical moments that show up in my teaching practice?

We turn next to the other two circles in Figure 22.1 above – the ethical landscape of the mindfulness-based teaching context and the wider societal context. We draw on the metaphor of a tree to depict the multiple components and layers involved. The roots represent the foundational ethical principles, the trunk addresses the teaching itself, whilst the branches depict the main structures that feed into and support the teaching. The canopy symbolises the wider systemic and societal issues that influence the whole structure.

The mindfulness-based teaching context

The roots: mindfulness ethics, professional ethics and the attitudinal foundations

When teaching MBPs, our ethical anchor points are both the ethics and the integrity that are inherent within the practice of mindfulness, and the ethical frameworks that are part of our mainstream institutions and professional practice contexts (Crane, 2016).

Kabat-Zinn's first implementation context for MBSR was health care and medicine:

> From the start, originating within a hospital and academic medical center, MBSR was of necessity rooted in the ethical soil of the Hippocratic Oath, namely, to first do no harm. This truly noble vow that each doctor takes upon graduating from medical school, has undergirded medicine and health care ... from their very beginnings ... the patient's needs come first, before the needs of the doctor and other caregivers. There is a foundation of selfless action built into this medical ethos .... akin to the Bodhisattva Vow, namely, to work for the liberation of others with all one's energy, putting their liberation above one's own.
>
> (2017, p. 6)

There is a significant and ongoing debate around the creative opportunities and challenging tensions that appear at the intersection between the contemplative roots of MBPs and mainstream delivery contexts (e.g. Baer & Nagy, 2017; Husgafvel, 2019). From a practice perspective it helps to think about the anchor points that support our ethical practice from both these roots. Thus the practice of mindfulness itself has an inherent embodied ethical orientation towards self, others, and the wider world (Grossman, 2015); and alongside this we embed ourslves in the long tradition of professional ethics that have arisen within our mainstream public service contexts (Baer, 2015).

The attitudinal foundations that Kabat-Zinn articulated are one way of navigating the intersection of Eastern philosophies and practices, alongside the pragmatic importance of needing to contextualise the teaching within the culture of our mainstream institutions (Kabat-Zinn, 2013). Since these attitudinal foundations are central to the pedagogical approach of MBPs, they are also central to embodied teaching. In Figure 22.3, their foundational nature is depicted as part of the roots.

The trunk: curriculum, participants and context

Curriculum

Fidelity to the particular form of MBP you are delivering is vital in maintaining integrity and quality (Chapter 2). It takes time in the early stages of teaching to get to know the curriculum. As familiarity builds we become more skilful in pacing the session, and in

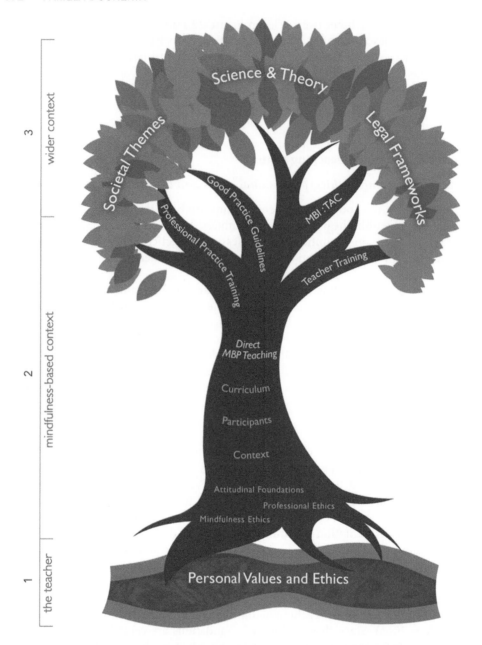

Figure 22.3 Tree model representing the teacher, the elements of the mindfulness-based context, and the wider societal context

using the curriculum in ways that are responsive to the moment, and to the group. The TLC (Chapter 19) may help you to reflect on this theme. More broadly, we need to understand the essential and variant ingredients of MBPs (Crane, 2017). This enables us to appreciate what it is that makes our teaching mindfulness-*based*. This depth of understanding is vital when adaptations to the curriculum are being made (Chapter 2).

Participants

Practising safely and preventing harm is our primary ethical duty. This requires knowledge about how harms might arise as well as know-how about the means to mitigate them. Baer et al. (2019) offers useful reminders of how MBPs are structured, taught, and held in ways that reduce the likelihood of harm to participants. For example:

- Careful assessment of potential participants is carried out using well considered inclusion and exclusion criteria. Teachers need to understand the theoretical and empirical foundations for using MBPs with their population and context, and to communicate this information to potential participants via a pre-program orientation as part of an informed consent process (Chapter 16)
- Teaching both the *what* and the *how* elements of MBPs. This needs to include the rationale for practices, emphasising the invitational aspect, and supporting participants in responding skilfully to intensity and difficulty
- Systematic monitoring to recognise when unusual or unexpectedly distressing experiences arise and knowing how to respond appropriately (Chapter 23)
- The teacher is alert to themes arising for individuals during the session and is available outside the sessions for consultation

Essentially, offering the overall course and all the elements within it in a way that is safe and accessible to the group is the primary priority for the teacher. Much of this book is an articulation of ways of doing this.

Context

The organisational and cultural context within which the MBP is offered, such as clinical, corporate, online or an educational setting, will influence the particular characteristics of the teaching space. This requires the teacher to explore how the curriculum and pedagogy can best be fine-tuned to meet these particular settings and cultures (McCown et al., 2016). Different settings will require particular ethical and professional considerations, which in turn are held alongside the values and ethos of MBPs. There is a growing body of literature examining this ongoing co-creation of the pedagogy within different contexts (e.g. Sanghvi, 2019).

The branches: teacher training, professional practice training and good practice

Teacher training

Robust teacher training, including training on professional issues and ethics, is crucial for protecting the safety and wellbeing of the public accessing MBPs (Baer & Nagy, 2017; Crane, 2017; Crane & Reid, 2016). Different training organisations offer a range of training options including post graduate programmes, structured training pathways, stand-alone courses, and apprenticeships. There is a growing consensus on the key ingredients of a quality training process, standards for good practice and for the assessment of training and teaching competency (BAMBA, 2019; Crane et al., 2013)

Professional practice training

It is also important that MBP teachers take generic training in other areas that they are not familiar with. For example we recommend that teachers who do not have a training in mental health attend the two-day Mental Health First Aid course (Mental Health First Aid Australia, 2019). Other important areas of training are equality, diversity and inclusion, safeguarding, and legal frameworks such as data protection (Chapter 24).

Good practice guidelines

As the practice of MBPs becomes established, regions and countries are developing national governance bodies. Globally, there is an International Integrity Network (2020). Within the UK, the British Association of Mindfulness-Based Approaches (BAMBA, 2019) provides Good Practice Guidelines and an ethical code for MBP teachers, trainers and supervisors. This includes guidance on personal mindfulneess practice, training, supervision, and ongoing development. It also provides a listing where the public can find an appopriately trained MBP teacher, who adheres to recommended ongoing good practice. Two elements are considered essential for ongoing practice – Mindfulness-Based Supervision and annual attendance on mindfulness retreats. Supervision serves a number of different functions including educational, supportive and managerial (Chapter 21). Developing your personal practice through regular daily practice, and annual attendance on retreat serves to deepen the embodied experience of mindfulness as a path and practice for life (Chapter 20).

Reflecting on the mindfulness-based teaching context

- How does the context I deliver within, and the participants I deliver to, shape my teaching practice?
- What ethical moments have shaped my practice?
- Is my assessment and orientation process appropriate?
- Do I have knowledge and skills to support safe practice including minimising harm and managing risk?
- How do I nourish my ongoing development?

The wider context: societal themes, legal frameworks and science and theory

In the tree model (Figure 22.3), the wider context is depicted as the canopy of the tree. Since the canopy offers shelter and sustenance essential for the survival of the tree, it is crucial to pay attention to the health of the canopy. This metaphor could help us to consider the relationship between the mindfulness-based context and this wider context: being aware of and keeping in touch with wider societal issues supports mindfulness-based work; with an intention to stay responsive and inclusive. Treleaven (2018) argues that understanding social context is part of offering safe practice (Chapter 24). Another important theme here is good governance, including adherance to the relevant legal requirements such as health and safety regulations, information governance, safeguarding, and having adequate indemnity insurance.

Britton (2016) wrote that scientific research and the building of an evidence base is largely responsible for the successful implementation of mainstream MBPs. MBP teachers therefore play a crucial role by engaging in evidence-based practice and, through their direct contact with the public, are key in maintaining trust in the field. Therefore, foundational scientific literacy is considered a key competency for MBP teachers (Chapter 25).

Personal values and professional ethics work together to ensure safety and integrity (Baer & Nagy, 2017). Our personal values influence how we apply the standards that are framed within codes of ethics. In the tree model the teaching of MBPs (the trunk) is influenced:

- By our own values, and the ethos of MBPs (the ground and water nourishing the roots)
- From the bottom up through foundational ethical principles (the roots)
- By the quality of teacher training and professional regulation (the branches)
- From the top down by wider systemic issues (the canopy of leaves)

As with a living tree, there is a dynamic interdependent relationship between the various elements, with each reliant on the other for growth and survival. Using the metaphor of the tree can also be a useful way of considering our personal relationship with the different elements. It may be, for example, that in the early phase of teaching, we don't feel ready to 'branch out'. We are perhaps naturally more focused on the 'trunk'- understanding the curriculum, developing materials and making decisions about assessment and orientation of participants. As a new teacher, the 'branches' can feel more complicated and out of reach, the canopy even more so. Perhaps once we become more established in our teaching, we can look up and take in a wider perspective, looking into the 'canopy' of the wider influences on our work. And when we become lost or unsteady, we can come back to the roots, the mindful attitudes, and to our values and intentions.

SUMMARY

Stay deeply rooted while reaching for the sky
From *Think Like a Tree*,
K.I. Shragg (Spencer, 2019)

In the developing field of mindfulness-based teaching, there are a number of waymarks to support teachers in practicing safely with integrity.

- Rather than following a set of rules and regulations, this dynamic and emergent process requires ongoing dialogue and exploration, staying open to what we know and do not know, and listening deeply and sensitively to our participants, the wider communities we serve, our fellow mindfulness practitioners and ourselves.
- As well as being concerned with the 'what' and the 'how' of teaching, it is important to turn our attention to ourselves, the 'who' that is teaching.
- The invitation is to engage in reflective practice, to notice one's own relationship to the subject and to consider how best to explore the vast terrain of professional issues and ethics in mindfulness-based teaching.

RESOURCES

The roots

Baer, R. & Nagy, L.M. (2017). Professional ethics and personal values in mindfulness-based programs: A secular psychological perspective. In L.M. Monteiro, J.F. Compson, & F.M. Musten (Eds.) *Practitioner's Guide to Ethics and Mindfulness-Based Interventions* (pp. 87–111). Springer

Feldman, C. & Kuyken, W. (2019). Ethics and integrity in mindfulness-based programmes. In *Mindfulness: Ancient wisdom meets modern Psychology* (pp. 202–234). The Guilford Press.

The trunk

Crane, R.S., Brewer, J., Feldman, C., Kabat-Zinn, J., Santorelli, S., Williams, J.M.G. and Kuyken, W. (2016). What defines mindfulness-based programs? The warp and the weft. *Psychological Medicine, 47*(6), 990–999. doi:10.1017/s0033291716003317

McCown, D.A. (2013). *The ethical space of mindfulness in clinical practice.* Jessica Kingsley.

The branches

BAMBA (2019). Good practice guidelines for teaching mindfulness-based courses [PDF File]. https://bamba.org.uk/wp-content/uploads/2019/12/GPG-for-Teaching-Mindfulness-Based-Courses-BAMBA.pdf

Crane, R.S., Soulsby, J.G., Kuyken, W., Williams, J.M.G., & Eames, C. (2018). *The mindfulness-based interventions: Teaching assessment criteria (MBI-TAC) manual, summary and addendum.* Retrieved from http://mbitac.bangor.ac.uk/

Crane, R.S., Kuyken, W., Williams, J.M.G., Hastings, R.P., Cooper, L., & Fennell, M.J.V. (2012). Competence in teaching mindfulness-based courses: Concepts, development and assessment. *Mindfulness, 3*(1),76–84, doi:10.1007/s12671-011-0073-2

The canopy

Brown, C.G. (2017). Ethics, transparency, and diversity in mindfulness programs. In L.M. Monteiro, J.F. Compson, & F.M. Musten (Eds.) *Practitioner's guide to ethics and mindfulness-based interventions* (pp. 45–85). Springer

Kabat-Zinn, J. (2017). Too early to tell: The potential impact and challenges- Ethical and otherwise- Inherent in the mainstreaming of dharma in an increasingly dystopian world. *Mindfulness, 8*(5), 1125–1135. doi:10.1007/s12671-017-0758-2

23
Trauma-sensitivity

Eluned Gold

Trauma is becoming more widely recognised as having an underpinning effect on people, communities, and societies (van der Kolk et al., 2007). Much of the current writing about trauma and mindfulness has a clinical perspective and, as MBP teachers are not expected to be clinicians, a translation is needed for MBP teachers. This chapter aims to inform MBP teachers (particularly those who teach in non-clinical settings), to teach with sensitivity to trauma, and to feel better equipped to support participants who may have symptoms of trauma.

Trauma-sensitive methods of teaching MBPs are also supportive to everyone in the teaching space. Offering trauma-sensitive practice options as part of routine guidance is useful to everyone (e.g., opening the eyes, standing up, changing position, moving to walking practice if stillness is triggering). We can thus normalise the range of nervous system responses, from being 'spaced out', to being overwhelmed, and acknowledge that this can arise in practice for anyone. This strengthens the sense of participant agency in knowing what one might need, moment to moment, both in practice and in life. As Treleaven (2018, p. xxvi) wrote: 'It is essential to foster an awareness of trauma in order to respond appropriately in our teaching relationships'.

AIMS OF CHAPTER

1 To increase awareness of the prevalence and degree of trauma within the general populations we teach.
2 To increase understanding of trauma, its effects on the human organism, and how mindfulness practice can impact these effects.
3 To offer succinct guidance and skills to enable the MBP teacher to approach each session and participant with trauma-sensitivity.
4 To signpost to further resources.

DEFINITIONS OF TRAUMA

As befits such a complex issue, there are many definitions of trauma, and the range of definitions points to differing ways of perceiving and addressing trauma, both as individuals experiencing trauma and professionals who seek to understand trauma. The following definitions address the ways in which trauma, known or unknown, may be present in an MBP teaching space.

- 'Any experience that is stressful enough to leave us feeling helpless, frightened, overwhelmed or profoundly unsafe is considered a trauma' (Ogden & Fisher, 2015, p. 66). This definition offers a broad account of trauma. Many of us may identify with a, or multiple, experience(s) in our lives when we have felt profoundly unsafe.
- 'Trauma is a fact of life but it doesn't have to be a life sentence'. Levine emphasises the effect of trauma on our natural inclination for connection and describes the impact of trauma as a 'loss of connection, to ourselves, our bodies, families and the world around us' (Levine, 2005, p. 4).
- van der Kolk (1994) suggests that trauma occurs when a person's natural defensive reaction to an experience overwhelms the central nervous system and changes the way the experience is remembered. This results in a failure of integration of the experience. Thus, van der Kolk's definition focuses on how the experience is received and understood by the individual and can help us understand how different people may experience and integrate the same event in different ways. For some there might be a lasting effect, whilst others seem to be able to shrug it off. Trauma experience and resilience is influenced by personal history, familial history, genetic inheritance, cultural history, and political and organisational systems.

In recent years, there has been an increased understanding of trauma due, in part, to greater knowledge of human neurophysiology. This new knowledge has been accompanied by an increased awareness of the prevalence of trauma in society. We used to consider trauma as the enduring impact of an event or a series of events on an individual. However, we should consider the possibility that trauma can also arise from our organisational, political and cultural structures. As suggested by Wineman (2003, p. 171) 'Oppression, which is the systematic abuse of power, renders people powerless. In turn, powerlessness is the hallmark of traumatic experience. It is therefore inevitable that trauma will be pervasive in a society organised around domination, both because oppression creates countless discrete acts of domination and because institutionalised oppression itself creates powerlessness and trauma'. This kind of systemic domination and institutional oppression is often pervasive and subtle, looking more like 'life as we know it,' than what we might think of as 'Capital-T Trauma'. Implicit biases, including sexism, racism, ageism, and homophobia, to name a few, are so interwoven into our milieu, as to be almost invisible. Over time, these biases become the water we swim in, unremarkable and seemingly unimportant. However, they operate powerfully in ways that may show up as trauma, but without a singular event to point to.

FRAMEWORKS FOR UNDERSTANDING TRAUMA

From the above definitions of trauma, we can summarise that trauma occurs when the emotion regulation system is overwhelmed, either temporarily or over time. The emotion regulation system is an internal conversation between the brain, the gut, the heart, and body.

Polyvagal theory

Polyvagal theory has provided new insights into the link between psychological experiences and physical manifestations (Porges, 2017, p. xiii). Much of our reaction to external and internal experiences occurs outside of awareness, through a process that Porges termed 'neuroception'. This is a 'process of responding at a neural level, to features in our environment with physiological shifts' (Porges, 2004, p. 19). Polyvagal theory describes three branches of a mammal's autonomic nervous system (ANS):

1 *Dorsal vagal branch* (a branch of the parasympathetic system) connects the gut and the brain and regulates digestive processes, basic relaxation and the 'freeze' response in times of perceived extreme danger.
2 *Sympathetic nervous system* that mobilises the body to fight or flight.
3 *Ventral vagal branch* (another branch of the parasympathetic system), sometimes known as the 'smart vagus'. The latter is the more recently evolved branch that connects the heart, lungs, muscles of the face and voice, and is active in human bonding, social communication, facial expressions, voice tone and prosody, and recognising emotions (Porges, 2011).

We are 'wired' for survival, and our external and internal experiences are monitored by structures within the ANS. Information is received from the sensory organs of the body via the neuroception system, and there is a rapid and simplistic assessment of the situation as 'safe' or 'not safe'. This system, adapted for survival, has no capacity for complex or nuanced appraisal of the situation. In the event of a 'not safe' appraisal then the rapid, but non-flexible system, mobilises the body to fight or flee, or immobilises the body to 'freeze' if it is deemed impossible to escape or fight. In the event of a 'safe' assessment then other responses become possible (see Figure 23.1).

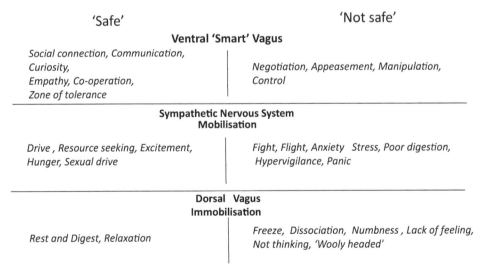

'Safe'	'Not safe'
Ventral 'Smart' Vagus	
Social connection, Communication, Curiosity, Empathy, Co-operation, Zone of tolerance	*Negotiation, Appeasement, Manipulation, Control*
Sympathetic Nervous System Mobilisation	
Drive , Resource seeking, Excitement, Hunger, Sexual drive	*Fight, Flight, Anxiety Stress, Poor digestion, Hypervigilance, Panic*
Dorsal Vagus Immobilisation	
Rest and Digest, Relaxation	*Freeze, Dissociation, Numbness , Lack of feeling, Not thinking, 'Wooly headed'*

Figure 23.1 The Autonomic Nervous System, in normal states and states of stress/trauma (adapted from Porges, 2011)

The parts of the brain that make a more sophisticated appraisal of the situation, the executive system, take longer to become activated. Porges (2004) describes these cognitive responses as secondary to neuroception. These are the parts that engage cognitive processes, can make use of available resources including emotional memory, problem solving capacity, seeking help, reassurance or social connection, and can help put experiences into perspective. These two systems act together in a process of neuroception and perception.

Recently, in addition to fight, flight, and freeze, a fourth instinctive reaction to danger has been recognised, that of 'tend and befriend' (Taylor, 2006). Tend and befriend behaviour is a complex response to a threat where an individual can become overly anxious to please an aggressor or oppressor. Tend and befriend may also be responsible for the phenomenon where group members move to protect and care for more vulnerable members, sometimes at the expense of their own safety. It is possible that tend and befriend behaviours arise from activation of the ventral vagal branch and sympathetic systems together.

Window of tolerance

The 'window of tolerance' (Siegel, 1999) refers to a zone of autonomic and emotional arousal that is optimal for wellbeing and effective functioning. Falling between the extremes of hyper- and hypo-arousal, this is a zone within which 'various intensities of emotional and physiological arousal can be processed without disrupting the functioning of the system' (Siegel, 1999, p. 253). When arousal falls within this window, information received from both internal and external environments can be integrated. Arousal contained within this window is available to the ventral vagal branch. When that window is exceeded or overwhelmed, other systems are activated – i.e. sympathetic fight or flight or the dorsal vagus to move into freeze (see Figure 23.2).

Self-Regulation and the integration of trauma

Integration is the capacity to recognise traumatic events or memories of events without getting overwhelmed. The process of integration can take moments, or years and

Hyper-arousal Zone

Increased sensation, Emotional Reactivity, Hypervigilance, Intrusive Imagery, Disorganised Cognitive processing

Window of Tolerance
Optimal Arousal Zone

Hypo-arousal Zone

Relative absence of sensation, Numbing of emotions, Disabled Cognitive processes, Reduced physical movement

Figure 23.2 Window of Tolerance (adapted from Ogden et al. 2006)

sometimes may never be completed, if the process itself feels too threatening. Siegel (2009) described integration as 'an internal attunement', it is the linkage of differentiated elements of a system and leads to the flexible, adaptive, and coherent flow of energy and information in the brain, mind, and body. Integration depends on the capacity for self-regulation.

Self-regulation is the facility to regulate one's emotions such that one is less easily disturbed by emotions (Lutz et al., 2007). Traumatic stress has a dysregulating effect, momentarily and/or longer term. The individual has the sense that their attention has been hijacked and the sympathetic fight/flight responses become activated. Alternatively, the system may move directly into dorsal vagus immobilisation, and the individual can feel disconnected or dissociated.

Integration is blocked when somatic experience is overwhelming and perpetuates trauma by triggering self-judging memories and negative cognitive processes; for example, when an abuse survivor considers themselves responsible for the abuse, or a victim of an accident berates themselves for being in the wrong place at the wrong time. When integration is blocked or incomplete, there is a tendency to be hyper-vigilant and/ or avoidant of difficult experiences associated with a traumatic event. Music (2014) wrote that bad experiences can lead to bodies and nervous systems that are programmed in expectation of a scary and unpleasant world.

MINDFULNESS AND TRAUMA

Mindfulness practice supports the processes of self-regulation and integration in a number of ways. One way of framing this is that the practice supports an expansion of the 'Window of Tolerance' (see Figure 23.3). Mindfulness practice may reduce the activity of the amygdala, through a top-down or bottom-up mechanism, which could lead to reduced activity to potential triggers (Hölzel et al., 2011). Rose et al. (2017) described how this model can be integrated into the experiential pedagogy of MBP teaching.

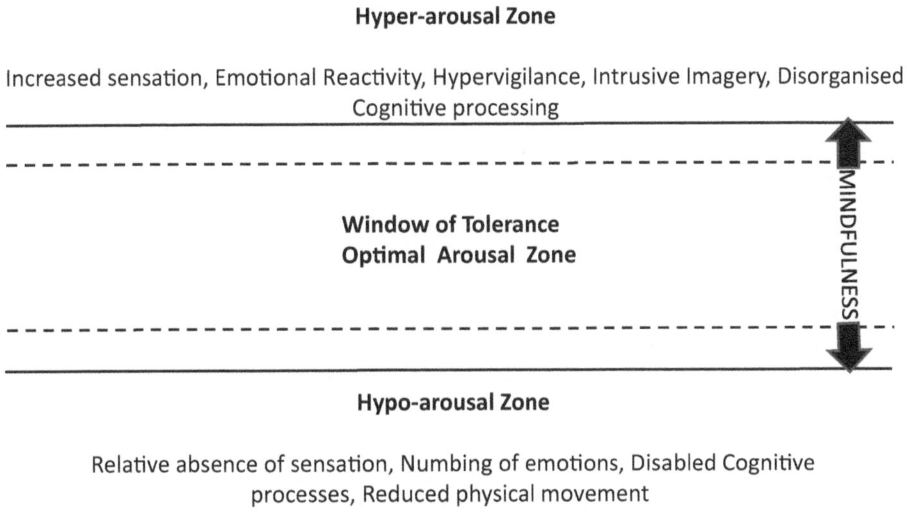

Hyper-arousal Zone

Increased sensation, Emotional Reactivity, Hypervigilance, Intrusive Imagery, Disorganised Cognitive processing

Window of Tolerance
Optimal Arousal Zone

MINDFULNESS

Hypo-arousal Zone

Relative absence of sensation, Numbing of emotions, Disabled Cognitive processes, Reduced physical movement

Figure 23.3 Window of Tolerance expanded with mindfulness practice (Adapted from Ogden et al. 2006)

Shapiro et al.'s IAA model (2006) offers a helpful example of how mindfulness may support regulation (see Chapter 3 for a description of the model), and this framework of intention, attention, and attitude may help with offering trauma-sensitive mindfulness.

> **Intention:** can include an aspiration to take care of oneself in the midst of difficult experience.
>
> **Attention:** participants can be trained to direct attention in ways that support stability with a focus on present moment sensing. When we are stressed, overthinking, or caught in memories of difficult experiences, skills to bring us into the present moment can be helpful. The use of pendulation (Levine, 2005) is critical here, where the participant is taught how attention can be moved towards or away from difficulty. When trauma symptoms are present there is the potential for these mechanisms to be impeded, in which case, a slower introduction is needed.
>
> **Attitude:** can include various qualities that are inherently regulating and adaptive, such as an orientation of curiosity, discernment and non-judgement. These can help to bring a kindly orientation to trauma-related experiences.

Decentering (or metacognition), the mechanism by which we can observe our thoughts without being emotionally caught by them, is recognised as an important skill that is cultivated during MBP training (Segal et al., 2019). When we increase awareness of our own internal experience and bring an attitude of acceptance and kindness to these observations then we are able to reduce the intensity of the experience and feel more regulated (Lutz et al., 2007).

There is much evidence of the benefits of mindfulness for people who have experienced trauma, if it is taught when conditions are appropriate. For example, evidence suggests that MBCT provided protection against depressive relapse for participants with a history of childhood trauma (Williams et al., 2014). However, mindfulness may not be the right approach for everyone. In the early stages of trauma-recovery, individual work with a skilled therapist may be most effective. With this foundation, a mindfulness practice can often take root more effectively, building on a growing sense of capability. Trauma can make one fearful of one's own experience, and it can be reactivated by any number of subsequent experiences. The process of paying close attention to internal experiences that may have been carefully avoided for years risks triggering further overwhelm. Britton has collated evidence of how intensive practice in retreat contexts have had harmful or unhelpful effects for some people. She wrote: 'We have all heard of the benefits of meditation ... yet the notion that mindfulness and meditation might be a cure-all for countless conditions and problems, including trauma, has had some unintended consequences (...) Those that do not share the benefits can feel deeply ashamed and convinced of their own brokenness.' (Treleavan, 2018, p. xi)

Shame can be a response to the human need to belong, and can be triggered by generalised and internalised systematic oppression. We can be threatened by real or imagined perceptions of 'what others will think of me', and the threat can be exacerbated by internal evaluations or self-attacking thoughts. When trauma or traumatic memories are triggered, they are often accompanied by shaming thoughts such as 'I should be over this by now', or 'what's the matter with me?' Our ability to engage with others may thus be compromised as patterns of connection are replaced with patterns of protection (Porges, 2017).

Treleaven (2018) quotes the startling figure that in the United States, 90% of the population have experienced some trauma. Of these, between 8% and 20% will develop a post-traumatic stress disorder, and for some in this category, mindfulness practices as taught in the 8-week curriculum, may be unhelpful or harmful. He wrote: 'What is triggering for one person can be beneficial for another'. It may not always be possible to know if someone on our course has trauma symptoms. We may have gained some information through a robust assessment process (Chapter 16), however, it is also possible that the participant themselves will not recognise their experiences as arising from trauma, and in fact, they may not arise from a single event or circumstance. Systemic oppression and implicit bias influence behaviour and the nervous system in ways that we are only beginning to understand. It is important, therefore, that MBP teachers develop skills in recognising trauma symptoms, and bring sensitivity to trauma into MBP teaching so that it is inclusive and safely available to all.

TRAUMA-SENSITIVITY IN THE MINDFULNESS TEACHING SPACE

The Center for Trauma Informed Care in the US offers a definition of a trauma-sensitive system which highlights the 4 R's: 'A program, organisation or system that is trauma informed **realises** the widespread impact of trauma and understands the potential paths for recovery; **recognises** the signs and symptoms of trauma in clients, families, staff and others involved with the system; **responds** by fully integrating knowledge about trauma into policies, procedures and practices; and seeks to actively resist **re-traumatising**' (Substance Abuse and Mental Health Service Administration's Trauma and Justice Strategic Initiative 2014, p. 9). This offers a useful basis for considering whether we are sensitive to trauma in our teaching spaces.

As MBP teachers we are thus called on to:

> **Realise** the possible prevalence of trauma in the cultures of our course participants as well as the individual and societal sources of trauma. We should also realise the potential for mindfulness practice to do harm to some individuals and to operate a robust assessment process (Chapter 16).
>
> **Recognise** the potential symptoms of trauma as they show up during and around the teaching sessions. This is not to say the teacher needs to diagnose trauma, or trauma symptoms, but rather to remain open to the possibility that some behaviours or reactions to the teaching may be adaptations to trauma.
>
> **Respond** with sensitivity, kindness and genuine curiosity to the individual and their experiences, resisting any impulse to diagnose or try to 'fix'.
>
> **Resist re-traumatising**. We can resist re-traumatising by maintaining an accepting, friendly and invitational orientation, and by integrating trauma-sensitive practices into our approach.
>
> **Referral**. A fifth 'R' should be added in the context of MBP teaching. We should be alert to the need to refer, and aware of resources in our locality that we can refer course participants to if they need more specialised help with trauma symptoms.

The key to all of this is that our role is to support the participant to skilfully manage and understand the responses they are experiencing here and now – and does not extend to helping the participants understand the potential traumatic event, for that, participants need to be referred to a specialist.

Box 23.1 Case example

A man who was a dedicated runner came to my MBSR class. He returned to session two after a week of practicing the body scan, in quite an agitated state. During the home practice inquiry, he said that practicing the body scan had caused him to have heart palpitations. Further inquiry revealed that as he was running, he had noticed his heart beat and he had never been aware of it before. This had led him to believe that something was very wrong. Applying the principles of trauma informed care to this situation:

Realise – the possibility of trauma or a trauma triggered response, even though the man himself was convinced this was a physical problem.

Recognise – the possible signs of trauma. The man was quite agitated and seeking reassurance. He was not calm and curious about this new state.

Respond – The appropriate response here was not to engage him in a discussion of his symptoms, or to attempt a deeper inquiry, but rather to provide the reassurance he was seeking and, as a teacher, to stay grounded in the face of his agitation (*embodiment*). To stay connected (*relational*), through voice tone and eye contact (Porges, 2017). Extend genuine curiosity about his experiences and not jump to conclusions or try to fix. It was also necessary to stay aware of and connected to the group (*managing group process*), who were also affected by his agitation.

Resist retraumatising – It was important to respond seriously to his distress, and to offer alternative practices (*guiding practices*) that would help him manage his agitation, in the moment (e.g. a pause or a Three-Step Breathing Space, or bringing awareness to the body in its entirety, encouraging groundedness), and in his personal practice if the anxiety returned. Whilst supporting him individually, I also helped him to stay connected to the whole group. Connection and social support are important for recovery and re-establishing equilibrium following a trauma experience. It can help to use a horizontal inquiry if appropriate (Part 1.5), or invite the whole group to breathe together or connect into a grounded area of the body for stability. It's important to offer alternatives as the breath may not always be a stable or accessible focus, even for those who have not experienced trauma. After the formal session the man and I had a one-to-one conversation in which we fine-tuned his mindfulness practice plans. I encouraged him to contact me by phone and/or email during the week to check in about his experiences.

Referral – The man was advised to visit his GP and to get checked out for any possible physical causes of the palpitations. I followed up with him individually in the subsequent week to check how this had gone and how he was doing.

TRAUMA-SENSITIVE TEACHING METHODS

This summary guidance to teaching with sensitivity to trauma is offered within the structure of the MBI:TAC domains (Crane et al., 2018). The key throughout is to fold trauma-sensitive teaching into how the course is offered so that it is not an add-on, but is simply good teaching. Note that it may be that group-based MBPs may not be suitable for people with high levels of PTSD, who would be ideally taught by someone with specialist training, in a one-to-one setting.

Domain 1 – Coverage pacing and organisation of session curriculum

One key to trauma-sensitivity is flexibility. It can be challenging to meet the curriculum demands in the session timeframe. However, trauma-sensitive teaching involves a willingness to adjust the pacing to the session, rather than getting too attached to meeting curriculum demands. This could be offered quite simply by sharing with participants a simple framework for understanding how intensity and difficulty can arise early on in the programme (for example, the window of tolerance diagram) (see Figures 23.2 and 23.3), along with a talk about how we can make choices to take care of ourselves.

Domain 2 – Relational skills

Our relational skills are perhaps the most potent resource we have in our intentions to be trauma-sensitive. 'Social engagement is a two-way process: ventral vagal branch systems are alert to signs of safety by monitoring facial expression, voice tone and prosody' (Porges, 2017, pp. 48–49). By maintaining a consistent, accepting and kindly attitude, the MBP teacher can convey a sense of safety for the course participants. 'A neuroception of safety is triggered by the other person's social engagement system' (Porges, 2017, p. 147).

Domain 3 – Embodiment

'Only when we are in a calm physiological state can we carry signals of safety to another' (Porges, 2017, p. 50). If relational skills are our ally in trauma-sensitive teaching, then embodiment of mindfulness is the best support for our relational skills. Through our own steadiness and embodiment of mindfulness, we not only convey a sense of what is possible, but also a deep intention for wellbeing for individuals on the course. Embodiment of mindfulness includes authenticity, and by owning our own struggles with mindfulness practice, we can often reduce striving and shaming self-reflections, and work towards rebalancing the power-imbalances that are inherent in a teacher-learner relationship. In addition, it is important to recognise that embodiment does not preclude dysregulation in ourselves that might arise in response to an exchange or person on the MBP course. In the above case study, for instance, it would not be unusual, even within a strong personal practice, for the teacher to experience a sense of activation as they received the participant's report. To recognise when we may *not* be in a calm physiological state, *is* embodiment. If we harden to these signals, we effectively close the door on the fluidity of the moment. Knowing what is arising, being able to skilfully draw upon one's own wholeness and resources, and meeting the participant in a mutually grounded space exemplifies embodiment in a dynamic, responsive, alive way. Even when we cognitively know it is not from anything we have or have not done, a sense of failing our participants can arise when we become aware of our own reactivity.

Domain 4 – Guiding mindfulness practices

Trauma-sensitised systems are finely tuned to detect signs of safety (and lack of it). For these individuals, bodily signals (i.e. facial expression, voice tone and prosody) are as important as language. It is important to inclusively offer choices from the beginning of each practice, including posture, options for focus/attentional anchor, a different mindfulness practice altogether, or even choosing not to practice in that specific moment. Noticing participants' responses *while practicing* gives important feedback, e.g., flushing or loss of colour in the face, agitation or restlessness can all indicate discomfort or overwhelm. Active monitoring of our participants creates opportunities for 'on the spot' adjustments to guidance. Moving the body is an instinctive way that we integrate intense affect (Ogden et al., 2006); and acknowledging restlessness can be very supportive during practices. We can also aid integration by offering short movement practices at any time during a session, or a moving practice as an alternative to a static one (See Box 23.2).

Box 23.2 Practical ways of guiding practices with trauma sensitivity

Posture.

Whilst there is a rationale for each of the postures we teach in a MBP, it is possible to engage with any of the practices from alternative postures, either standing, sitting or lying. Lying down may feel particularly unsafe for some participants and we can offer sitting or even standing as an alternative.

Alternative anchors for the attention.

Alternatives to the breath as an anchor, could include a focus on the contact of feet on the floor, hands with the body (e.g. hand on belly), or something external (e.g. a cold metal chair leg). Focusing on senses other than touch can also be a helpful steadying focus for some (e.g. sound, or a smell such as a favourite essential oil). Slowly tracking the horizon with the eyes or finding a pleasing spot for the eyes to rest (a particular colour or shape), is also supportive of present-moment experience. Importantly, when we offer alternatives, we encourage the individual to discover for themselves what is most helpful for them.

Movement

Movement can be introduced at any point during the course. Inviting everyone to stand and stretch or 'have a wriggle', can regulate intensity without drawing attention to an individual who may be struggling to be still. Movement can be subtle, such as tracing the fingers of one hand with one finger of the other hand or, if the room allows, an individual can be invited to walk even during a sitting meditation. In addition, brisk or strong movements can ameliorate a sense of 'freeze' that may arise in response to threat or lack of safety. Mindful movement does not have to be slow or gentle. Jumping, shaking, brushing the body off with strong sweeps of the hands can support presence and relate to the natural responses we see in the animal kingdom. This relates to Sapolsky's (2004) stress physiology and the natural healing response of the nervous system when allowed to respond in its most basic way.

Domain 5 – Conveying themes through interactive inquiry and didactic teaching

In essence, the inquiry process is teaching people to be curious about their own internal experience. A self-regulated individual is able to be curious and to approach their experience. Through human connection and acceptance, we can help our course participants to witness their own internal processes and to integrate them with cognitive understanding – a bottom-up and top-down process. For the trauma-sensitive individual, both the attention to internal experiences and the cognitive concepts may make it challenging to maintain a sense of safety. A skilful teacher brings patience and understanding, recognising that pace of learning and integration is entirely individual.

Domain 6 – Holding the group-learning environment

We have seen that accepting human connection is key to trauma resilience. The mindfulness-based teacher can cultivate safety and connection by the skilful holding of the group-learning environment. Inquiring in skilful ways, recognising our common humanity, and normalising emotions, biological and physiological responses as part of the range of being human, supports the process of welcoming and allowing all that is in the room. In some situations, social connectivity also carries a risk of shame and rupture of connection. The skilful mindfulness teacher can be alert to these possibilities and move to repair and soothe if this occurs. Bringing mindfulness to the group process supports a strengthening of each participants' ability to meet themselves and others, just as they are. This in itself reduces shame and supports integration.

TRAUMA AND THE MINDFULNESS-BASED TEACHER

Given the prevalence of trauma in our societies, as MBP teachers we must also acknowledge our own trauma histories, and the implicit biases that cloud or alter our perception. As we move deeper into our own practice, we will connect with the tender aspects of our own histories. Like all humans, we are prone to shame and defensive blocks. It is a matter of self-care, authenticity and ethical integrity that we look deeply at the personal impact of individual and societal trauma and seek to address these through relationships with our supervisors, meditation teachers, therapists, families and ultimately with ourselves (Chapters 20–22).

The ethos of MBPs begins with a sense of the innate integrity and wholeness of a human being – no matter what may be happening that seems otherwise. 'As long as you are breathing, there is more right than wrong with you' (Kabat-Zinn, 2013, p. xlix). Recollecting this in the face of trauma – our own or others – is essential. The human capacity to creatively meet trauma to survive in the moment, even when these strategies are unhelpful long-term, can be viewed as the ultimate elegance of a neurological system that is still in refinement. What might arise in an MBP teaching space is a natural longing to live from that wholeness. As such, awareness, especially as it may be accessed within the steady frame of MBP practice, can be a primary inner resource for healing and growth.

SUMMARY

- Trauma is prevalent in our societies and its origins are both individual and societal.
- In order to offer trauma-sensitive MBP teaching, we must familiarise ourselves with definitions of trauma and frameworks to understand its impact on the human organism.
- MBP teachers, as part of standard teaching practice, should integrate trauma-sensitive guidance when teaching MBPs.
- Group-based MBPs may not be suitable for people with high levels of PTSD, who would be ideally taught by someone with specialist training, in a one-to-one setting.
- Self-regulation and integration are key to trauma resilience, and mindfulness practice can offer skills that enhance these. For some individuals, however, mindfulness practice can exacerbate trauma symptoms. Robust assessment and trauma-sensitive teaching are required to avoid re-traumatising.
- Trauma-sensitivity requires the 5 'R's: realising, recognising, responding, resisting re-traumatising and being aware of resources for further referral.
- Addressing our own trauma history is matter of self-care and ethical integrity for mindfulness-based teachers.
- Trauma-sensitive practice is "an ongoing orientation to practice and a commitment to being a continual learner" (Treleaven, 2018, p. 203).

RESOURCES

Gilbert has written extensively about the concept of shame and its role in trauma and depression. – e.g. Gilbert, P. (2010). *Compassion focused therapy: Distinctive features*: Routledge.

Treleaven's website includes a range of resources and a helpful summary of how to recognise trauma activation. Trauma Informed Education (n.d.). David Treleaven: Making mindfulness safe and effective for people who've experienced trauma. https://davidtreleaven.com/

Treleaven, D. A. (2018). *Trauma-sensitive mindfulness: Practices for safe and transformative healing*. WW Norton & Company.

Window of Tolerance is a concept developed by Siegel (Siegel, D. J. (1999). *The developing mind* (Vol. 296). New York, NY: Guilford Press) and adapted by Ogden (Ogden, P., Minton, K., & Pain, C. (2006). *Norton series on interpersonal neurobiology. Trauma and the body: A sensorimotor approach to psychotherapy*. W W Norton & Co.).

24
Societal themes

Bethan Roberts and Rebecca Crane

Neither the life of an individual nor the history of a society can be understood without understanding both.

Mills (2000, p. 3)

This chapter offers a broad-brush view of the vast territory of societal themes and the interface of these with MBP teaching, and is therefore necessarily limited in scope. We offer it within the context of this book to stimulate exploration of these themes by MBP teachers; and with a recognition that explicit links between these themes and MBP teaching is underdeveloped on multiple levels – personal, organisational, and in the wider field. These issues represent a frontier for our work, and we are learners in this space.

MBPs have at their root the desire to reduce suffering. This chapter highlights that suffering is not solely an individual phenomenon: it is both deeply individual and personal, and socially and contextually situated; and that mindfulness has a role in supporting people to become socially mindful as well as individually mindful. There is currently an active inquiry within the mindfulness field on these issues (e.g. Harrington & Dunne, 2015). This is catalysing an examination of the potential limits of current MBP curriculum models in terms of their dominant emphasis on the inner personal causes of suffering, and lesser emphasis on contextual and social causes. We aim in this chapter to examine both how this can begin to be rebalanced within the existing forms of MBSR and MBCT, and to highlight other MBP developments that emphasise social context from the outset. Within all of this, we emphasise the need for ongoing inquiry into our own 'personhood' as MBP teachers, with a particular priority on examining the influence of our situated conditioned experience. We strongly encourage a practice of increasing our personal awareness of biases, prejudices, and taken for granted assumptions so that we as teachers are less likely to inadvertently *cause or perpetuate* suffering through lack of awareness. We consider the broader questions of how we can play our part in reducing social inequalities, and in reducing suffering caused by global challenges such as climate change, economic inequality and disease. The views offered within this chapter are necessarily from the lens of our own particular individual and contextual positions, and to make this visible we briefly share some of this here.

Prior to entering the world of mindfulness teaching, my work (BR) was in the field of equality and diversity. My professional working life started in the late 1980s as a researcher in the AIDS and HIV field, which I was drawn to largely because of the anti-gay prejudice that the epidemic fuelled. This was hard on the heels of my 'coming out' as a gay woman within the context of a traditional Welsh speaking family in North Wales, who reacted with deep shame and bitter disappointment. The overwhelming pain and confusion I experienced in the wake of this reaction, together with the anti-gay discrimination I was subjected to in my first professional job, and the pervasive hostility within British society towards gay people at that time, fuelled my need to better understand prejudice, discrimination and exclusion. I wanted to make some sense out of why having a same-sex relationship had such a profound influence on seemingly every aspect of life. I returned to university to study and then spent 15 years working in three UK statutory equality commissions. The 'awareness raising' of the mechanisms that drive various types of oppression that came through studying and working in this field, as well as living with a British-Asian partner for 25 years, helped enormously in terms of my journey to self-respect and appreciation of the marginalised communities of which I am part. I discovered there was space for me in these diverse communities. It was also a disturbing (in the best sense of the word) journey as it shone a light on my own conditioning and biases which opened a door to greater freedom from these toxins. Yet 'awareness raising' was not enough for me. My heart needed to be healed from the hurt that I had experienced, not only within my family and at work, but also from day-to-day living, including being spat at on the street by strangers, drivers passing by winding their windows down to hurl homophobic abuse, and neighbours sending anti-gay hate mail. These social sources of suffering undoubtedly affected my inner world. Mindfulness practice offered a way to transform this. In 2010, my MSc dissertation explored whether mindfulness could potentially reduce the damage to health caused by social inequalities. There was very little literature on this topic at that time, so it is heartening to find a growing energy and focus gathering around this theme now. The themes are being strongly highlighted now as we write this in 2020, with the coronavirus epidemic further spotlighting social inequalities, and the anti-racism movement gathering momentum.

I (RC) lead CMRP, and my working life has been spent in the health service and then in academia. My personal experience of developing and leading novel and unrecognised work in an academic context where more of my peers and senior leaders are male has offered me some insight into the experience of marginalisation. However, I also recognise my multiple privileges and my whiteness, and that these will influence my taken for granted assumptions. I proactively locate myself as a learner not an expert on the themes we are investigating here. I have always seen the core mission of CMRP as being about enabling broad accessibility to MBPs through enabling its uptake in mainstream institutions such as the health service and education settings. However, it has also become clear over the years that there are both potentials and limits to enabling social change from within the mainstream (Kucinskas, 2019). On both a personal and an organisational level, I am on a journey in terms of considering the place of MBPs in relation to broader contextual challenges. I am proactively engaging in training and practice to enable greater consideration of how the influence of context can be skilfully included in our understanding of human struggles. This is both a personal process, and one that we are engaging in collectively within the CMRP core training team, and with colleagues in the wider field. This includes reflecting deeply on my own formative conditioning, along with reflecting on the particular collective challenges and pressures we are experiencing socially and environmentally at this moment in time.

We structure the chapter by first, describing some of the issues within this territory; second, we examine how skilful recognition and understanding of societal and contextual issues can influence how we practice and teach MBPs; and third, we highlight our legal responsibilities in relation to inclusive practice, and consider how understanding of non-discriminatory practice shapes how we relate to and support participants in and around the sessions.

MINDFULNESS-BASED PROGRAMMES AND SOCIAL-ENVIRONMENTAL CONTEXT

At the heart of teaching MBPs is an engagement with the reality of suffering, a commitment to understand and be awake to its causes, and a recognition that there are skilful ways of relating that enable greater freedom, and that release capacities for healing and creative engagement with experience. MBPs are fine-tuned to help us recognise the causes and conditions that tend us towards distress. Some of these vulnerabilities are general – all humans experience them – and some are more particular to certain groups. Some emanate from inner habit patterns, whilst some emanate from the external context and systems. Examples of general human vulnerabilities are: our use of language which helps us make sense of, but also separates us from the immediacy of our experience; our tendency to live in automatic pilot habit mode; a tendency to not be present because, wanting control, we live conceptually in the future or past; our evolutionary survival mechanisms that do not discriminate between real and imagined threats, nor between internal and external stressors; and our tendency to over-rely on thinking, seduced by a misguided sense that it provides more control than our intuition and senses (Crane, 2017). An example of general contextual vulnerability that we (as a species) are all facing is our changing relationship to the natural world, the reality of climate breakdown, pandemics and predictions of accompanying social instability in years to come; and the increasingly polarised political discourse, which is creating increasing levels of uncertainty and fear.

The surrounding social context is profoundly implicated in generating personal vulnerability to distress and harm. Indeed, in countries that are more unequal, outcomes are worse for almost everyone in areas such as public health, education, obesity and social mobility (Wilkinson & Pickett, 2018). Marginalised groups (e.g. Black, Asian and minority ethnic (BAME) groups; cultural and/or religious groups; women; disabled people; lesbian, gay, bisexual, transgender, intersex, queer or asexual [LGBTQIA] people; older people, and people with a working-class background) disproportionately experience harm and suffering which come from discrimination, stigma, hate crimes, exclusion, and inequality. Harm is generated by the social, economic, historical and political context, which still privileges some groups (i.e. white, male, non-disabled, cis-gendered, heterosexual, upper and middle class), and oppresses others. The suffering caused by discrimination and stigma leads to people in marginalised groups living shorter lives and spending many more years in poorer health than those higher up the social ladder (Pickett & Wilkinson, 2009). For example, the suicide rates amongst sexual minority youth are more than three times higher than their heterosexual peers; and youths who are transgender (sexual orientation unknown – this data was not collected in this study) are nearly six times as likely to attempt suicide as their cisgender and heterosexual peers are. Bullying has been shown to be a significant contributing factor (di Giacomo et al., 2018).

Various factors play a part in these adverse effects on physical and mental health. First, there are the obvious material factors such as income, occupation, and housing which have undoubtedly played their part in BAME groups being at a higher risk of dying from coronavirus than white people in the UK (Office for National Statistics, 2020).

Second, there is an enormous psychosocial consequence to the reality of living with daily discrimination, prejudice and injustice, including how people *feel* about their social status. Common feelings that arise from low social status are anxiety, hostility, inferiority, shame, not feeling valued, depression, and lack of control over one's circumstances. MBPs focus on how these types of feelings trigger the stress-reaction cycle. This inner reaction to adverse circumstances creates bodily changes that in turn can further damage health and reduce length of life (Pickett & Wilkinson, 2009). In some, depression can be linked to low social status as people feel devalued, defeated, inferior to others, subordinated, worthless and 'at the bottom of the pile' (Gilbert, 2009). Negative self-judgment through to self-rejection and self-loathing seep inside one's heart and mind from a discriminatory external environment.

Some groups are given power and others are disempowered by the system of institutionalised oppression within which we are all embedded. However, ultimately it creates suffering to some degree for all (Pickett & Wilkinson, 2009). There is increasing exploration regarding how mindfulness training could open a way to enable participants from all backgrounds within society to build awareness of and capacities to skilfully engage with and influence social injustice (Mindfulness and Social Change Network, n.d.; Wreford & Haddock, 2019). For those who benefit from the unequal, discriminatory social and economic system, mindfulness may be one part of a journey of recognition that empowers ways of acting to transform the system of oppression we are all part of. For individuals and groups who are disempowered by oppression, mindfulness has the potential to build capacities to relate differently to harmful inner patterns born of toxic social contexts. It may offer inner protection in the face of hostility and exclusion, and help heal inner wounds caused by societal oppression.

Theories underpinning mindfulness practice in the MBP context have tended to draw on those that emphasise how suffering is created on an individual level. However, there is also a strong body of teachings that situate mindfulness within an organisational and societal level (e.g. Loy, 2019; Magee, 2019; Petty, 2017). We can recognise how, on a systemic level, the ways human societies operate are often not in the service of human flourishing. Over time, aspects of our global societal system have developed patterns of relating which are driven by greed, hatred, fear, anger, and misunderstanding of what is needed to enable peace and ease. In turn this has led to overconsumption in many parts of the world, to widening social hierarchies, and inequity of access to resources. Our relationship with the natural world is dominated by a tendency to take what we can in the short term without consideration of the needs of other species, or of our own descendants in generations to come. Of course, it is important to balance all this with recognition that there are inspiring organisations, leaders and individuals who are proactively engaged with these issues, and that extraordinary progress has been made internationally to acknowledge and address poverty, inequality and exclusion.

In short, a key part of the personal work that we need to do as MBP teachers, individually and collectively, is to have a commitment to ongoing inquiry on the causes and conditions that lead to suffering and distress on an individual *and* a societal level, and to develop insight into the causes and conditions that lead to flourishing on all levels.

MINDFULNESS-BASED PRACTICE AND TEACHING WITH AWARENESS OF SOCIAL CONTEXT

MBPs can be skilfully adapted in a range of ways to support a range of outcomes. Some are now pioneering MBP adaptations that arise from a fine-tuned analysis of the social context which generates suffering. This understanding is integrated with mindfulness training to enable participants to attune to their interrelationship with the conditions of their lives (e.g. Rupprecht et al., 2019; Whitehead et al., 2014). Others (including ourselves) are working within existing models such as MBSR with an expanded understanding of the multiple causes of distress and suffering embedded into the teaching process. There is a continuum rather than a polarity here – it is important within any MBP delivery to include awareness of contextual influences on distress, and it is important within MBPs that have a greater focus on social contexts to give space for individuals to make their own discoveries about their internalised patterning. In this emergent field, the diversity of MBP developments from a range of perspectives and contexts are important contributors to our understanding about how to skilfully influence on both individual and systemic levels.

MBSR was developed to enable participants to discover new relationships to life challenges. Jon Kabat-Zinn also had a wider vision. In his first book – Full Catastrophe Living (Kabat-Zinn, 2013) – he described a vision for the potential for the practice of mindfulness to influence our lives on all levels including the societal. Specifically, he had the aspiration that the work would influence the paradigm and systemic underpinning of how health care is delivered. As the MBP field evolves and expands, and the world context changes (in both challenging and encouraging ways), there is appropriately stronger questioning of the issue of the relationship between MBPs and social change. We do know from research that participants of MBSR and related MBPs are more likely to engage in behaviours that are pro-social and pro-environmental such as random acts of kindness, recycling etc (e.g. Baer, 2015). However, many practitioners question the proposition that if enough people engage in mindfulness training it will create a critical mass that will lead to a tipping point of greater levels of awareness, which in turn will naturally lead to systemic change. There is also increasing recognition that MBPs internationally have to date largely been delivered to and by those who are privileged by the social hierarchy, which from the outset nullifies the potential of these programmes to influence change on a systemic level (Kucinskas, 2019). The MBP developments to date offer a strong foundation of research and practice, and established recognition within the mainstream, which hopefully provides the ground from which new creative developments can emerge. As MBP teachers, we each work in different ways, in different contexts, and this influences what is possible, and how we situate our work. Below are some examples of ways of engaging with these themes, which align our MBP teaching practice more closely with the changes we would like to see on a societal level.

Ensuring that MBP teaching embraces a wide understanding of the causes and conditions that lead to suffering

A key responsibility of MBP teaching is to understand and hold the teaching on human suffering in a wide container. We aspire to support participants to both grow in understanding of the ways in which we inadvertently deepen our personal distress due to inner habit patterns; and simultaneously to recognise that the causes of suffering impact unequally across different groups. The latter is particularly critical in ensuring that MBP teachers do not inadvertently give the message that if participants were skilful in managing their personal process they would experience ease and wellbeing. There are clearly multiple causes and conditions of suffering that are beyond our control and immediate influence.

If we take a fresh look at the MBP curriculum from this broader perspective, we can reflect on how an understanding of the breadth of causes and conditions that cause suffering can be interwoven throughout the MBP. The first contact with participants is in the orientation and assessment meeting either in a group or individual context. We convey here the underpinning aims of the practice and the course. There is scope here to communicate that we will be bringing awareness to inner habits that cause distress in our lives, and discovering ways to do things differently; and we will also be recognising that some of our life difficulties are caused by the reality of the conditions we live within; and we will be exploring how we can relate as skilfully as possible to the forces that are both within and beyond our control. This theme can then be acknowledged when it emerges naturally in the inquiry conversations within the sessions. The group exercises that investigate perception (session 2), depression or stress (sessions 4–5), communication (MBSR session 6) and lifestyle factors (session 7) can all include wider systemic themes. For example, when drawing from the group what the stress triggers are in their lives, it is important to give space to both inner and outer stress triggers – and as teacher to name examples of external influences on stress that may not emerge naturally in the group discussion such as air pollution, racism, disability hate crimes etc. Another example is to weave unconscious bias into the explorations around perception. This can bring awareness to when we unknowingly exclude or discriminate against others. This clearly needs to be held with sensitivity and care. These themes can stimulate guilt and shame which needs compassionate holding within the teaching space.

A key challenge for MBP teachers working within mainstream institutions such as health care or schools is navigating the tension of offering a programme whose pedagogy rests on non-instrumentality within organisations that are heavily oriented around instrumentality. Furthermore, the model, which predominates in significant parts of our health service, is a medical one. For example, MBCT was developed, researched and positioned within the NHS as a depression prevention approach. The challenge for the teacher is to create and sustain a learning environment that parks the aspiration of depression prevention, and enables participants to open into a willingness to meet whatever experience is showing up with kindly curiosity. Of course, we want change on both personal and systemic levels, but from a mindfulness perspective, how we orient towards this aspiration is as important as what we do. These themes are explored further in Chapters 1 and 26.

Creating safety within the 'container' of MBP teaching

MBPs are rooted in psychological and neuroscientific evidence. In our view, the overwhelming scientific evidence of the causal links between (a) human activity and global warming and (b) social inequalities and health inequalities should also underpin the delivery of MBPs. Given that discrimination, stigma, and harassment cause harm and suffering, the MBP teacher has a responsibility to create as much safety as possible within the learning space. Setting ground rules at the outset is key, but the teacher needs to continue to maintain a container that has clear boundaries throughout the MBP (Chapter 13). There will be a diversity of views and opinions within any group, and the ethos of inclusivity is central to MBPs, but when harmful perspectives are expressed the teacher has a responsibility to be proactive in protecting safety. For example, if an MBP teacher was faced with a participant who told another participant who has a history of mental illness, such as depression, that their illness was caused by demons and they were 'possessed', how would the teacher respond? With kindness and compassion hopefully, but also by laying down clear boundaries that expressing such views is not permitted because it creates an unsafe environment. Taking time with the individual to explain the reasons for setting this boundary and to raise awareness is important, but if such beliefs continue to be deeply held, it is vital to be clear that they cannot be expressed in the teaching space because they undermine trust, safety and the potential for learning. In this way, it is not the individual that is excluded but the harmful behaviour. In other words, creating such ethical boundaries *is not about excluding people with prejudicial views* but being clear about what is unacceptable behaviour. Sometimes setting such boundaries needs to be done within the whole group, and at other times it is more appropriate to address the issue on a one-to-one basis. The MBP teacher has a duty not to silently stand by if discriminating and stigmatising beliefs are expressed, which are harmful to other participants and/or to the MBP teacher themselves. Teachers are stewards of the groups they teach, and by default, have responsibility for taking care of the ethical container of that group.

Teaching from a pro-social/pro-environmental orientation

As the paragraph above illustrates, within existing curriculum forms such as MBSR, the teacher is the carrier of the ethical system within which the teaching is embedded (Chapter 22). We propose that a key part of this is a proactive orientation within the teacher and the teaching towards pro-environmental and pro-social ways of being. The baseline inquiry that guides the teacher's ethical stance is – what is in the service of wellbeing inwardly and outwardly, on personal, collective and ecological levels? The teacher's inner compass on these becomes a baseline norm that finds expression across the teaching process. For example, although the emphasis in MBPs has tended towards exploration of mindfulness as an inner orientation, it is very possible to expand this to encourage inquiry into how we behave and act pro-socially in the world. Small examples of this include: when giving suggestions for informal mindfulness practice, there is an important distinction between being mindful of 'taking the rubbish out' vs 'sorting the recycling', or 'driving your car' vs 'walking to work' or 'taking the bus'; when exploring kindness and compassion, naming that we are both cultivating an internal orientation, and also one that becomes proactively expressed in our actions in the world; exploring to whom we find ourselves offering kindness and who is excluded (shining a light on our conscious and/or unconscious bias); and exploring how we can skilfully relate to and influence social justice issues when reflecting on external stress triggers, or lifestyle factors.

Reflecting on the underpinning assumptions that drive the contextual positioning of the courses we teach

Many MBP teachers have a strong and wholesome wish to open access to the teaching to communities and populations who are marginalised. There is important work to be done in this arena, *and* there are important perspectives and sensitivities about how to develop and situate programmes in ways that are responsive to the social and political context of individual stress, wellbeing, and change. In particular, it is important to reflect on how an MBP delivery could inadvertently give back to members of marginalised communities the responsibility for managing the impact of oppression, when in reality the responsibility for the circumstances they are compelled to operate within lies elsewhere. As a general direction of travel, we encourage teachers who have lived experience of particular populations, cultures, and communities to offer MBPs within these contexts. In this way, there will be embodied knowledge of context and cultural issues within the delivery. In order for this to happen there needs to be greater access to training, delivered by a greater diversity of trainers.

It is important for all MBP teachers to inquire around how to sensitively and skilfully adapt to culture, context, and population. These are large themes that we encourage you to investigate. We recommend the Mindfulness Initiatives 'Field book for Innovators' which includes analysis of these issues and the implications for programme design (Sanghvi, 2019). This question about how to skilfully adapt and situate the delivery of MBPs in ways that open the potential for meeting both individual and collective patterns of suffering is a key frontier in the ongoing development of this field.

Offering follow-up MBPs that explicitly invite engagement with social-environmental issues

Many MBP teachers are creatively developing models for follow-up courses in these areas. MBSR and MBCT participants have a thorough grounding and training in the development of a personal practice and are often hungry for development opportunities. The 8-week course is just the beginning of a path of exploration. A vital aspect of this journey is an inquiry into the ways in which our personal practice informs a whole life path that values all living beings. Linked to this are the ways in which awareness can be harnessed to build understanding of the deeper causes of social suffering, and an inquiry into what is possible for me to do within my circle of influence.

Designing and delivering an MBP that is explicitly aimed at cultivating pro-social awareness and behaviours, compassion and awareness of personal bias and prejudice

Some practitioners are developing and researching MBPs that are explicitly designed to address implicit and unconscious bias and prejudice, and develop more skilled ways of relating to each other. These are often integrated with theories from behavioural insights and are being delivered in workplace contexts to support changes in practice towards greater sustainability and conscious engagement with ethical practice (Whitehead et al., 2014).

NON-DISCRIMINATORY PRACTICE

Everyone working in the service of others has a responsibility to develop understanding of their own patterns of unconscious bias and prejudice; and to learn about their own racial, cultural and family history, and the implications this has for inherited conditioning. As MBP teachers, the responsibility to do our own work in this area is particularly strong because our entire 'raison d'être' is to create learning environments that enable relief from suffering. If we inadvertently perpetuate in the MBP classroom the oppressive and discriminatory practices that some participants experience in their everyday lives, the sense of betrayal can be deep and the missed opportunities for the individuals concerned can have long reaching implications. There is therefore an imperative that we all participate in training on, and proactively raise our awareness of, equality, diversity, inclusion, and conscious and unconscious bias; and, in an ongoing way, recognise that engagement with these themes on a deeply personal level are a critical aspect of our mindfulness practice. This inner work is a process of education, learning and bringing 'on radar' the patterns within ourselves that sustain external conditions that perpetuate social justice. Our mindfulness practice combined with proactive engagement with training and education on these issues enables a way of honestly seeing this 'off radar' inner conditioning. Practice then also supports us in meeting the emotional impact of recognising our own patterning, which can be challenging. This also enables us to cultivate greater empathy for, and understanding of, any of our participants who hold prejudicial views and to know from direct experience that these views are not solid, and can be worked with in similar ways to the way we work with other self-limiting and harmful habitual thought patterns

Our unconscious mind is led by automatic, reactive patterns that are in turn driven by deeply conditioned emotional and intuitive feelings. Logic and reason do not stand much chance in the face of quick patterns of mind that favour people *most like us*, (or for some individuals in discriminated groups this can mean favouring people 'not like us' if oppression has been internalised). Aspiring to live in a more humane and just society and holding values that align with this are not enough. If we want to bring our actions and choices in line with our values, we have inner work to do.

One aspect of our development work as MBP teachers is to investigate our motivations for engaging in this work. Clarifying and regularly reconnecting to our aspiration for the ease of suffering of all living beings is inspiring, nourishing, and an important bedrock for our work (Chapter 18). These issues are also a key part of the ethical foundation for MBP teaching practice (Chapter 22).

We are also supported in our intention to align to non-discriminatory practice by legal frameworks. These will vary across the world and it is important to operate within the law of the country within which you practice. In the UK, we operate within the Equality Act 2010 (Government Equalities Office & Equality Human Rights Commission, 2013) that lays out the human characteristics that are protected by law from discrimination, defines what unlawful discrimination and positive action is, and the legal duty conferred upon the public sector to promote equality (see Figure 24.1). The Act applies to the responsibilities of education and service providers, and employers; therefore, MBP teaching clearly falls within its scope. Part of your learning about issues of equality, diversity and inclusion therefore needs to include familiarisation with the Equality Act in the UK context, or the equivalent legal context for teachers in other countries. For those operating in countries without equality legislation we recommend developing personal frameworks of practice that align with the core values and professional ethics underpinning MBP teaching. The principles of equality and non-discrimination are enshrined in international law including the United Nations international human rights legal framework (United Nations, n.d.).

If you are working as an MBP teacher within an organisation, it should have policies that provide guidance on non-discriminatory practice, and you should be able to access training on non-discriminatory practice through your employer. If you are working freelance, it is important that you independently attend training, reflect on non-discriminatory practice and the practical steps you can take. This needs consideration across the breadth of your practice – the ways you market your courses, the ways you assess and orientate participants, the ways you teach and where you teach. We recommend formulating an equality, diversity and inclusion policy for your practice, making it explicit to your participants, and regularly reviewing how the policy is enacted in your work through supervision and other means.

Discrimination often happens unintentionally so it is important this this is an ongoing area that we bring attention to. MBP courses are not currently populated by groups that reflect the diversity that is represented in the general population, so it is clear that there is much work to be done in this area. The British Association of Mindfulness-Based Approaches (BAMBA, 2019) has an Equality, Diversity and Inclusion Policy and a

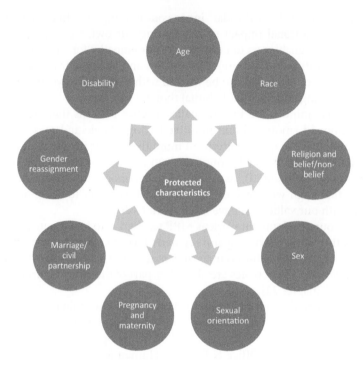

Figure 24.1 Protected Characteristics within the UK Equality Act

working party, and encourages all member organisations to have their own policy. These are important steps in ensuring that the issues are on the table.

SUMMARY

The themes touched on in this chapter are developmental frontiers for the MBP field. Mindfulness is not a panacea for tackling social injustice and oppression, global uncertainty, pandemics, and climate change, but it can play a part, and developing clearer understanding of methodologies that enable this is important.

- Reflecting on the theme of diversity and inclusion can inspire us and shape the directionality of our MBP teaching practice.
- Suffering is contextually situated. Some of the causes of suffering are universally experienced; but many experience suffering generated by their social or economic contexts. Through this understanding, mindfulness teachers can support people in becoming socially and contextually mindful, as well as individually mindful.
- Supervision and peer support can facilitate the ongoing inquiry into the 'person of the teacher', of their situated/conditioned experience enabling increased awareness of bias and taken for granted assumptions.
- MBP teachers have a responsibility to develop an understanding of non-discriminatory practice, social context, and legal duties through training and ongoing development.

- These understandings need to underpin and inform how MBP classes are framed and marketed; how participants are assessed and oriented; how the teaching is offered and how the ethical container of the group is established and protected.
- There is much room for the community of mindfulness teachers, trainers and supervisors to proactively engage with and support the creative work that has begun in influencing social justice and environmental issues.

RESOURCES

Gilbert, P. (2009). *Overcoming Depression: A self-help guide using cognitive behavioural techniques.* Robinson.

Irving, D. (2014). *Waking Up white, and finding myself in the story of race.* Elephant Room Press

King, R. (2018). *Mindful of race: Transforming racism from the inside out.* Sounds True Inc

Magee, R. (2019). *The inner work of racial justice: Healing ourselves and transforming our communities through mindfulness.* Bantam Dell Publishing Group

Mindfulness and Social Change Network (n.d.). https://mindfulnessandsocialchange.org

Petty, S. (Ed.). (2017). Social justice, inner work, & contemplative practice: Lessons & directions for multiple fields [Special Issue]. *Initiative for Contemplation, Equity, & Action (ICEA) Journal, 1*(1).

Pickett, K. & Wilkinson, R. (2009). *The Spirit level: Why more equal societies almost always do better.* Penguin Books.

Wilkinson, R. G. and Pickett, K. (2018). *The inner level: How more equal societies reduce stress, restore sanity and improve everyone's well-being.* Penguin Books.

25

Science and theory

Gemma Griffith and Karunavira

In this chapter, we discuss the way theory and science informs and supports our teaching. In the 'warp and weft' paper that maps the essential ingredients of MBPs, the first principle is that MBPs are "Informed by theories and practices that draw from a confluence of contemplative traditions, science and the major disciplines of medicine, psychology and education" (Crane et al., 2016. p. 990). The aim of this chapter is to outline some core principles of how you might engage in theoretical and scientific underpinnings, and to signpost you to further resources. The key point to underline is that it is important that we study the various roots of MBPs, so that our teaching is informed by and framed within a clear context of understanding. Here we offer a broad outline of these theoretical underpinnings, followed by a practical demonstration of how theories and empirical evidence offer an underpinning to our MBP teaching.

A key distinguishing feature of MBPs is that they are a meeting place between divergent ways of understanding human experience. They integrate contemplative practices and teaching that arose in the East (particularly within the context of Buddhism), with western empiricism (particularly stress physiology, neuroscience, cognitive psychology, and psychology). This interface is a rich and fertile ground for investigating human experience, and the source of creative tensions for MBP implementers (Chapter 26). There are robust debates in the literature on the potential for compromises to the integrity of the work if MBP teachers and researchers are naïve to the sources from which they draw (Grossman & Van Dam, 2011).

Research and theory development are interlinked. Research is often designed to test theories that have developed through engagement with the practice of MBP teaching. In this way, an empirically informed understanding of the mechanisms of mindfulness is gradually built. Figure 25.1 offers a diagrammatic representation of the epistemological sources we draw on at the roots of MBPs. In this chapter, we will focus on these roots: first, pedagogical theory and contemplative traditions will be explored, and second, scientific underpinnings.

PEDAGOGICAL THEORY AND CONTEMPLATIVE TRADITIONS

This confluence of understanding offers models and frameworks which inform how and why humans experience distress, what conditions are needed to enable flourishing, and what part mindfulness may play in this. Additionally, we draw on theories that inform

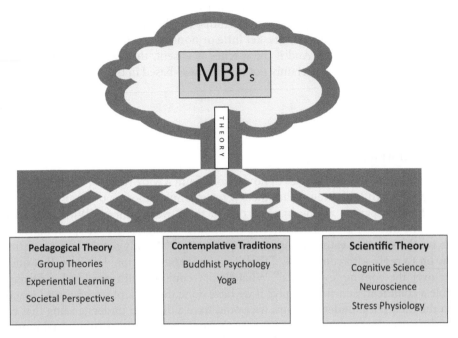

Figure 25.1 Mapping some of the main theoretical roots of MBPs

ways of teaching MBPs skilfully. Examples include the IOG model (Griffith et al., 2019a), the three layers of inquiry (Crane, 2017), and trauma-sensitive pedagogies (Chapter 23).

Buddhist psychological understandings underpin the content and approach of the 8- week course (Feldman & Kuyken, 2019). When creating MBSR, Kabat-Zinn was strongly influenced by the Buddhist psychological understanding about suffering, and its causes. There is a clear mapping of an early Buddhist teaching called the 'Four Noble Truths' within the pedagogical development of the programme (Crane, 2017). The term 'Truth', in this context, does not imply dogma but rather four essential observations or premises about how to better understand and work with suffering. The 1st Truth is that our everyday experience is *essentially* unsatisfactory (Pali: dukkha). This can be understood in terms of how we are impermanent organisms, designed and orientated to seek permanence. This gives rise to the 2nd Truth of *craving* (Pali: tanha) i.e. wanting things to be different to how they essentially are. Recognising and understanding this truth of the *cause* of suffering points to the 3rd Truth, i.e. that there *is* a way to free ourselves from this essential suffering. The 4th Truth details the various ways in which this 'work' can be undertaken i.e. by working *with* our *relationship* towards and with our experience. The orientation and pedagogy of MBPs arises from this understanding, i.e. that we can re-perceive our relationship to experience and in so doing, *let go* of the tension arising from needing it to be different (Shapiro et al., 2006). This theory – from Buddhist psychological understandings – is not explicitly mentioned in the secular setting of MBPs but the confidence derived from perceiving its natural logic infuses everything the teacher does and does not do. Many of the teachings of the world religions and philosophies share aspects of this theory, but in Buddhism it is explicitly articulated. The significance of this theoretical underpinning is illustrated by the words of its founder Jon Kabat-Zinn (2011).

It can be hugely helpful to have a strong personal grounding in the (Buddhist) teachings ... In fact, it is virtually essential and indispensable for teachers of MBSR and other mindfulness-based interventions. Yet little or none of it can be brought into the classroom except in essence. And if the essence is absent, then whatever one is doing or thinks one is doing, it is certainly not mindfulness-based in the way we understand the term.

(p. 281)

Theory-informed teaching

Next we illustrate a few examples of how theory from a wide range of disciplines informs and supports MBP teaching. What theory, for example, informs our reply to the work-stressed, single parent, asking in week one of the 8-week course, "Why, when what is driving me into the ground are my endless circular thoughts, are we spending so much time on the senses ... eating a raisin, this endless *@**?* body scan?" What is it that we draw on to reply with confidence, "That is a very good question, let's keep that question alive over the coming few weeks!" What theory conjoins with our lived experience to enable a confident, non-fixing reply? If we have done the work of studying and practising with the theoretical underpinnings, we would have a digested understanding that enable us to bring to the fore the relevant theory without moving into a conceptual mode that could disconnect us from our participants. First and foremost, we would know that the entire MBP, in all its various iterations, is soundly based on an ancient empirical study of how to practice and establish mindfulness, the 'Four Foundations of Mindfulness' (Nanamoli & Bodhi, 1995). This demonstrates the importance of a progression of *objects of attention* starting with 'the body and its senses', the 1st Foundation; then, building on this through paying attention to 'feeling-tones', the 2nd Foundation; and then, to 'thoughts and objects in the mind', the 3rd Foundation. We would know how this ancient teaching formed the theoretical backbone to Kabat-Zinn's creation of MBSR. We would also know that for several millennia this approach to the easing of suffering has stood the test of time.

Similarly, if we have studied developmental psychology, we would understand how this early theory has parallels in Piaget's seminal work which places sensing, or the 'pre-operational' as the building block for thinking, or 'abstract-operational' (Ginsburg & Opper, 1988). And, we would be informed by Mark William's seminal work on how sensing being-mode diverts attention from thinking doing-mode, enabling a way to skilfully move beyond the clutches of negative rumination (2008). Beyond this we might draw on the wealth of theory from cognitive science that demonstrates how ruminative thinking can often be maladaptive, feeding into discrepancy-based monitoring, the 'driven-doing' mode, and how this, together with 'experiential avoidance', can contribute strongly to lowering mood, stress, and depression (Crane, 2017; Williams, 2008). So, learning how to first pay attention to our senses forms a valuable basis for wellbeing and for later working with unhelpful thinking, including our tendencies to be 'driven into the ground' by overthinking! None of this theory is spoken as we face the confusion and frustration of the single parent who is demanding to know what the point of all this sensing and body focus is, but without this understanding, how authentically can we reply, "Let's wait and see?"

The MBP then tackles the knotty problem of learning *how* to relate less reactively in our lives by, in session 2, inviting attention to *perception* (i.e. to how we *make sense* of our sensing), how we relate to the experience arriving from our senses. Then, in sessions 3 and 4 we explore our perceptions as *pleasant* and *unpleasant* experiences. This sequence follows the 1st and 2nd 'Foundations of Mindfulness' mentioned earlier. We become able to recognise how we habitually *react* to pleasant experiences by wanting more of them and to unpleasant ones by pushing them away. In learning to recognise these automatic (reactive) patterns, especially as body-felt reactions, participants are offered the possibility of conscious choice (i.e. *responding*) rather than reactive, unconscious habit patterns. This process of stepping back and recognising reactivity draws strongly on the Buddhist teaching of the two darts (Bodhi, 1997). The first dart is the direct physical or emotional pain, which is unavoidable (for example a sharp pain from stepping on a pin), and the second dart is how we add to our suffering by the way we react to or think about the event (for example, feeling very angry towards the person who dropped the pin, with thoughts about how clumsy or irresponsible they were). The practice of mindfulness trains us to step back and notice how we are feeding this second dart – expressed in contemporary cognitive scientific theory as 'reperceiving' or 'decentering' (Shapiro et al., 2006). The essential theory here is that if we can step back from being 'fused' to our perceptions, cognitions and emotions (Hayes et al., 2012), we can learn to 'defuse' the situation, by reducing the 'second darts' of fretting, blaming, catastrophising and so on.

Another powerful example of the way theory informs teaching might arise in session 5 of the 8-week course. It is at this point that we may invite participants to carefully *stay with* and *allow* difficult thoughts, emotions or sensations. I (KV) recall one particular incident, working with the mother of a child with severe autism and physical disabilities, when at this point, she said to me in tears, "This is the absolute worst thing you could do to me". My heart sank and my stomach twisted. But then she said, "This is also the best thing you can do to me". At such moments, the teacher needs to comprehensively know *why* staying-with, rather than suppressing or avoiding a difficulty may, when approached with mindfulness, be helpful, and potentially transformative. Participants often only express the first sentiment and we, as teachers have to hold this upset and anger with confidence. Holding and skilfully managing such strong upset is supported by many theoretical underpinnings, including all that was outlined above in connection with 'experiential avoidance' and also, all that is unpacked in the chapter on trauma-sensitive mindfulness (Chapter 23), and on societal perspectives (Chapter 24). From the contemplative tradition we might recall the motivating and insight filled poetry of surrender by thirteenth century poet, Rumi, or the teaching of 'The two darts' from the Buddhist tradition mentioned above. We might also recollect the work on cognitive *reappraisal* and *extinction* by Hölzel et al. (2011).

Less emotively, theory can be helpful when simply meeting the frustration of a participant struggling with a wandering mind. At such times we might draw on broader models of mindfulness such as the Intention, Attention, and Attitude (IAA) model (Shapiro et al., 2006). If a participant is giving themselves a hard time about not being able to keep their *attention* on the breath, a fruitful discussion can arise about the *attitude* that they have towards their experience or the absence of a clear *intention* during the practice. Such theoretical understandings of MBPs can underpin and inform specific moments in our teaching.

To recap briefly, the earliest writing on the cultivation of mindfulness describes how we start by learning to pay attention in the present moment to our sense experience (i.e. the 1st Foundation of mindfulness) and then, in the 2nd Foundation (feeling-tones) to discern these impressions as 'pleasant', 'unpleasant' or 'neutral' (i.e. basically as either opportunities or as threats). The theory illustrates how we can either prevent unskilful (maladaptive) mental states, thoughts, and emotions arising, by seeing how they are conditioned by 'feeling-tones', or, work to bring mindful awareness to the arising thoughts and emotions

(3rd Foundation) and begin to see that they are not 'facts' (Segal et al., 2013). In this way we can learn to relate to thoughts more adaptively, seeing them for what they are and seeing how they naturally change or dissipate. This basic theory is central to the structure and pedagogy of MBPs. It describes a developmental sequence of steps by which we learn to work creatively with our relationship to our senses, feeling-tones, and thoughts and emotions, and so towards our 'self' and others. When teaching (or researching) mindfulness remembering how the underpinnings draw from and integrate both modern and ancient sources provides a fundamental ground of understanding and confidence.

THE USE OF SCIENTIFIC PRINCIPLES WHEN TEACHING MINDFULNESS-BASED PROGRAMMES

Part of the reason that MBPs have become accepted in mainstream settings is because they are based upon sound scientific research; likewise, some participants are drawn to MBPs precisely because of the strong evidence base. As both a researcher and a mindfulness-based teacher, I (GG) spend much of my professional life navigating between the worlds of MBP teaching and scientific research. The translation of research into practice is challenging. As a teacher of MBPs, how can I possibly keep up with the numerous mindfulness studies published each week, and how can I translate these into my teaching practice?

This section aims to help you orientate to how science can inform practice. This is also known as evidence-based practice. Equipped with some knowledge about how to interpret scientific papers, and some guidance around how can draw upon science to teach MBPs, we can align our teaching practice with scientific principles. Part of good MBP teaching practice is to stay aligned with the science (Britton, 2016), and the relationship between research and our teaching can be fruitful and rewarding. The intention of this section is to help you to align your MBP teaching to scientific literature; to give you the confidence to be curious about the latest developments in research, and how keeping up to date with research can inform how you teach MBPs.

Learning about science is like learning a language

Learning about scientific principles may not have been what you 'signed up for' when you first decided to teach MBPs. Understanding the theoretical underpinnings of MBPs, and keeping up to date about scientific and pedagogical developments is however, an essential aspect of delivering MBPs. People who train as MBP teachers come from many different backgrounds. Some may have training on the principals of science and are able to critically read scientific peer-reviewed articles. For others, science and research can be intimidating.

How to interpret scientific research is a skill that is honed over many years, and is beyond the scope of this chapter, but has been written about extensively and well elsewhere. If you would like to learn more about how to understand research articles, an excellent book is 'How to read a paper' by Greenhalgh (2019). As I often tell my research students at Bangor University, interpreting scientific research is like learning a new language, so takes time to learn how to engage with it well. For now, here are some general broad principles to bear in mind when reading scientific studies.

- If you read a single study that makes a claim, remember, it is just that, a single study conducted at one time point, and the findings cannot usually be generalised. Many people make this error – assuming that because a study is published, the results it presents must be applicable to everyone. Remember that a single study is only a tiny fragment of the whole picture, and unless you know the broader research area well, you will not know if it supports or contradicts other research on the same topic. Likewise, I have heard about MBP teachers having read one article showing that MBPs were *not* useful for a particular population, which has then stopped them entirely from teaching that population. Although caution is helpful, it is important to have a clear understanding of the field as a whole before making such a decision. Remember that an article is just one part of a vast research field.

- The only time that you can potentially generalise from a single paper to your teaching practice, is if that paper is reviewing lots of other studies – so is presenting synthesised evidence from many studies to give you an overall view of the field. Even then, you will notice that authors of reviews will often be cautious about their conclusions, and you also need to adhere to the principles outlined below on translating research into teaching practice.

How to use research to inform your teaching practice

Empirical evidence

My colleagues who were MBP teachers in the 1990s tell me that back then, it was possible to have read every research paper on mindfulness and have a solid grasp of the entire literature on MBPs. Now, with thousands of studies on mindfulness published every year, it is impossible to do this: I find it challenging to keep up to date with my small areas of particular research interests (mindfulness for people with learning disabilities and their families, pedagogical research, and group process research). Given competing pulls on our time, how can we keep abreast of developments without becoming overwhelmed?

Tips to keep up to date with mindfulness research:

- Regularly attend mindfulness-based conferences where research is being presented
- Sign up for email alerts so you will get periodic updates about new research articles as they are published (e.g. American Mindfulness Research Association, 2020, https://goamra.org/publications/mindfulness-research-monthly/)
- Become familiar with popular search engines and how to find research articles. For example 'Google Scholar' is free, and is intuitive to use. Practice finding articles you are interested in by typing in "Mindfulness and xxx" into the Google Scholar search engine and seeing what you find! We introduce this to our students by asking them to search for 'Mindfulness and chocolate'
- When using search engines to find articles on a particular subject, search for a review. If one has been published in your area of interest this saves you a lot of time by giving a broad overview of the area. For example, to see if there is a review about mindfulness and chocolate, I would type something like "Mindfulness chocolate review"
- A special issue in Current Opinion in Psychology in 2019 gives a snapshot of current research areas in mindfulness (Bernstein et al., 2019).

How to use science when teaching MBPs

This section contains some information about how to use empirical evidence and scientific principles when teaching MBPs, before, during, and after the course.

Before the course starts

An important thing to know is that science can never *prove* anything to be true. Findings can simply *suggest* a phenomenon is likely to be true. When describing the potential impact of an MBP course in your participant recruitment materials, use language like 'Many studies have reported that MBPs can help lower anxiety' rather than 'It is proven that MBPs lowers anxiety'. It is also important that you are familiar with the empirical literature in the particular populations that you are working in (e.g. MBCT for depression prevention, MBSR for general populations etc).

During the course

It is not surprising, given the mind-body separation in many western cultures, that some people find the mind-body connection presented in MBPs difficult to understand. This is where our clear explanations of biological and neurological processes (such as the stress-reaction cycle) can help. Tables 25.1 and 25.2 list the main biological, neurological, and cognitive processes taught in a typical MBP course, alongside recommendations for how to find out more about each of these topics. To make it as easy as possible for you to find more information, the list is limited to a few core books, plus two journal articles. MBP teachers are often surprised to find that they are using numerous scientific principles already in their teaching.

When describing scientific or theoretical underpinnings of MBPs, keep it simple, using as few technical terms as possible to optimise the potential for meaningful learning. Making the same main point a number of times throughout the MBP is likely to be more helpful than giving a lot of detail on a single point. Remember to gauge how your group is doing with science-based information to determine how detailed you go.

Knowing what we teach is grounded in scientific principals can also be helpful in moments of wobble while teaching, for example, the principle of turning towards difficulty, is often counter-intuitive, and we can encounter reluctance to do so both within ourselves and in participants we teach. Equipping ourselves with knowledge of these mechanisms – including trauma-informed principles which indicate when turning towards is not helpful, or needs to be approached with trauma-informed principles at the fore (Chapter 23) – helps us become more confident in how we teach if we encounter tears or annoyance in the teaching space.

After the course

As part of our practice as MBP teachers, it is important to evaluate how our courses are experienced by those we teach, and to do this with participant safety and wellbeing at the fore. Gathering feedback from participants is particularly important if you are a new teacher, or have adapted a standard MBP course for a new setting, or with a population you have not worked with before.

Please note that this section is aimed at teachers who teach courses to the general public (i.e. non-clinical populations), which may well include specific groups, such as workplace settings, schoolteachers etc. This is not an exhaustive 'how to' evaluate your courses, but instead offers broad suggestions. Further resources to guide the process of course evaluation for a range of settings are given at the end of the chapter.

Table 25.1 Cognitive psychology: scientific and theoretical underpinnings that are explored in MBPs

Cognitive psychology	Further reading	
Automatic-pilot Doing vs Being	Crane, R. (2017). *Mindfulness-based cognitive therapy*. (2nd ed.). Routledge.	Chapters 4–6
	Feldman, C. & Kuyken, W. (2019). *Mindfulness: Ancient wisdom meets modern psychology*. The Guilford Press.	Chapter 3
Rumination	Crane, R. (2017). *Mindfulness-based cognitive therapy*. (2nd ed.). Routledge.	Chapters 8, 10
Decentering/ Re-perceiving	Crane, R. (2017). *Mindfulness-based cognitive therapy*. (2nd ed.). Routledge.	Chapter 9
	Shapiro, S. L., Carlson, L. E., Astin, J. A., & Freedman, B. (2006). Mechanisms of mindfulness. Journal of clinical psychology, 62(3), 373–386.	
Taking action to self-care Behavioural Activation	Segal, Z. V., Williams, J.M.G. & Teasdale, J. (2013). *Mindfulness-based cognitive therapy for depression* (2nd ed). The Guilford Press.	Chapter 16
Discrepancy monitoring	Segal, Z. V., Williams, J.M.G. & Teasdale, J. (2013). *Mindfulness-based cognitive therapy for depression* (2nd ed). The Guilford Press.	Chapter 4
	Williams, J. M. G. (2008). Mindfulness, depression and modes of mind. *Cognitive Therapy and Research, 32*(6), 721–733.	
Turning towards the difficult.	Crane, R. (2017). *Mindfulness-based cognitive therapy*. (2nd ed.). Routledge.	Chapters 10–12
	Feldman, C. & Kuyken, W. (2019). *Mindfulness: Ancient wisdom meets modern psychology*. The Guilford Press.	Chapter 5
Respond vs react	Crane, R. (2017). *Mindfulness-based cognitive therapy*. (2nd ed.). Routledge.	Chapter 9
What makes an emotion?	Williams, M., & Penman, D. (2011). *Mindfulness: a practical guide to finding peace in a frantic world*. Piatkus.	Chapter 2

208 • GEMMA GRIFFITH AND KARUNAVIRA

Table 25.2 Biological and neurological scientific and theoretical underpinnings that are explored in MBPs

Biological and neurological	Further reading	
Stress reaction cycle	Kabat-Zinn, J. (2013). *Full catastrophe living, revised edition: How to cope with stress, pain and illness using mindfulness meditation.* (Revised ed.). Piatkus.	Chapters 17–20
	Sapolsky, R. M. (2004). *Why zebras don't get ulcers: The acclaimed guide to stress, stress-related diseases, and coping.* Holt paperbacks.	All chapters
Flight, fight, freeze	Sapolsky, R. M. (2004). *Why zebras don't get ulcers: The acclaimed guide to stress, stress-related diseases, and coping.* Holt paperbacks.	All chapters
Negativity bias	Crane, R. (2017). *Mindfulness-based cognitive therapy.* (2nd ed.). Routledge.	Chapters 10, 26
	Hanson, R. (2009). *Buddha's brain: The practical neuroscience of happiness, love, and wisdom.* New Harbinger Publications, Inc.	Chapter 4
Neuro plasticity	Hanson, R. (2009). *Buddha's brain: The practical neuroscience of happiness, love, and wisdom.* New Harbinger Publications, Inc.	Part 1
The role of the amygdala and the prefrontal cortex	Hanson, R. (2009). *Buddha's brain: The practical neuroscience of happiness, love, and wisdom.* New Harbinger Publications, Inc.	Part 1

There are three main ways to gather feedback:

1. A bespoke feedback form given during the last session
2. Recording attendance/dropout rates
3. Measures/Scales (e.g. self-compassion scale)

1. Bespoke feedback form

One of the simplest ways of getting feedback is to create a unique feedback form that asks for information you would find most useful. Feedback forms generally have a combination of open-ended questions and scaled items. The most helpful information is likely to come from open-ended questions. Because participants can respond how they like, this feedback will give you a real sense of how the course went for participants and allow them to offer suggestions for improvement. A general guideline is to keep feedback forms short, no more than two pages, as participants can lose interest when completing forms. Make sure each question is distinct and will elicit different information from participants, such as:

- What did you find most useful about the course?
- What did you find most challenging about the course?
- What would have improved the course?
- How likely are you to carry on a regular mindfulness practice? Why/Why not?

Scaled items: Another simple way of gathering information is to ask participants to rate their experience on a scale of 1–10. This will give you quick information about how your course was perceived. For example:

How likely would you be to recommend this course to other people?
Very unlikely   Maybe   Very likely
1 2 3 4 5 6 7 8 9 10

Practical tips: It is good to hand feedback forms out during a session and give a space of about 10 minutes to complete them. The return rate will be lower if you seek feedback after the course has ended. Remember not to ask for names on the sheet, this keeps it anonymous for your participants and they may be more inclined to offer honest feedback. Do be aware of bias though – feedback written during a feel-good session 8 is likely to be positively biased. If you can find a way to capture feedback from those who dropped out of your course (such as emailing them with a request to complete feedback) this will give you valuable information from those for whom the course may have presented significant challenge.

2. Recording attendance and dropout rates

It is important to keep a written record of attendance so you can monitor individual participants' commitment during the course, so if someone misses a week without making contact, you can then follow this up. It also helps to monitor patterns of drop out over several courses. If you notice consistent dropouts after session 1, for example, you can perhaps reflect on why this is (are there practical issues, or is there something you could improve in session 1 or in the orientation process?). Research has found that those who dropped out of an MBCT course for depression had high scores of cognitive reactivity, brooding, and depressive rumination (Crane & Williams, 2010). These are also the very participants who benefit most from MBCT when they are able to stay with the training process. The information was therefore used to improve later MBCT practice and research trials, as researchers prepared participants for the inevitable challenge of meeting aversive experience during and around the practices during the orientation.

3. Measures and scales

It is not necessary to use validated measures or scales to evaluate a typical MBP course delivered to a general public population outside of a clinical service. Most measures (for example the Five Facet Mindfulness Questionnaire (Baer et al., 2008) have been designed for use in research, and to use them correctly takes quite a bit of statistical knowledge and time.
   Issues to consider:

- Is your participant group (sample size) large enough to detect any meaningful (statistically significant) differences in scores? Generally, you need at least 30 participants.
- Do you understand the scoring system of the measure (i.e. reverse scoring rules; what to do with missing items)? Look up the original article written by the developers of the measure to find out how to score correctly if this is not included on the measure.
- Do you know what statistical test to use to measure any pre-post differences, and how to use statistical software packages?

- Is it worth participant's time (and yours) to know the results? Will the results be meaningful to your practice (i.e. not just collected for the sake of collecting)? Think carefully about what you will do with this data and weigh up whether it is worth collecting, bearing in mind that if we are asking participants to spend time completing a questionnaire, we need to have a good reason for doing so.

Ethical issues

It can be tempting to want to measure clinical outcomes such as anxiety or depression in your participants, however, we would strongly counsel against this outside of a clinical service or research project. This is because ethical issues may arise if you start to measure clinical outcomes. For example, if you use a depression scale and discover that a participant meets the clinical threshold for depression (and the participant is not aware of this), what will you do with this information? Likewise, a participant may guess that they score highly on a depression scale whilst completing it and become distressed. Remember that the purpose of your MBP evaluation is not to suggest a clinical diagnosis, so ensure that any data you collect are not used as such. Therefore, due to ethical reasons, it is best practice to avoid measures that look at clinical diagnoses or outcomes when working in non-clinical contexts. Examples of good measures for non-clinical contexts are the WHO-5 wellbeing index (1998), or the self-compassion short form (Raes et al., 2011).

Data protection is another ethical issue, be sure to be familiar with data protection laws in your country and never share any data you have collected about your participants with a third party (without explicit, signed permission from your participants). The data you collect is to enable you to evaluate the service you are providing only.

EVIDENCE-INFORMED TEACHING

In this section, I (GG) use my experience as an example to demonstrate how scientific evidence can inform one's practice as an MBP teacher. This augments the earlier examples by KV on theory-informed teaching. Before we begin, a note of caution: this chapter was written in the first half of 2020, and by the time you read this book the literature will have expanded. This is part of the fun (and challenge) of being an evidenced-based practitioner! Here, I explore a question I have often grappled with as a teacher of MBPs:

> How many minutes of home mindfulness practice per day is optimum for participants on an MBP?

This question arises in my mind every time a participant asks me if a 20-minute practice can be done as a replacement for a 45-minute practice. As an MBP teacher, I am faced with a dilemma – should I encourage or discourage this person doing 20-minute practices?

What research tells us: Do MBP participants actually practice for the recommended time?

Before looking at how much practice is optimum, it is useful to first know how much practice participants actually report doing on an MBP course. We all know that participant engagement varies widely, from those who do no home practice at all to those that diligently follow the home practice guidelines. The most robust evidence I could find is a recent review that combined data from 59 studies (Parsons et al., 2017). The authors examined: 1) how much home practice participants reported doing, and 2) whether more home practice led to improved psychological outcomes (lower stress, anxiety etc). We will examine the evidence for each of these below.

Forty-three of the 59 reviewed studies required participants to engage in the standard 45 minutes of home practice a day, six days a week. The finding that most participants did not follow these requirements will be of little surprise to most of us teachers (!); it was found that participants reported engaging in 64% of the recommended home practices, which is equivalent to about 29 minutes per day.

What about MBPs that required participants practice less than the standard 45 minutes per day? It seems that the less practice that is asked of participants, the less they do. In ten studies, participants engaged in about 84% of the requested amount, which was about 151 minutes per week, equivalent to about 25 minutes per day.

Some caveats on these findings to consider: We do not know whether these findings are generalisable to other courses. The data was based on participants self-reports and they also knew that their practice time was being recorded by researchers. This may have meant that participants in these studies were more likely to engage in practice, or report that they had done so. There is some evidence that people who do not practice much at home are less likely to report this (Parsons et al., 2017).

What research tells us: Does more home practice lead to better outcomes?

Twenty-eight studies required the standard home practice of 45 minutes a day and reported on participant wellbeing outcomes. Parsons et al. (2017) combined this data and found that participants who reported practicing more were *significantly more likely* to report psychological benefits, although the strength of this correlation was fairly small. There was no evidence of a linear relationship though, so psychological benefits were *not directly dependent* on the amount of time a participant practiced.

At this point, I would also like to bring in a recent study by Segal et al. (2019) which has also shaped my thinking on this matter. They found that, among MBCT participants with recurring episodes of depression, those who kept engaging in formal practice for two years after the course were *significantly less likely* to have a depressive relapse than those who stopped regular mindfulness practice. Now, this is where it gets a bit complicated: the association between amount of meditation practice and depression relapse was not a direct association. In between this was the factor of *decentring* (i.e. observing thoughts and emotions without getting caught up in them, Shapiro et al., 2006). Those participants who practiced more were more likely to approach their experience from a decentred perspective, and so decentring may be a key factor which leads to positive psychological outcomes. *It suggests that participant's ability to decentre is a key factor in preventing depressive relapse, rather than amount of meditation practice per se.* At the same time, the more someone practices meditation, the more likely they are to decentre.

Another interesting finding by Segal et al. (2019) is that the amount of home practice during the 8-week MBCT course was not correlated with later depressive relapse, but participants who reported high levels of practice during the course were *more likely* to continue practice after the course.

Translating the evidence to teaching practice – core principles to consider

Before we delve into how research can be translated into our practice as MBP teachers; here are some suggested core principles to abide by:

- Ensure that changing your teaching practice will do no harm to participants
- Ensure that studies that influence any changes in your teaching are supported by the wider literature on the theoretical underpinnings or pedagogy of MBPs.
- Do not change your teaching practice based upon a single study or review that is unsupported by wider literature.
- Ensure that no changes you make contradict the training you received. If you are unsure on this point, bring this as a topic of discussion with your mindfulness supervisor.
- Check to see what population the study was based upon. The findings from a study examining participants with anxiety may or may not be applicable to participants with depression, for example.
- Be prepared to tweak your teaching methods again when new research emerges – hold it lightly!

The review by Parsons et al. (2017), and the longitudinal study by Segal et al. (2019) both offer new information to help answer the question: 'How many minutes of home mindfulness practice per day is optimum for participants on an MBP?' After reading these studies, this is how I adapted my teaching practice:

- I found out there is no 'magic' amount of home practice that leads to greater wellbeing. I often wondered how strongly to encourage participants to do the full 45 minutes of practice, and how encouraging or discouraging to be towards participants who would feedback in sessions that they used a 20-minute practice found online instead of the 45 minutes. The evidence from the review does suggest that the more a participant practices, the more likely they are to experience improved outcomes (Parsons et al., 2017). However, this relationship is not linear or strong, and when this relationship was examined more closely in another study, it seemed that the relationship between amount of practice and improved outcomes was influenced by the factor of decentring (in people with depression, Segal et al., 2019). Essentially, there is currently no specific evidence that people regularly practicing for (say) 20 minutes vs. 45 minutes will strongly differ in outcomes (although note that this has not been directly tested in research). I take this to mean that any length of practice is to be strongly encouraged during the 8-week course, of course with an emphasis on the curriculum standard.
- A key factor in people with depression reporting improved outcomes seems to be whether a participant is able to decentre (Segal et al., 2019). So, I hold an intention to teach with a greater emphasis on the theme of decentring during inquiry and practice guidance – i.e. I explicitly underline the importance of holding or witnessing thoughts (and all aspects of experience) within wider awareness.
- I knew before this research that encouraging participants to establish a home practice was important and placed most of my emphasis on encouraging participants to practice *during* the 8-week course. Now there is some evidence that future wellbeing is linked to *maintaining* a practice after the course is finished (Segal et al., 2019). I do not leave it until session 8 to emphasise the importance of continuing practice after the course, but thread it into the course right from the start (i.e. from session 1 saying "This is the start of a continuing relationship with mindfulness practice"). I also give out resources about continuing practice in session 6, rather than the very last thing in session 8, so participants have a chance to prepare for continuing mindfulness practice after the course, and have a look at them and ask questions/ share experiences about them during sessions 7 and 8.

You may have noticed that I have changed my teaching based upon a single study that looked at people with depression, which differs from the general public population I teach. This contradicts some of the core principles outlined above, so why do I think generalising to a different population in this instance is ok? First, because the other core principals outlined above are being followed. The changes are to do with *emphasis*, not any shifts in the core curriculum. They are not dramatic or fundamental changes to the curriculum. This is very unlikely to be harmful to participants and are likely to be of benefit. Second, the findings from the Segal et al. (2019) study match broader theoretical underpinnings of the mechanisms of mindfulness (e.g. Shapiro et al., 2006).

There are often no definitive, clear-cut answers to pedagogical queries, and the original question I asked of the research literature – *"How many minutes of home mindfulness practice per day is optimum for participants on an MBP?"* was not directly answered. This is often the case with research, it can (and indeed, probably will) feel messy as we navigate our way through it. However, this will help avoid getting stuck in a rut as a teacher and helps us keep an attitude of curiosity to what new evidence tells us. Indeed, we owe it to our participants to teach in the most evidence-informed way as possible. Thus, theory and science, including from the contemplative traditions, constitute the most deeply implicit layers of the MBP curriculum.

SUMMARY

- Pedagogical theory and contemplative traditions underpin teaching MBPs. A deep familiarisation with the literatures is important as a teacher of MBPs.
- Familiarising yourself with how to read and interpret scientific papers is a useful skill to develop as an MBP teacher
- MBPs are based upon scientific evidence and theoretical underpinnings, it is important that you are comfortable translating these concepts to your participants (e.g. the stress-reaction cycle, decentring etc)
- It is important to be aligned with the latest scientific and theoretical developments as an MBP teacher – to be an evidence-based practitioner

RESOURCES

Feldman, C. & Kuyken, W. (2019). *Mindfulness: Ancient wisdom meets modern psychology.* The Guilford Press.

Greenhalgh, T. (2019). *How to read a paper: The basics of evidence-based medicine.* John Wiley & Sons.

McCown, D., Reibel, D., & Micozzi, M. S. (2010). *Teaching mindfulness. A practical guide for clinicians and educators.* Springer.

Measures for evaluating your MBP course

The below measures are short and easy to use, and do not measure clinical outcomes:

WHO5 wellbeing index (WHO Collaborating Centre in Mental Health, 1998): www.psykiatri-regionh.dk/who-5/Documents/WHO5_English.pdf

Self-compassion short form: Raes, F., Pommier, E., Neff, K. D., & Van Gucht, D. (2011). Construction and factorial validation of a short form of the Self-Compassion Scale. *Clinical Psychology & Psychotherapy, 18*(3), 250–255. https://doi.org/10.1002/cpp.702

26

Implementing mindfulness-based programs

Rebecca Crane and Heledd Griffiths

In the early days of developing training within CMRP, I (RC) had a naïve and optimistic sense that if we enabled our trainees to develop their skills as MBP teachers, they would be able to go back to their organisation and make this work available to their clients. What became increasingly clear to us was that the process of implementation is complex, because it involves the vagaries of human behaviours within complex and demanding organisational systems. We include the process of implementation in this book because there are skilful ways to relate to the processes involved in the implementation journey: ways of being proactive in influencing barriers and facilitators to catalyse the implementation process; and times when it is best to conserve energy!

In 2011 together with my colleague Willem Kuyken, I conducted a survey of graduates from our MBP teacher training programmes asking them about their implementation experiences. We were particularly interested in MBCT in the UK health service because it had been recommended for inclusion in care pathways since 2004. The findings have relevance to the implementation of all MBPs. What we discovered was a very mixed picture of service availability with a small number of well developed services, and a larger number of lone practitioners and services struggling to make MBCT implementation happen (Crane & Kuyken, 2013). This picture is not unique to MBP implementation. There is a research practice gap for many new interventions. It was though clear that the particular nature and culture of MBPs posed unique challenges to implementers. The first sentence of our first paper on this issue of implementation reads: 'Even if a psychosocial intervention has compelling aims, has been shown to work, has a clear theory-driven mechanism of action, is cost-effective and is recommended by a government advisory body, its value is determined by how widely available it is in the health service' (Crane & Kuyken, 2013, p. 246). In summary, even though there seem to be compelling reasons to implement, the process of implementation is still uphill work!

These issues are also of concern from a wider field perspective. Dimijian and Segal (2015) in their analysis of the status of the MBP research, reported that there are some discrete areas where the research is well developed through the various stages of research from early concept to implementation; but that there is also a mass of early but underdeveloped evidence that does not translate into accessibility to MBPs for ordinary people. Linked to this is the risk of an 'implementation cliff' in which the potency of the MBP is gradually diluted as it moves from the clinical science process to routine service delivery – in which resource constraints set the bar for training providers at ever lower levels.

It was clear to us that this issue is an important area for us to understand and investigate. In 2012, we secured funding from the National Institute for Health Research to investigate MBP implementation further. The ASPIRE project (Accessibility and Implementation in UK services of MBCT) was led by Professors Jo Rycroft-Malone (an Implementation Scientist then at Bangor University), and Willem Kuyken (Director of the Oxford Mindfulness Centre). RC was a co-applicant and HG one of the researchers who spent many months on the road across the UK interviewing stakeholders about MBCT implementation. Our aim was to understand the MBCT implementation process within the health service across the four nations of the UK. The research was in three phases: first, a broad-brush scope of MBCT uptake across the UK to map out where and how MBCT was being offered; second, conducting eight in-depth case studies of MBCT services at different stages of the implementation process and in varied geographical regions, with an aim to understand the facilitators and barriers to implementation; and third, a phase of dissemination. This chapter makes the findings of the study available in a practical way to support your work of implementing in your context. Although the study was anchored into the experience of MBCT implementation in the UK health service, a large proportion of the findings are relevant to the implementation process of MBPs for a range of populations, contexts, and regions. There was a particular focus in the research findings on delivering MBPs from within mainstream organisations, but much of the material will also be relevant to you if you are working as a freelance MBP teacher. The study website (https://implementing-mindfulness.co.uk) will give you more practical pointers and materials to support implementation, and you can read an in-depth presentation of the findings in the main outcome paper (Rycroft-Malone et al., 2019).

The first part of this chapter describes the key factors that influence the creation of an MBP service, and the second draws out a series of recommendations. The analysis of these stories enabled us to draw out common themes. Our hope is that awareness of these will facilitate implementation processes in your context. Remember as you read that this data is drawn from a careful analysis of multiple interviews with MBP teachers, service users, and managers from 40 UK service providers, detailing their experiences of the MBP implementation process. We intersperse in italics some of the voices from these interviewees.

THE IMPLEMENTATION JOURNEY

One of our key interests was to discover why some sites had a more embedded MBCT service than others did. We found that implementation of MBPs is a *process and a journey* – each MBP service had its own journey, which was unique, but that there were some common patterns.

The next section unpacks six interdependent themes we identified within the data that help us understand why some sites were further along in their journey (the presence of an implementer, making it fit, context, drive, adherence to good practice, and pivot points), that influence the process of the MBP implementation journey. Awareness of these themes will empower you to guide the implementation process more skilfully.

Presence of an implementer

For an implementation journey to start and progress, a necessary condition is that there is an implementer. Importantly though, it was what these implementers do and/or how they do it which has an effect on implementation. Some implementers have characteristics that support successful implementation. These include a certain level of passion and drive, and the ability to skilfully engage stakeholders at all levels of the organisation (senior managers, decision makers, colleagues and service users). We saw that lone enthusiasts struggled to build momentum on their own. More successful implementation happens when a site has a combination of different implementers, with a variety of seniority and skills, all working towards the same agenda.

Spend a moment reflecting: Who are the implementer(s) in my context developing the delivery of MBPs? What work are they doing? What skills, passions and characteristics do they have?

Making it fit

The research showed that implementation is more successful and sustainable when the implementer shapes the alignment between the intervention, the health service context, existing local service strategy, priorities, and care pathways. MBCT is represented as a depression prevention intervention delivered at the end of a treatment pathway, but the health service setting historically is largely based on a medical 'quick fix' model. The intervention is not therefore a straight forward 'fit'. Implementers necessarily have to widen the inclusion criteria to reflect the clients they have on the ground.

> *If I stuck tightly to the NICE guidelines, we wouldn't have anybody I don't think.*
> *As time has gone on, we've expanded to take people with a more moderate level of depression at the start, so it's become more MBCT for active depression .... we've been evaluating it as closely as we can ... We've run about 12 programmes in each area, and what we've found every time is almost exactly the same results – a 50% reduction in pre-post measures of depression and anxiety from the start to the finish of the programme. So that, along with qualitative feedback from people about how they find the programme, and other evidence showing how helpful MBCT can be for active depression, has given us confidence that this is a helpful and reasonable thing to do.*

In addition, in a very target driven culture, implementers need to be aware of the particular target issues that their managers are interested in. They have to engage with these colleagues, and frame the intervention in ways that meet these issues in order to get institutional support. The challenge for implementers is to discern when to adapt and flex the delivery to fit the needs of the service, and when to hold a line to maintain personal integrity and the integrity of MBPs.

Spend a moment reflecting: What are the systems and structures within which my MBP practice sits? How do these facilitate or pose barriers to developments? What skilful ways of working with these are possible?

Context

A supportive context (e.g. financial, practical, and human) is key. Organisational culture is an important aspect of this – the presence of supportive colleagues who welcome the implementation activities makes a tremendous difference. Often these supportive cultures need to be deliberately cultivated by the implementer through a range of activities (see below). It is particularly important to have explicit support from middle and senior management. Factors such as reorganisations, change in staff/management, cuts in funding, and competing priorities inevitably hinder developments.

Another aspect of organisational culture that influences MBP implementation is the philosophical values base to the overall service. For example, in some sites, recent shifts in culture from a medical to a wellbeing model enabled MBPs to find their place within the overall service structure. There was evidence also that the presence of MBP delivery within the organisation had influenced this shift in culture. A strong theme in the data was the tension between the culture of the health service and the ethos underpinning MBPs.

Quite a struggle ... to deliver the program in a mindful way ... because the culture of IAPT [Improving Access to Psychological Therapies] and primary care therapy ... tends to be therapy on roller skates, that's the whole culture, its bums on seats, quickly in, quickly out, have we got to recovery, off we go, quick team meeting, you know, rush, rush, rush.

Finding ways to honour the non-instrumental or implicit curriculum emphasis within MBPs in contexts which have an overriding emphasis on instrumentality is deeply challenging. Our data showed the importance of the implementers keeping their links to supervision, collegial support, and connected to their personal mindfulness practice, to enable them to hold their own truth in the midst of these pressures. There are very real tensions between holding to a line around integrity and meeting the demands of the organisational setting. There was clear evidence that settings that had held to high standards of integrity ultimately had a more sustainable and integrated service. There was also evidence of implementers deciding *not* to implement because they were being put under pressure to deliver in ways that compromised standards.

> Spend a moment reflecting: What barriers and facilitators does the surrounding context for my MBP practice present? Are there ways I can influence these? How do I both fit my MBP practice to the context, and maintain my integrity and the integrity of the work?

Successful implementers had a vision for the service they want to develop, and a lot of commitment, drive and passion to bring this about. In our data, all implementation started bottom up, but bottom-up drive on its own would only reach a certain point. For it to become further embedded implementation needed to be met by top-down strategic drive, support, and investment. Without this, we saw that implementation got as far as raising awareness at a local level, or running groups under the radar of the organisation's management. If lone implementers left their role, the service they had built up ceased. Sustainability relies on building a team.

If I was to leave tomorrow, essentially the mindfulness service would die with me.

A combination of top-down and bottom-up engagement from staff within the organisation is thus necessary to drive implementation. The level of personal engagement and drive in the process of implementation by the successful implementers in our data was striking.

Spend a moment reflecting: Are there ways to widen out the engagement with the MBP innovation I am driving so that it is more sustainable? How do I keep resourcing myself within the energy that is needed to drive implementation?

Adherence to good practice

Another important element of the MBP implementation journey, particularly in relation to sustainability, was the nature of the MBP teacher-training pathway and supervision arrangements. In some sites, lack of resources meant that training and supervision provision were compromised and sometimes fell below good practice guidance. This meant that some staff were in the position of delivering MBPs even though they did not have the necessary skills and understanding. As a result, the quality of provision was diluted, less sustainable, and tended to drift away from the evidence.

Where there were good training and supervision arrangements, implementers felt more confident in their skills and had support around them to work through the inevitable challenges of implementing and delivering. Within the sites where the MBP service was embedded, training and supervision were funded by the organisation, there was a greater emphasis on quality and adherence to good practice guidelines, and an emphasis on nurturing clinicians' personal mindfulness practice. In sites where implementation was fragile and patchy, many implementers were paying for their own training and external supervision.

There was considerable evidence of the tension between providing gold standard and 'good enough' training within resource constrained services. One place where this issue frequently cropped up in the data was in relation to the good practice requirement to attend an annual retreat:

> *This [resourcing of retreats] is a sticky point at the moment, the requirements for the best practice ... I end up negotiating with the service managers about: we'll pay for it or we'll let people have time off and then you have to compromise with the staff to do that ... previously we would have funded everything but just at the moment there isn't the money available.*
>
> *Speaking as somebody who's been in involved in commissioning ... one of the things I have to marry up here is the gold standard mindfulness training, versus working out the politics of financing all of that and for us to be happy with an imperfect but nevertheless good enough level of provision.*

Being an MBP practitioner is not a role that is confined to ones working life. There is a significant personal engagement with the process that influences the entirety of our lives. One of the issues this raises is the balance between how much personal resources and how much organisational resources are dedicated to engagement with training and ongoing good practice adherence.

Spend a moment reflecting: How do I resource myself as an MBP implementer and teacher? How does my practice align with recognised good practice guidance?

Pivot points

During the implementation journeys, events/activities occur which help MBCT get further implemented in the service or, conversely hinder or halt progress. Over the years, the level of embeddedness can change dramatically in positive or negative directions due to a change in organisational priorities, structures and conditions. Even an MBP service that seems established and solid can in reality be fragile. Effective implementation involves proactive engagement with both these downward and upward pivot points.

One of the themes that emerges for myself (RC) as I reflect on this is the reality that there are inherent challenges to working within large organisations such as the health service and universities (the two organisations I am familiar with – but it applies to others). There are organisational forces that are beyond our control. What is not beyond our control is the way we relate and orientate to these dynamics. In our personal mindfulness practice, we are discovering how to relate to inner experience in skilful ways – to understand the inherent unsatisfactory nature of experience, to know the conditions that promote wellbeing and those that perpetuate distress, and to influence how we respond accordingly. The same themes are relevant on an organisational level – after all an organisation is the creation of a number of human minds attempting to work together. Organisations are therefore naturally subject to the same conditions that our own body-mind is subject to. It is not personal – it is all phenomena. Yet of course, it feels intensely personal when an MBP service we have poured our energy into creating is threatened by a re-organisational process. How can our mindfulness practice be of service in these moments of organisational intensity? There is no single answer to this. It is clear though that these are the times we dig deep, and draw on our inner resources for responding wisely and skilfully. There are times to hold our ground and push back, there are times to join the direction of the organisational forces, and there are times to step back and not participate.

> Spend a moment reflecting: How am I relating to the bigger organisational dynamics that influence the development of my MBP teaching practice?

Implementation recommendations

Through engaging with these themes during the research process, we have discovered a lot about what facilitates MBP implementation. Together we can now use this knowledge to inspire sustainable development of MBPs in our health service, and in other mainstream settings. The implementation recommendations below arose from this process, and are split into two sections; 'Starting your implementation journey' and 'Maintaining and sustaining your implementation journey.'

STARTING YOUR IMPLEMENTATION JOURNEY

Make a case

MBPs are not interventions that provide 'a quick fix' – they place people as active agents in their own recovery and promote mental health and wellbeing. The ethos of MBPs can sometimes be at odds with the pace and pressure of current services. Making the case can be a challenge and requires proactive engagement in activities, see Figure 26.1:

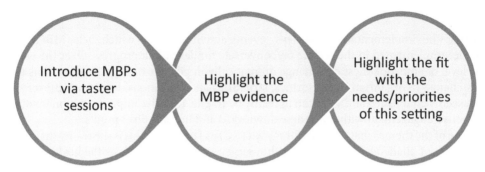

Figure 26.1 Making a case

Establish your networks

Seek out and/or establish a network of multiple stakeholders to strengthen your support system and access resources. Build formal and informal networks; online networks locally, regionally and nationally; and platforms for sharing ideas, learning, finding solutions and sharing expertise. Start small by building local relationships with colleagues and managers, before establishing wider links with external regional and national implementers, training and supervision networks, and research networks, see Figure 26.2:

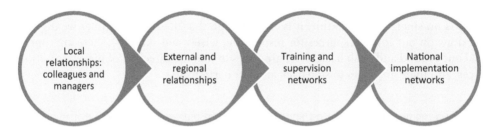

Figure 26.2 Establishing your networks

Training MBP teachers

One of the most substantive facilitators supporting successful implementation is ensuring good pathways to train MBP teachers, and ensuring access to ongoing supervision, retreats, and training. Sustainable implementation relies on practitioners who can deliver the intervention competently, and in time go on to supervise and train others to do so, see Figure 26.3:

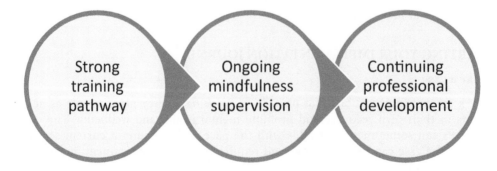

Figure 26.3 Training MBP teachers

MAINTAINING AND SUSTAINING YOUR IMPLEMENTATION JOURNEY

The following elements will support your journey of creating, maintaining and sustaining an MBP service. Further detail and resources to support you in each of these areas are available in the study website (https://implementing-mindfulness.co.uk). These points have been developed by analysing the common characteristics of an embedded MBP service.

Making it 'fit' the service you are working within

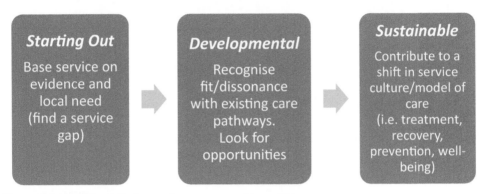

Figure 26.4 Making it fit the service you are working within

Developing an evaluation approach, using it and learning from it

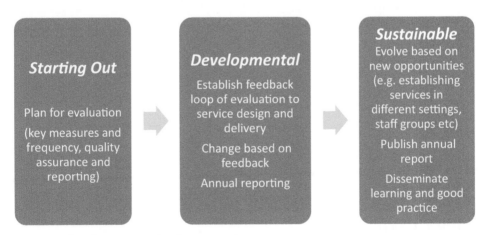

Figure 26.5 Developing an evaluation approach

Creating your networks and building a culture

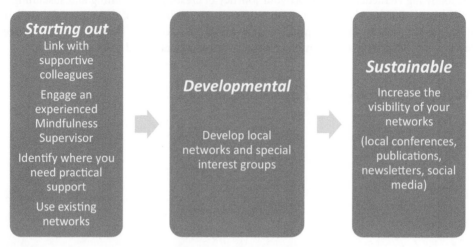

Figure 26.6 Creating your culture and building your networks

Building a team to deliver

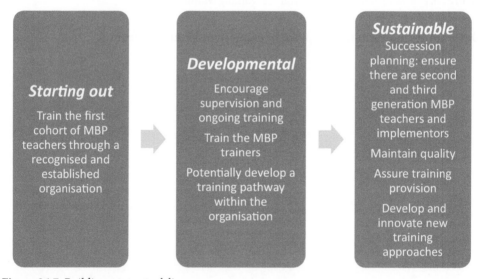

Figure 26.7 Building a team to deliver

Getting top-down buy in

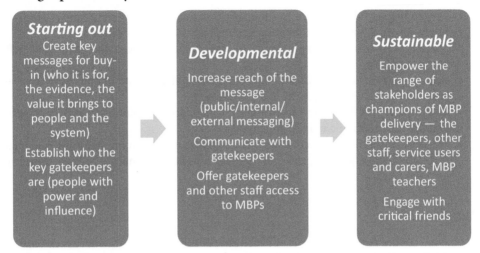

Figure 26.8 Getting top-down buy in

Creating a fit for purpose structure and governance

Figure 26.9 Creating a fit for purpose structure

Nourishing and sustaining yourselves and your colleagues

Figure 26.10 Nourishing and sustaining yourself

SUMMARY

- Developing an MBP service is a journey that takes many years, requires clarity of intention, and persistent individual and organisational commitment,
- Various activities involving a range of stakeholders support the process of MBP implementation
- Both bottom-up and top-down engagement are needed in an organisation to create sustainable change in the form of MBP delivery
- The process of MBP service development is an ongoing evolution as both the context and the intervention changes and adapts
- Personal mindfulness practice is a deep support in resourcing MBP implementers through the long journey, and inspiring them to keep connected to their intentions for their work

RESOURCES

- The study website (www.implementing-mindfulness.co.uk) has a wealth of resources to support the implementation journey including guidance on such issues as evaluating your courses, making a business case, marketing etc.
- Mindfulness-Based Supervision is an important arena for exploring some of the challenges, tensions, and dilemmas that emerge in the MBP implementation process – see Chapter 21
- See Chapter 18 for a summary of the practical things to bear in mind when setting up an MBP course.
- This paper: Crane, R.S. (2017). Implementing Mindfulness in the Mainstream: making the path by walking it, *Mindfulness*, doi:10.1007/s12671-016-0632-7 – explores the inherent tensions of implementing MBPs in the mainstream and how we can find a place to stand in the midst of this.

References

American Mindfulness Research Association (AMRA) (2020). *Monthly bulletin.* https://goamra. org/publications/mindfulness-research-monthly/

Atkins, S. & Murphy, K. (1993). Reflection: A review of the literature. *Journal of Advanced Nursing, 18*(8), 1188–1192. https://doi.org/10.1046/j.1365-2648.1993.18081188.x

Baer, R. (2015). Ethics, values, virtues, and character strengths in mindfulness-based interventions: A psychological science perspective. *Mindfulness, 6*(4), 956–969. https://doi.org/10.1007/s12671-015-0419-2

Baer, R., Crane, C., Miller, E., & Kuyken, W. (2019). Doing no harm in mindfulness-based programs: Conceptual issues and empirical findings. *Clinical Psychology Review*, 71, 101–114. https://doi.org/10.1016/j.cpr.2019.01.001

Baer, R. & Nagy, L. M. (2017). Professional ethics and personal values in mindfulness-based programs: A secular psychological perspective. In L. Monteiro, J. Compson, & F. Musten (Eds.), *Practitioner's guide to ethics and mindfulness-based interventions* (pp. 87–111). Springer Cham.

Baer, R. A., Smith, G. T., Lykins, E., Button, D., Krietemeyer, J., Sauer, S., Walsh, E., Duggan, D., & Williams, J. M. G. (2008). Construct validity of the five facet mindfulness questionnaire in meditating and nonmeditating samples. *Assessment, 15*(3), 329–342. https:/doi.org/10.1177/1073191107313003

BAMBA (2019). British Association for Mindfulness-Based Approaches. https://bamba.org.uk/

Bartley, T. (2017). *Mindfulness: A kindly approach to being with cancer.* Wiley-Blackwell.

Bernstein, A., Vago, D.R., & Barnhofer, T. (Eds.) (2019). Mindfulness [Special issue]. *Current Opinion in Psychology, 28*, 1–326. Retrieved from www.sciencedirect.com/journal/current-opinion-in-psychology/vol/28/suppl/C

Berry, W. (2013). *New collected poems.* Counterpoint Press.

Britton, W. B. (2016). Scientific literacy as a foundational competency for teachers of mindfulness-based interventions. In McCown, D., Reibel, & M. Micozzi (Eds.) *Resources for teaching mindfulness* (pp. 93–119). Springer Cham.

Britton, W. B. (2019). Can mindfulness be too much of a good thing? The value of a middle way. *Current Opinion in Psychology, 28*, 159–165. https://doi.org/10.1016/j.copsyc.2018.12.011

Bruner, J. S. (1966). *Toward a theory of instruction.* Harvard University Press.

Burch, V. (2010). *Living well with pain and illness: The mindful way to free yourself from suffering.* Sounds True Inc.

Center for Mindfulness. (2017). Mindfulness-based stress reduction (MBSR) authorized curriculum guide. www.umassmed.edu/globalassets/center-for-mindfulness/documents/mbsr-curriculum-guide-2017.pdf

Chadwick, P. (2014). Mindfulness for psychosis. *The British Journal of Psychiatry, 204*(5), 333–334. https://doi.org/10.1192/bjp.bp.113.136044

Chapman, M. J., Hare, D. J., Caton, S., Donalds, D., McInnis, E., & Mitchell, D. (2013). The use of mindfulness with people with intellectual disabilities: a systematic review and narrative analysis, *Mindfulness*, 4(2), 179–189.

Cladder-Micus, M. B., Speckens, A. E., Vrijsen, J. N., T. Donders, A. R., Becker, E. S., & Spijker, J. (2018). Mindfulness-based cognitive therapy for patients with chronic, treatment-resistant depression: A pragmatic randomized controlled trial. *Depression and Anxiety*, 35(10), 914–924.

Collins, B. (2001). *Sailing alone around the room: New and selected poems*. Random House.

Covey, S. (1989). *The 7 habits of highly effective people: Powerful lessons in personal change*. Simon & Schuster.

Crane, C. & Williams, J. M. G. (2010). Factors associated with attrition from mindfulness based cognitive therapy in patients with a history of suicidal depression. *Mindfulness*, 1(1), 10–20. https://doi.org/10.1007/s12671-010-0003-8

Crane, R. S. (2014). Some reflections on being good, on not being good and on just being. *Mindfulness*, 6(5), 1226–1231. https://doi.org/10.1007/s12671-014-0350-y

Crane, R. S. (2016). Implementing mindfulness in the mainstream: Making the path by walking it. *Mindfulness*, 8(3), 585–594. https://doi.org/10.1007/s12671-016-0632-7

Crane, R. (2017). *Mindfulness-based cognitive therapy* (2nd ed.). Routledge.

Crane, R. S., Brewer, J., Feldman, C., Kabat-Zinn, J., Santorelli, S., Williams, J. M. G., & Kuyken, W. (2017). What defines mindfulness-based programs? The warp and the weft. *Psychological Medicine*, 47(6), 990–999. https://doi.org/10.1017/s0033291716003317

Crane, R. S., Eames, C., Kuyken, W., Hastings, R. P., Williams, J. M. G., Bartley, T., Evans, A., Silverton, S., Soulsby, J.G., & Surawy, C. (2013). Development and validation of the mindfulness-based interventions – teaching assessment criteria (MBI: TAC). *Assessment*, 20(6), 681–688. https://doi.org/10.1177/1073191113490790

Crane, R. S. & Kuyken, W. (2013). The implementation of Mindfulness-Based Cognitive Therapy: Learning from the UK health service experience. *Mindfulness*, 4(3), 246–254. https://doi.org/10.1007/s12671-012-0121-6

Crane, R. S. & Reid, B. (2016). Training mindfulness teachers: Principles, practices and challenges. In D. McCown, D. Reibel, & M. Micozzi (Eds.), *Resources for teaching mindfulness: A cross-cultural and international handbook* (pp. 121–140). Springer.

Crane, R. S., Soulsby, J. G., Kuyken, W., Williams, J. M. G., & Eames, C. (2018). *The universities of Bangor, Exeter and Oxford manual of the mindfulness-based interventions teaching assessment criteria (MBI-TAC) (version 2018)*. Mindfulness Teaching Skills. http://mbitac.bangor.ac.uk/documents/MBITACmanualsummaryandaddendums0517.pdf

De Silva, P. (1990). Buddhist psychology: A review of theory and practice. *Current Psychology*, 9(3), 236–254.

di Giacomo, E., Krausz, M., Colmegna, F., Aspesi, F., & Clerici, M. (2018). Estimating the risk of attempted suicide among sexual minority youths: A systematic review and meta-analysis. *JAMA Pediatrics*, 172(12), 1145–1152. https://doi.org/10.1001/jamapediatrics.2018.2731

Dimidjian, S. & Segal, Z. V. (2015). Prospects for a clinical science of mindfulness-based intervention. *American Psychologist*, 70(7), 593–620. https://doi.org/10.1037/a0039589

Dreamer, O. M. (2001). *The dance: Moving to the rhythms of your true self*. HarperCollins.

Dreyfus, H. L. & Dreyfus, S. E. (1986). *Mind over machine: The power of human intuition and experience in the age of computers*. The Free Press.

English, B. (2019). *Does retreat experience contribute to the development of mindfulness teachers?* [Unpublished master's Thesis]. Centre for Mindfulness Research and Practice, Bangor University.

Evans, A. (2019). *Supervisors' and supervisees' perspectives of mindfulness-based supervision: A grounded theory study* [Manuscript in Preparation]. Clinical Education Development and Research, Exeter University.

Evans, A., Crane, R., Cooper, L., Mardula, J., Wilks, J., Surawy, C., Kenny, M., & Kuyken, W. (2015). A framework for supervision for mindfulness-based teachers: A space for embodied mutual inquiry. *Mindfulness*, 6(3), 572–581. https://doi.org/10.1007/s12671-014-0292-4

Evans, A., Griffith, G.M., Crane, R.S., & Samson, S.A. (2021). Using the Mindfulness-based interventions: Teaching Assessment Criteria (MBI:TAC) in supervision. *Global Advances in Health and Medicine, 10*, 1–6. https://doi.org/10.1177/2164956121989949

Feldman, C. (2016, June). *The long view- perils and possibilities* [conference session]. The Centre for Mindfulness Research and Practice, Bangor University -Mindfulness in Society: Chester.

Feldman, C. & Kuyken, W. (2019). *Mindfulness: Ancient wisdom meets modern psychology*. The Guilford Press.

Gilbert, P. (2009). *Overcoming depression: A self-help guide using cognitive behavioural Techniques* (3rd ed.). Robinson.

Gilbert, P. & Choden (2013). *Mindful compassion: Using the power of mindfulness and compassion to transform our lives*. Robinson.

Ginsburg, H. P. & Opper, S. (1988). *Piaget's theory of intellectual development* (3rd ed.). Prentice-Hall, Inc.

Government Equalities Office & Equality Human Rights Commission (2013). *Equality act 2010: Guidance*. www.gov.uk/guidance/equality-act-2010-guidance

Greenhalgh, T. (2019). *How to read a paper: The basics of evidence-based medicine and healthcare* (6th ed). Wiley-Blackwell.

Griffith, G. M., Bartley, T., & Crane, R. S. (2019a). The inside out group model: Teaching groups in mindfulness-based programs. *Mindfulness, 10*(7), 1315–1327. https://doi.org/10.1007/s12671-019-1093-6

Griffith, G.M., Hastings, R.P., Burke, C., Charlesworth, P., Chapman, M., Fothergill, S., McGarry, J., Noone, S., Pert, C., Steele, K., Ward, A., & Wright, G. (2019b). *Good practice guidelines: Mindfulness-based programmes for people with learning disabilities*. BAMBA. https://bamba.org.uk/teachers/good-practice-guidelines/

Grossman, P. (2015). Mindfulness: Awareness informed by an embodied ethic. *Mindfulness, 6*(1), 17–22. https://doi.org/10.1007/s12671-014-0372-5

Grossman, P. & Van Dam, N. T. (2011). Mindfulness, by any other name … : Trials and tribulations of sati in western psychology and science. *Contemporary Buddhism, 12*(1), 219–239. https://doi.org/10.1080/14639947.2011.564841

Hanson, R. (2009). *Buddha's brain: The practical neuroscience of happiness, love, and wisdom*. New Harbinger Publications, Inc.

Harrington, A. & Dunne, J. D. (2015). When mindfulness is therapy: Ethical qualms, historical perspectives. *American Psychologist, 70*(7), 621–631. https://doi.org/10.1037/a0039460

Hayes, S. C., Strosahal, K. D., & Wilson, K. G. (2012). *Acceptance and commitment therapy: The process and practice of mindful change* (2nd ed.). The Guilford Press.

Hölzel, B. K., Lazar, S. W., Gard, T., Schuman-Olivier, Z., Vago, D. R., & Ott, U. (2011). How does mindfulness meditation work? Proposing mechanisms of action from a conceptual and neural perspective. *Perspectives on Psychological Science, 6*(6), 537–559. https://doi.org/10.1177/1745691611419671

Hopwood, T. L. & Schutte, N. S. (2017). A meta-analytic investigation of the impact of mindfulness-based interventions on post traumatic stress. *Clinical Psychology Review, 57*, 12–20. https://doi.org/10.1016/j.cpr.2017.08.002

Husgafvel, V. (2019). The 'universal dharma foundation' of mindfulness-based stress reduction: Non-duality and Mahayana Buddhist influences in the work of Jon Kabat-Zinn. *Contemporary Buddhism, 19*(2), 275–326. https://doi.org/10.1080/14639947.2018.1572329

International Integrity Network (2020.). IMI network in the world. http://iminetwork.org/

Jinpa, T. (2016). *A fearless heart: How the courage to be compassionate can transform our lives*. Avery.

Kabat-Zinn, J. (2003). Mindfulness-based interventions in context: Past, present, and future. *Clinical Psychology: Science and Practice, 10*(2), 144–156. https://doi.org/10.1093/clipsy.bpg016

Kabat-Zinn, J. (2010) Foreword. In D. McCown, D. Reibel, & M.S. Micozzi, *Teaching mindfulness: A practical guide for clinicians and educators* (pp. ix–xxii). Springer.

Kabat-Zinn, J. (2011). Some reflections on the origins of MBSR, skillful means, and the trouble with maps. *Contemporary Buddhism, 12*(1), 281–306. https://doi.org/10.1080/14639947.2011.564844

Kabat-Zinn, J. (2013). *Full catastrophe living, revised edition: How to cope with stress, pain and illness using mindfulness meditation* (Revised ed.). Piatkus.

Kabat-Zinn, J. (2015). Foreword. In Mindfulness All-Party Parliamentary Group (MAPPG), *Mindful nation UK* (p. 10). The Mindfulness Initiative. www.themindfulnessinitiative.org/Handlers/Download.ashx?IDMF=1af56392-4cf1-4550-bdd1-72e809fa627a

Kabat-Zinn, J. (2017). Too early to tell: The potential impact and challenges – ethical and otherwise – inherent in the mainstreaming of dharma in an increasingly dystopian world. *Mindfulness, 8*(5), 1125–1135 https://doi.org/10.1007/s12671-017-0758-2

Kabat-Zinn, J., Koerbel, L., & Meleo-Meyer, F. (Eds.). (2021). *Mindfulness-Based Stress Reduction (MBSR) Training and Curriculum Guide 2021.* [Unpublished manuscript].

Khoury, B., Knäuper, B., Schlosser, M., Carrière, K., & Chiesa, A. (2017). Effectiveness of traditional meditation retreats: A systematic review and meta-analysis. *Journal of Psychosomatic Research, 92,* 16–25.

Killingsworth, M. A. & Gilbert, D. T. (2010). A wandering mind is an unhappy mind. *Science, 330*(6006), 932–932. https://doi.org/10.1126/science.1192439

Kolb, D. (1984). *Experiential learning: Experience as the source of learning and development.* Prentice-Hall Inc.

Kramer, G. (2007). *Insight dialogue: The interpersonal path to freedom.* Shambhala Publications.

Kramer, G., Meleo-Meyer, F., & Turner, M. L. (2008). Cultivating mindfulness in relationship: Insight dialogue and the interpersonal mindfulness program. In S. F. Hick & T. Bein (Eds.), *Mindfulness and the therapeutic relationship* (pp. 195–215). The Guilford Press.

Kucinskas, J. (2019). *The mindful elite: Mobilizing from the inside out.* Oxford University Press.

Lakey, G. (2010). *Facilitating group learning: Strategies for success with diverse adult learners.* Jossey-Bass.

Levine, P. (2005) *Healing trauma: A pioneering program for restoring the wisdom of the body (book and audio).* Sounds True Inc.

Loy, D. R. (2019). *Ecodharma: Buddhist teachings for the ecological crisis.* Wisdom Publications.

Luft, J. & Ingham, H. (1955). The Johari window: A graphic model of interpersonal awareness. In *Proceedings of the western training laboratory in group development.* Los Angeles, CA: University of California Los Angeles.

Lutz, A., Dunne, J. D., & Davidson, R. J. (2007). Meditation and the neuroscience of consciousness. In P. D. Zelazo, M. Moscovitch, & E. Thompson (Eds.), *The Cambridge handbook of consciousness* (pp. 499–555). Cambridge University Press. https://doi.org/10.1017/CBO9780511816789.020

Magee, R. V. (2016). The way of ColorInsight: Understanding race and law effectively through mindfulness-based ColorInsight practices. *Georgetown Law Journal of Modern Critical Race Perspectives, 8,* 251–304. https://papers.ssrn.com/sol3/papers.cfm?abstract_id=2638511

Magee, R. V. (2019). *The inner work of racial justice: Healing ourselves and transforming communities through mindfulness.* Penguin Random House.

McCown, D.A. (2013). *The ethical space of mindfulness in clinical practice: An exploratory essay.* Jessica Kingsley Publishers.

McCown, D.A. (2016). Stewardship: Deeper structures of the co-created group. In D. McCown, D. Reibel, & M.S. Micozzi (Eds.), *Resources for teaching mindfulness: An international handbook* (pp. 3–24). Springer.

McCown, D., Reibel, D., & Micozzi, M. S. (2010). *Teaching mindfulness: A practical guide for clinicians and educators.* Springer.

McCown, D., Reibel, D., & Micozzi, M. S. (2016). *Resources for teaching mindfulness: An international handbook.* Springer.

McGonigal, K. (2013, June). *Katie McGonigal: How to make stress your friend* [Video] TED. www.ted.com/talks/kelly_mcgonigal_how_to_make_stress_your_friend

Mental Health First Aid Australia (2019). Mental health first aid australia: Learn the skills to make a difference. https://mhfa.com.au

Mills, C. W. (2000). *The sociological imagination.* Oxford University Press.

Mindfulness and Social Change Network (n.d.). https://mindfulnessandsocialchange.org

Music, G. (2014). *The good life: Wellbeing and the new science of altruism, selfishness and immorality.* Routledge.

Nanamoli, B. & Bodhi, B. (Trans.) (1995). Satipatthana Sutta: The foundations of Mindfulness. In *The middle length discourses of the Buddha: A translation of the majjhima nikaya* (pp. 145–155). Wisdom Publications.

Neff, K. & Germer, C. (2018). *The Mindful self-compassion workbook: A proven way to accept your-self, build inner strength, and thrive.* The Guilford Press.

Nye, N. S. (1998). *The words under the words: Selected poems.* Far Corner.

Office for National Statistics (2020). Coronavirus-related deaths by ethnic group, England and Wales methodology. www.ons.gov.uk/peoplepopulationandcommunity/birthsdeathsandmarriages/deaths/methodologies/coronavirusrelateddeathsbyethnicgroupenglandandwalesmethodology

Ogden, P. & Fisher, J. (2015). *Sensorimotor psychotherapy: Interventions for trauma and attachment.* W. W. Norton & Co.

Ogden, P., Minton, K., & Pain, C. (2006). *Norton series on interpersonal neurobiology. Trauma and the body: A sensorimotor approach to psychotherapy.* W. W. Norton & Co.

Oliver, M. (1992). *New and selected poems: Volume 1.* Beacon Press.

Oxford Mindfulness Centre (n.d.). Oxford mindfulness centre MBCT app. https://development.oxfordmindfulness.org/news/oxford-mbct-app/

Palmer, P. J. (1998). *The courage to teach: Exploring the inner landscape of a teacher's life.* Jossey-Bass.

Palmer, P. J. (2007). *The courage to teach: Exploring the inner landscape of a teacher's life.* (10th anniversary ed.) Jossey-Bass.

Parsons, C. E., Crane, C., Parsons, L. J., Fjorback, L. O., & Kuyken, W. (2017). Home practice in Mindfulness-Based Cognitive Therapy and Mindfulness-Based Stress Reduction: A systematic review and meta-analysis of participants' mindfulness practice and its association with outcomes. *Behaviour Research and Therapy, 95,* 29–41. https://doi.org/10.1016/j.brat.2017.05.004

Petty, S. (Ed.). (2017). Social justice, inner work, & contemplative practice: Lessons & directions for multiple fields [Special Issue]. *Initiative for Contemplation, Equity, & Action (ICEA) Journal, 1*(1).

Piaget, J. & Inhelder, B. (1969). *The psychology of the child.* Basic Books.

Pickett, K. & Wilkinson, R. (2009). *The spirit level: Why equality is better for everyone.* Penguin Publishers.

Place, P. (2019). *The role and impact of retreat experiences on the training and development of mindfulness teachers.* [Unpublished master's Thesis]. Centre for Mindfulness Research and Practice, Bangor University.

Porges, S. W. (2004). Neuroception: A subconscious system for detecting threats and safety. *Zero to Three, 24*(5), 19–24. https://eric.ed.gov/?id=EJ938225

Porges, S. W. (2011). *The Norton series on interpersonal neurobiology. The polyvagal theory: The neurophysiological foundations of emotions, attachment, communication, and self-regulation.* W. W. Norton & Co.

Porges, S. W. (2017). *Norton series on interpersonal neurobiology. The pocket guide to the polyvagal theory: The transformative power of feeling safe.* W. W. Norton & Co.

Raes, F., Pommier, E., Neff, K. D., & Van Gucht, D. (2011). Construction and factorial validation of a short form of the Self-Compassion Scale. *Clinical Psychology & Psychotherapy, 18*(3), 250–255. https://doi.org/10.1002/cpp.702

Rilke, R. M. (2012). *Letters to a young poet* (C. Louth, Trans.). Penguin Classics.

Rose, S. A., Sheffield, D., & Harling, M. (2017). The integration of the workable range model into a mindfulness-based stress reduction course: A practice-based case study. *Mindfulness, 9*(2), 430–440. https://doi.org/10.1007/s12671-017-0787-x

Rumi, J. (1988). Two kinds of intelligence. In C. Barks & J. Moyne. (Trans.), *This longing: Poetry, teaching stories, and selected letters of Rumi.* Threshold Books.

Rumi, J. (1994). Personal intelligence. In J. Moyne & C. Barks (Trans.), *Say I am you.* MAYPOP.

Rumi, J. (1995). *The essential Rumi* (C. Barks & J. Moyne, Trans.). Harper Collins.

Rupprecht, S., Koole, W., Chaskalson, M., Tamdjidi, C., & West, M. (2019). Running too far ahead? Towards a broader understanding of mindfulness in organisations. *Current Opinion in Psychology, 28,* 32–36. https://doi.org/10.1016/j.copsyc.2018.10.007

Russell, S. (2018). *Evaluating the use of Mindfulness-Based interventions: Teaching Assessment Criteria (MBI:TAC) in training programmes internationally* [Unpublished master's Thesis]. Centre for Mindfulness Research and Practice, Bangor University.

Rycroft-Malone, J., Gradinger, F., Owen Griffiths, H., Anderson, R., Crane, R. S., Gibson, A., Mercer, S.W., & Kuyken, W. (2019). "Mind the gaps": The accessibility and implementation of an effective depression relapse prevention programme in UK NHS services: Learning from

Mindfulness-Based Cognitive Therapy through a mixed-methods study. *BMJ Open*, *9*(9), e026244. https://doi.org/10.1136/bmjopen-2018-026244

Sanghvi, M. (2019). *Fieldbook for mindfulness innovators* (R. Bell & J. Bristow, Eds.) Mindfulness Initiative. www.themindfulnessinitiative.org/fieldbook-for-mindfulness-innovators

Sapolsky, R. M. (2004). *Why zebras don't get ulcers: The acclaimed guide to stress, stress related diseases, and coping.* Holt paperbacks.

Segal, Z. V., Anderson, A. K., Gulamani, T., Dinh Williams, L., Desormeau, P., Ferguson, A., Walsh, K., & Farb, N. A. S. (2019). Practice of therapy acquired regulatory skills and depressive relapse/recurrence prophylaxis following cognitive therapy or mindfulness based cognitive therapy. *Journal of Consulting and Clinical Psychology*, *87*(2), 161–170. https://doi.org/10.1037/ccp0000351

Segal, Z. V., Williams, J. M. G., & Teasdale, J. (2013). *Mindfulness-based cognitive therapy for depression* (2nd ed). The Guilford Press.

Shapiro, S. L., Carlson, L. E., Astin, J. A., & Freedman, B. (2006). Mechanisms of mindfulness. *Journal of Clinical Psychology*, *62*(3), 373–386. https://doi.org/10.1002/jclp.20237

Shapiro, S., Siegel, R., & Neff, K. D. (2018). Paradoxes of mindfulness. *Mindfulness*, *9*(6), 1693–1701. https://doi.org/10.1007/s12671-018-0957-5

Sharpless, B. A. & Barber, J. P. (2009). A conceptual and empirical review of the meaning, measurement, development, and teaching of intervention competence in clinical psychology. *Clinical Psychology Review*, *29*(1), 47–56. https://doi.org/10.1016/j.cpr.2008.09.008

Siegel, D. J. (1999). *The developing mind: How relationships and the brain interact to shape who we are.* The Guilford Press.

Siegel, D. J. (2009). Mindful awareness, mindsight, and neural integration. *The Humanistic Psychologist*, *37*(2), 137–158. https://doi.org/10.1080/08873260902892220

Spencer, S. (2019). *Think like a tree: The natural principles guide to life* (G. Walker, Ed.) Swarkestone Press.

Strauss, C., Cavanagh, K., Oliver, A., & Pettman, D. (2014). Mindfulness-based interventions for people diagnosed with a current episode of an anxiety or depressive disorder: a meta-analysis of randomised controlled trials. *PLoS One*, *9*(4), e96110.

Substance Abuse and Mental Health Service Administration's (SAMHSA) Trauma and Justice Strategic Initiative (2014). *SAMHSA's concept of trauma and guidance for a trauma-informed approach.* https://store.samhsa.gov/system/files/sma14-4884.pdf

Taylor, S. E. (2006). Tend and befriend: Biobehavioural bases of affiliation under stress. *Current Directions in Psychological Science*, *15*(6), 273–277. https://doi.org/10.1111/j.1467-8721.2006.00451.x

Thornton, C. (2016). *Group and team coaching: The secret life of groups* (2nd ed.). Routledge.

Treleaven, D. A. (2018). *Trauma-sensitive mindfulness: Practices for safe and transformative healing.* W. W. Norton & Co.

Tricycle (2011). Human nature, Buddha nature: On spiritual bypassing, relationship, and the dharma. An interview with John Welwood/Interviewer: T. Fossella. *Tricycle Magazine*. https://tricycle.org/magazine/human-nature-buddha-nature/

Tuckman, B. W. (1965). Developmental sequence in small groups. *Psychological Bulletin*, *63*(6), 384–399. https://doi.org/10.1037/h0022100

United Nations. (n.d.). *Equality and non-discrimination.* www.un.org/ruleoflaw/thematic-areas/human-rights/equality-and-non-discrimination/

Van Aalderen, J. R., Breukers, W. J., Reuzel, R. P., & Speckens, A. E. (2012). The role of the teacher in mindfulness-based approaches: A qualitative study. *Mindfulness*, *5*(2), 170–178. https://doi.org/10.1007/s12671-012-0162-x

van den Brink, E., Koster, F., & Norton, V. (2018). *A practical guide to mindfulness-based compassionate living: Living with heart.* Routledge.

van der Kolk, B. A. (1994). The body keeps the score: Memory and the evolving psychobiology of posttraumatic stress. *Harvard Review of Psychiatry*, *1*(5), 253–265. https://doi.org/10.3109/10673229409017088

van der Kolk, B. A., McFarlane, A. C., & Weisæth, L. (Eds.). (2007). *Traumatic stress: The effects of overwhelming experience on mind, body, and society.* Guilford Press.

Wellings, N. (2016). *Why can't I meditate? How to get your mindfulness practice on track.* TarcherPerigee.

Whitehead, M., Lilley, R., Howell, R., Jones, R., & Pykett, J. (2014). (Re)inhabiting awareness: Geography and mindfulness. *Social and Cultural Geography*, *17*(4), 553–573. https://doi.org/10.1080/14649365.2015.1089590

WHO Collaborating Centre in Mental Health (1998). *WHO (five) well-being index (1998 version)*. Psychiatric Research Unit, WHO Collaborating Centre for Mental Health. www.psykiatriregionh.dk/who-5/Documents/WHO5_English.pdf

Whyte, D. (1990). *Where many rivers meet*. Many Rivers Press.

Wilkinson, R. & Pickett, K. (2018). *The inner level: How more equal societies reduce stress, restore sanity, and improve everyone's well-being*. Allen Lane.

Williams, J. M. G. (2008). Mindfulness, depression and modes of mind. *Cognitive Therapy and Research*, *32*(6), 721–733.

Williams, J. M. G., Fennell, M., Barnhofer, T., Crane, R., & Silverton, S. (2017). *Mindfulness-Based Cognitive Therapy with people at risk of suicide*. Guilford Press.

Williams, J. M. G. & Kabat-Zinn, J. (2011). Mindfulness: Diverse perspectives on its meaning, origins, and multiple applications at the intersection of science and dharma. *Contemporary Buddhism*, *12*(1), 1–18. https://doi.org/10.1080/14639947.2011.564811

Williams, J. M. G., Crane, C., Barnhofer, T., Brennan, K., Duggan, D. S., Fennell, M. J., ... & Russell, I. T. (2014). Mindfulness-based cognitive therapy for preventing relapse in recurrent depression: a randomized dismantling trial. *Journal of Consulting and Clinical Psychology*, *82*(2), 275.

Wineman, S. (2003). *Power-under: Trauma and nonviolent social change*. Author. http://traumaandnonviolence.com/files/Power_Under.pdf

Wreford, L. & Haddock, P. (2019, 6 August). *Mindfulness and social change*. Open Democracy: Free thinking for the world. www.opendemocracy.net/en/transformation/mindfulness-and-social-change/

Yalom, I. D. & Leszcz, M. (2005). *The theory and practice of group psychotherapy* (5th ed.). Basic Books.

Appendix 1
Further resources

If you are interested in taking your learning further, this section offers some suggestions for training as an MBP teacher, further reading, websites, and retreat centres.

THE MBP TRAINING JOURNEY

As can be seen from the emphasis throughout the book, MBPs are a *mindfulness-based* learning process. Given that the transformative potential of MBPs is reliant on gaining access to perspectives that arise during mindfulness meditation practice, it follows that the professional training process for MBP teachers should offer the particular conditions within which these perspectives can be cultivated and explored.

The learning trajectory that supports the teaching involves an engaged inquiry into what it means to be human, and so there are multiple pathways through which MBP teachers arrive at this work. There are, however, some consistent and common threads, and various training organisations who offer developmental processes that support the required learning. The following section offers an overview of a typical training pathway.

FOUNDATIONAL TRAINING

A primary qualification for teaching mindfulness-based approaches is that mindfulness has become a way through which we explore and engage with experience and life. Of course, this requires each person to test this out for themselves. The best approach is to take an 8-week MBSR or MBCT course, and then take a minimum of six months to consolidate a personal mindfulness practice. Following this, it will be possible to decide whether you would like to take this exploration and development further.

This foundation of personal mindfulness practice becomes the bedrock of the teaching process. Learning to teach an MBP in ways that allow the richness and potential of mindfulness-based learning to become accessible to participants involves a committed engagement to this long-term personal development process. However, the experience of MBP trainees is that the rewards of this engagement go far beyond the development of the ability to teach or integrate mindfulness within one's professional work.

It is necessary to have a professional training relevant to the context within which you intend to teach MBPs. If in a clinical context, it is important to also have specific clinical experience with the client group that the group will be offered to.

PRELIMINARY TEACHER TRAINING

Trainees enter preliminary MBP teacher training (sometimes termed Level 1) with:

- Sufficient depth of personal experience with mindfulness practice to begin the development towards teaching. This must include a regular engagement with the three main practices taught in mindfulness-based approaches (body scan, sitting practice and mindful movement practice).
- Familiarity with the MBP course structure and process.
- Professional training and experience in the context within which you plan to teach MBP.
- Knowledge of relevant underlying psychological processes, associated research and evidence-based practice, unless these are provided to an adequate level by the MBP training programme.
- Experience and skills in leading and teaching groups (unless these are provided within the training).

This training stage is offered in a range of formats usually involving 8 days of training. A container is needed which enables participants to access and develop their inner mindfulness practice-based exploration, alongside the development of theoretical knowledge and competencies in teaching. The practice-based learning context enables the outer and more visible learning processes to be informed and related to in a mindful way.

There are a number of processes which then support the initial and ongoing process of becoming a teacher. It is recommended that you have regular supervision with a trained mindfulness supervisor (Chapter 21), (The Mindfulness Network offers telephone supervision for mindfulness-based teachers (www.mindfulness-supervision.org.uk); and that you take some time to deepen personal mindfulness practice in a retreat context. Further training in specific skill areas is supportive – for example, you can take masterclasses in holding the group process, in facilitating inquiry, or in guiding mindful movement. It is also tremendously helpful to work as an apprentice to a more experienced teacher in the early stages of learning to teach MBPs. We also recommend taking a specialist training in the particular MBP curriculum form you are specialising in. This is generally offered as a 5 day training.

The Mindfulness-Based Interventions: Teaching Assessment Criteria (MBI:TAC) and the TLC (Chapter 19) in this book offers a useful framework for reflection on your development with your supervisor (mbitac.bangor.ac.uk). The British Association for Mindfulness-Based Approaches (BAMBA) offer good practice guidelines for mindfulness-based teachers on the necessary ingredients of a training pathway to help chart how far along in the process you are (https://bamba.org.uk/). If you practice in the UK, once this training stage is complete, and you are adhering to ongoing good practice, it is possible to apply to be publicly registered with BAMBA.

FURTHER TEACHER TRAINING

Following completion of preliminary teacher training, trainees enter further (sometimes termed Level 2) MBP teacher training with:

- Experience of having taught several MBP courses
- Commitment to attendance on regular mindfulness-practice retreats
- Engagement in a regular mindfulness supervision

Trainees at this level will have moved beyond the early explorations of the form and shape of the MBP programme and curriculum, and will developmentally be at the point of exploring ways to refine their existing skills and to deepen their understanding of mindfulness as a teaching and learning process. A key overall intention is to support trainees in developing the ability and confidence to teach from the immediacy of their own experience. This tends to grow out of a depth of experience with mindfulness practice, with the teaching process and with the form of the MBP programme. Developmentally, many teachers experience that their confidence of knowing what is needed develops to the point that they can let go of holding the teaching in a certain way, and relate to the process from a wider, more embodied, creative and spacious place. This Level 2 training is commonly structured as a week-long residential training within a retreat context, and there are online formats now available. In many training centres this training phase culminates in an assessment of competence using the MBI:TAC, via submission of a portfolio including audio-visual recordings of an 8-week course.

ONGOING TRAINING

One of the deep pleasures of teaching MBPs is that it links closely with one's own personal engagement with mindfulness practice, so sustaining the energy and interest to keep the inquiry alive becomes more natural. Various things can help keep the learning nourished:

- Sustaining an ongoing formal and informal personal mindfulness practice through attendance on retreat, practicing with friends, engaging with mindfulness teachers, and reading books;
- Building connections with colleagues who are engaged in mindfulness-based teaching as a means to share experiences and learn collaboratively; and co-teaching including scheduled mutual feedback sessions;
- Ongoing and regular supervision of teaching, and inquiry into personal practice by an experienced teacher of mindfulness-based approaches, which ideally includes receiving periodic feedback on teaching through video recordings, or through your supervisor sitting in on teaching sessions.

RESOURCES FOR DEVELOPING AND SUPPORTING PERSONAL PRACTICE

There are many mindfulness teachers and centres from which to choose. It is important to engage in teachings and participate in retreats which offer forms of meditation which are aligned with those taught in MBPs. In practice this will likely mean exploring teachings offered by centres related to the Western insight meditation tradition. The Mindfulness

Network offers retreats specifically designed to meet the needs of mindfulness-based teachers (retreats.mindfulness-network.org). Gaia House in Devon, UK (www.gaiahouse.co.uk), the Insight Meditation Society in Massachusetts, USA (dharma.org), Spirit Rock in California (spiritrock.org), and the Australia insight meditation network (dharma.org.au) all teach mindfulness practice in a spirit and form that is compatible with MBPs. The Bodhi College offers a training and retreat context for mindfulness-based teachers who wish to deepen their understanding of the Buddhist underpinnings (bodhi-college.org).

Recordings of guided mindfulness practices are an invaluable support when meditating at home. Meditation practices recorded by teachers at Bangor University are freely available to download (bangor.ac.uk/mindfulness/audio/index.php.en); Jon Kabat-Zinn's CDs are available through mindfulnesscds.com; and recordings are available through the Oxford Mindfulness Centre (oxfordmindfulness.org/learn/resources/).

There is an active alumni group within The Mindfulness Network which offers a community which supports personal and teaching practice and organises events throughout the year. There is also a peer-led community of mindfulness practitioners (Support for Integrity in Teaching and Training: SITT), see here for details: www.sitt.community.

PROFESSIONAL TRAINING

Training processes and organisations are developing rapidly. Within the UK there are two university-based training establishments that offer MBSR and MBCT teacher training, which both provide training in the experiential and theoretical elements, and the evidence base:

1 The Centre for Mindfulness Research and Practice (CMRP) (www.bangor.ac.uk/mindfulness/postgraduate-courses/) within Bangor University's School of Psychology trains students in both MBCT and MBSR. It offers two master's degrees (MSc or MA): one offers full MBP teacher training alongside a master's degree (MA in Teaching Mindfulness-Based Courses) and the other focuses on the theory and research underpinning MBPs (MA/MSc in Mindfulness-Based Approaches). The Mindfulness Network (in collaboration with the CMRP at Bangor University) provide full MBP teacher training via a Teacher Training Pathway (training.mindfulness-network.org).

2 Oxford University offers a Master of Studies in MBCT and other MBCT training events through the Oxford Mindfulness Centre (oxfordmindfulness.org).

BAMBA lists the other UK MBP training organisations, some of which offer MBCT/MBSR training, and some that offer training in other MBP models. The Mindfulness-Based Professional Training Institute at University of California San Diego (mbpti.org), and the Center for Mindfulness Studies in Toronto, Canada (mindfulnessstudies.com) both offer MBP professional training. The MBCT websites for North America (www.mbct.com) will give information on developments there and to some extent in Europe. Further details of MBSR teacher training opportunities are also available at Brown University in the USA (www.brown.edu/public-health/mindfulness/home).

BOOKS

Five books on MBCT are *Mindfulness-Based Cognitive Therapy for Depression* by Segal, Williams, and Teasdale (for a professional audience – describes the development of the approach, the theoretical underpinnings and offers a session-by-session outline); *The Mindful Way Through Depression* by Williams, Teasdale, Segal, and Kabat-Zinn (a self-help guide for those exploring mindfulness practice as a way of working with depression); *The Mindful Way Workbook* by Teasdale, Williams and Segal (a workbook which supports moving through the MBCT course independently, and a useful followup for participants at the end of the MBCT course); *Mindfulness-Based Cognitive Therapy with People at Risk of Suicide* by Williams, Fennell, Barnhofer, Crane & Silverton (recounts the development and research of MBCT for people vulnerable to suicidality, and also offers a window onto the process and experience of being an MBCT teacher); and *Mindfulness-Based Cognitive Therapy: Distinctive Features* by Crane (a succinct practical and theoretical guide to MBCT for teachers). All are invaluable – wonderfully written, informative and accessible.

Kabat-Zinn's first book *Full Catastrophe Living* describes the MBSR programme in an accessible and engaging way and is essential reading for those wanting the background to the development of the clinical applications of mindfulness. He has also written *Wherever You Go, There You Are* (published in the UK as *Mindfulness Meditation in Everyday Life*), which is a wonderful support to the development of personal practice; and *Coming To Our Senses* (now republished as four updated volumes) which offers a broad and wide ranging though deeply personal exploration of the potential for mindfulness within our lives and the world.

SELECTED FURTHER READING

Baer, R. A. (2005). *Mindfulness-Based Treatment Approaches: Clinician's Guide to Evidence Base and Applications.* Academic Press.

Goldstein, J. (2016). *Mindfulness: A Practical Guide to Awakening.* Sounds True

Kabat-Zinn, J. (2013). *Full catastrophe living: Using the wisdom of your body and mind to face stress, pain and illness.* Delacorte.

Kornfield, J. (2002). *A Path with Heart.* Rider.

McCown, D., Reibel, D., Micozzi, M.S. (2010). *Teaching Mindfulness, A Practical Guide for Clinicians and Educators*, Springer.

McCown, D., Reibel, D., Micozzi, M.S. (2016). *Resources for Teaching Mindfulness*, Springer

Salzberg, S. (1999). *A Heart As Wide As The World. Living with Mindfulness, Wisdom and Compassion.* Shambhala.

Santorelli, S. (2000). *Heal Thyself: Lessons on Mindfulness in Medicine.* Bell Tower.

Index

Page numbers in *italics* refer to figures. Page numbers in **bold** refer to tables.